T3-BEA-508

Does man have the power to mentally
control disease?

Perform complicated surgery by intuition?

Transmit thoughts to cure an illness—
or even kill by telepathy?

PSI-HEALING

An eye-opening, in-depth report of the amazing
medical discoveries being made by psychic healers
throughout the world.

Documented case histories, interviews and profiles
of the men and women who perform miracle cures
using their paranormal powers.

Including: the woman who "sees" disease with her
fingers • the healing cults of the Philippines • the
physician who practices by remote control • and
many, many others in

PSI-HEALING

A Complete Survey of the Incredible
World of Today's Miracle Doctors

BY ALFRED STELTER

PSI-HEALING

ALFRED STELTER

*Translated from the German
by Ruth Hein*

WITHDRAWN
by Unity Library

UNITY SCHOOL LIBRARY
UNITY VILLAGE, MISSOURI 64065

PSI–HEALING
A Bantam Book / October 1976

All rights reserved.
Copyright © 1976 Scherz Verlag.
Translation Copyright © 1976 by Bantam Books, Inc.
This book may not be reproduced in whole or in part, by
mimeograph or any other means, without permission.
For information address: Bantam Books, Inc.

ISBN 0–553–02505–8

Published simultaneously in the United States and Canada.

Bantam Books are published by Bantam Books, Inc. Its trade-mark, consisting of the words "Bantam Books" and the por-trayal of a bantam, is registered in the United States Patent Office and in other countries. Marca Registrada. Bantam Books, Inc., 666 Fifth Avenue, New York, New York 10019.

PRINTED IN THE UNITED STATES OF AMERICA

To Harold Sherman
with deep appreciation and admiration
for his pioneering work
in the field of psychic surgery

CONTENTS

Miracles happen, not in
opposition to Nature,
but in opposition to what
we know of Nature.

— ST. AUGUSTINE

This book is not written for scientific traditionalists,
for it deals with paraphenomena or psi phenomena,
processes which take place outside the natural laws
accepted and codified by science.

The reader may be reassured that ten years ago the
author too would not have accepted many of the
phenomena discussed in this book. "Common sense"
is relative; "reason" has estalished new norms in every
era, and just because one is a scientist one cannot trust
reason and common sense in every case. I can only
hope that, in spite of descriptions and theories of
parahealing which must still appear fabulous, I will
not be considered a fabulist.

1 / ESTABLISHED MEDICINE AND PARAMEDICINE

The belief that there can be no successful methods for the treatment of illness that differ fundamentally from established Western medicine has long been in need of revision. There are effective methods of diagnosis, treatment, and surgery that cannot be explained by our medical knowledge or any of our contemporary sciences.

To this day science is mystified by Sigrun Seutemann, a German healer who simply looked at the "aura" of a patient she had never met before. Within moments she had pinpointed the origin of severe paralytic symptoms—tetanus-serum poisoning—which had gone unrecognized even in a teaching hospital during a year and a half of neurological and psychiatric treatment.

We do not know what actually occurred when Ambrose Worral, an American healer, caused a tumor to dissolve remarkably quickly, simply by laying hands repeatedly on the affected part of the patient's body.

Neither medicine nor chemistry and physics can explain how a patient already certified as terminal by his doctors took a turn for the better (leading to a complete cure) at precisely the moment when a world-famous English healer, Harry Edwards, concentrated on him. Edwards was some miles away from the hospital—had been engaged by his relatives —and the patient had no knowledge whatever of the event.

We do not know how the Brazilian healer Zé Arigo, using an ordinary knife, managed to remove a small tumor on the arm of the renowned scientist and physician Andrija K. Puharich. The procedure was

1

painless, there was very little loss of blood, no infection set in, and the resulting scar was almost nonexistent. Reason is further challenged when we examine psychic surgery as practiced in the Philippines. What really happens during operations by psychic surgeons, who seem to penetrate the patient's body with their bare hands and often alleviate severe organic disturbances?

At this, our "common sense"—or what we think is common sense—goes on strike. Reason registers a protest, since what is not lawful cannot exist. Rather than allow our picture of the universe to be called into question, we prefer to suspect deception.

Trickery? So thought the secretary-general of the French Academy of Sciences in Paris when he and an illustrious body of scientists attended a demonstration of the first phonograph. Convinced that he was dealing with a ventriloquist, in order to unmask the demonstrator he gripped him by the throat and began to choke him. But to everyone's astonishment, the machine went on playing.[189]*

In 1893, Carl Ludwig Schleich, a young Berlin surgeon who later gained some renown, tried to demonstrate to a medical congress a procedure he had developed for local anesthesia. The medical leaders of his day drove him from the auditorium. And in 1910, when a discussion of psychoanalysis was announced at a Hamburg congress of German neurologists and psychiatrists, Professor Wilhelm Weygandt struck the table with his fist and shouted in outrage, "That is not a proper subject for a scientific meeting. It is a matter for the police courts."

If we think of all the scientific discoveries made during the last fifty years alone, we will have to admit the truth of the French scientist François Arago's statement, made 130 years ago, that great care must be taken in using the word "impossible" except in mathematics.

But is it not odd that our progress is restricted almost entirely to technical achievements? The sciences

---

*Numerals refer to the corresponding number in the References.

of the rational age have focused almost exclusively on the material world and have all too often relinquished any awareness of other realities that may concern the human race.

In every age people have believed that they have reached the pinnacle of what is humanly possible. At the end of the last century most scientists felt that nothing basically new remained to be discovered. They believed that all fundamental laws of nature were known; people who believed in things that could not be subsumed under the existing natural sciences were subjected to smiling condescension or to quiet, gentlemanly boycotts.

The nineteenth-century world view led to the neglect of—often attacks on—many realities we openly accept today. Hypnosis, for example, is no longer in dispute. Anyone who deals with the psychology of dreams need no longer fear being decried as a charlatan. We have long since come to take for granted the space rockets whose spiritual fathers, the pioneers Oberth and Goddard, were regarded as technical con men during the 1920s, when it was also held that the product of energy can never significantly exceed the output in coal burning.

The question is whether we have learned from the mistakes of our grandfathers. It does not look like it. Apparently, a hundred years is not long enough to fundamentally change mankind. It appears that every human being has an innate inertia which fights against anything that tends to lead him outside his accustomed trains of thought. Like most psychoemotional functions, this defense mechanism works quite unconsciously. A practicing psychologist and psychotherapist told me:

> Most people are only looking for confirmation of their attitudes, they don't want to learn. Even the psychopath who seeks out a psychotherapist doesn't want his attitudes changed, even though his false attitudes cause his difficulties. All of us are receptive to additional knowledge, but only if it does not conflict with our own basic views or call for entirely new ways of thought. Generally

we are barely aware that we are enslaved by our automatic thought patterns . . . This can be a considerable
obstacle to accepting ideas that call for a different mode
of thinking and new mental habits.

The person most strongly committed to very specific mental habits is the specialist, the authority in a
field. He knows like no one else what is possible in
his area. Therefore revolutionary new findings naturally meet with the most vehement opposition
from scientists working in the particular field, and it
is no accident that revolutionary discoveries are often
made by people with only relatively superficial
knowledge of the field, who take a bird's-eye view.

The discovery of nuclear fission—a process of nuclear *physics*—we owe to two *chemists*, Otto Hahn
and Fritz Strassmann. The actual experts in this field
had presented erroneous interpretations for four
years. Modern psychology received valuable impulses
from the cybernetic thought patterns created by en-
gineers and mathematicians. Sigmund Freud, the
founder of psychoanalysis and official discoverer of
unconscious psychic processes, was not a psychologist
but a medical doctor widely at variance with the
pure psychology of consciousness of his day.

Resistance to the young science of parapsychology
stems for the most part from official established
psychology. The most stubborn opponents of paramedicine may be found in the ranks of established
physicians, while many of its proponents come from
other scientific disciplines.

From the discoveries of Lister, Pasteur, and Robert
Koch in the last century to the modern chemothera-
pies and the use of laser beams, a single breathtaking
parade seems to march along. But many ailments
still linger on in spite of extensive use of the most
modern medical techniques. Many new illnesses have
appeared, which were never problematic before.

That established medicine has developed one-
sidedly is admitted by many doctors who are aware of
those avenues opened by, for example, psychosomatic
research. To this day it happens that patients are

treated for months, even years, at enormous cost in money and the most modern technical means but without success—until the patient experiences an astonishingly swift and lasting cure by a doctor using psychosomatic methods, a medical outsider, or a healer. Recall the successes of the French healer Maurice Mességué with herbal infusions. Many famous people—including even the judges who were forced to sentence him for healing without a license—sent him written testimonials.

Medical outsiders have always had a difficult time. Many physicians seem committed to the attitude that any method not theoretically justified within the contemporary status of medical science is quackery. The patient, on the other hand, will care less whether the method is already scientifically accepted.[199] The crucial factor for the patient will be whether he is taking a risk in employing a particular therapy and, finally, the success of the treatment. Therefore, are we ethically justified in ignoring or fighting methods—such as acupuncture and spiritual healing—which, pose no risk to the patient but have helped many a sufferer?

Besides official established medicine there is the extensive area of practical medicine. Some methods of therapy and diagnosis in this area have proven their usefulness in practical application, but it is not yet exactly understood how their effects are achieved. This realm includes homeopathy, founded at the beginning of the nineteenth century by the German physician Samuel Hahnemann; based on the principle of *similia similibus curantur* ("like is cured by like"), it is still not recognized by the prevailing tradition of allopathy.[74] There is also irisdiagnosis, established at the end of the eighteenth century by the Hungarian Dr. Ignaz Peczely;[116,117] it is still attacked by many men of medicine with passionate intensity.[196]

It is said that when he was a child, Peczely observed an owl breaking its leg while it clutched at the boy's arm; Peczely detected the development of some sign in the owl's eyes. This was the point of departure for irisdiagnosis, or eye diagnosis, which he later introduced. It has been employed by healers and various paraphysicians; it has led to astonishing diagnoses in a number of cases, but it requires a great deal of practical experience before it can give reasonably exact results. Interestingly, a number of Soviet physicians and scientists have kept an open mind on irisdiagnosis.[51]

Equally controversial is chirological diagnosis—diagnosis on the basis of particular markings on the hands or of the formation of the hands and fingers—a method that has also gone unexplained to this day.[14,107]

In the same way, practical healers have for years been utilizing the Chinese art of acupuncture,[55] which is still not taken seriously enough by official medicine. Many other methods belong in this category. Neural therapy,[53,54] developed in 1925 by Dr. Ferdinand Huneke, made possible instant cures in cases that had resisted all forms of therapy for years. Time and again, neural therapists note that scars can cause a variety of severe disorders at sites often far removed from the onetime seat of the dysfunction. Thus the German healer C. Dahn cured a patient of chronic renal colic, which had resisted all conventional treatment, by an injection of Impletol in an old scar.[179]

It is tempting to see certain parallels between neural therapy and acupuncture. In both, relatively simple or superficial treatment can effect cures in other parts of the body, even in internal organs. Though both are still surrounded by mystery, an explanation is forthcoming—not last, as will be shown, through the work of psi researchers, who are also on the trail of the phenomena of paramedicine, investigating all those methods of treatment and cure which cannot be explained. A system of determining acupuncture points on the skin by means of conductometric titration, for example, can contribute to acupuncture's becoming effectively incorporated into scientific medicine.

It is often held against researchers in psi healing

that, along with natural explanations, they offer supernatural ones. But the distinction between "natural" and "supernatural" has no place in scientifically practiced paramedicine and is probably a fiction based on the limitations of human thinking. Many things—if not, perhaps, everything—seem to suggest that the laws to be discovered by psi research are superordinate to the natural laws known so far: that is, the laws we have hitherto recognized will turn out to be special cases of superior laws.

Opponents insist that recognition of paranormal therapies would open the door to charlatanism. There are tricksters in every profession. But the best way to reduce quackery to a minimum would be an open-minded attitude by official medicine toward paramedicine, which draws more on observation and intuition and argues in terms of wholes and syntheses. The skilled physician stands somewhere *between* official medicine and paramedicine, for a good doctor must have more to show than purely rational-scientific qualifications. He also needs considerable intuition.

Intuition is often much more reliable than rational thinking on the road toward spiritual progress. Once they have been scientifically deciphered, many intuitively evolved methods of today's paramedicine may be conventional therapies of tomorrow.

2/THE LIMITS OF PSYCHOGENESIS

Reports of "miracle cures" are among man's oldest traditions. Prophets, founders of new religions, and saints have often sought to show spontaneous and spectacular healing of the sick. Hardly any para-medical process does not have precedents in the antiquity of the Near or Far East or in the Bible.

The laying on of hands on the affected part of the body was practiced on a large scale in ancient and early Christian times.[103,251] As medical science progressed, the method fell into disuse and, in the age of rational science, into disrepute; for Western medicine traced back to the "power of the imagination" all cures that did not fit the scheme of established medicine.

A patient's faith alone can bring about astonishing changes in physiological functions. The technical term for such manifestations is "psychogenesis." In one experiment people who claimed that coffee gave them coronary palpitations and insomnia were given intravenous injections of a solution of dextrose or sodium chloride. Told that the injections contained caffeine, the patients promptly experienced palpitations and had trouble falling asleep. Conversely, after they had been given a caffeine injection under the pretext that it was a sedative, most of them felt drowsy and fell asleep.

Pharmaceutical products, too, utilize the effect of the patient's expectations. Group experiments have tested the effectiveness of these products by administering the real drug to one group and treating another with a placebo, without the group's knowledge.

In many cases the outcome was positive, showing no difference between the effects of the genuine product and of the placebo. The patient's attitude of trust is enough to bring about an improvement in his condition; it may even effect a cure. Such successes primarily occur with purely functional disturbances, but organic ailments have also been relieved in this manner.

Modern psychosomatic medicine accepts that many organic illnesses have purely psychological causes—that is, arise from wrong emotional attitudes such as exaggerated, frustrated ambition; permanent anger that cannot be abreacted; constant fear of losses of some sort—any of these may bring on a great variety of illnesses.[170,308]

One young man experienced inexplicable paralytic symptoms in his right arm; it never crossed his mind that the mysterious cramps and paralyses were caused by his suppressed anger at his boss, whom he really wanted to punch in the nose. Physicians in the past were unable to recognize or admit such relationships. Over a hundred years ago, however, Samuel Hahnemann already suspected psychosomatic causes—and prescribed homeopathic medicines for the deleterious effects of anger, rage, and other negative emotions.[74]

Every responsible physician takes the interplay between our intellectual and emotional worlds and our physical bodies into consideration in prescribing treatment. A cure brought about *solely* by influencing the patient's emotional life or his belief that he will recover is a "psychogenic cure." How it works is still largely a mystery, which is why we must not explain away all such cures as psychogenic. Some inexplicable cures are more than conventional faith cures, even though an element of faith may contribute to the cure —such as the numerous cures at Lourdes, recognized as miracles by the Church as well as by doctors. Curing small children and infants of the most severe malformations can in no way be accounted for by the patients' will to believe.[81,224] Here we see a paranormal effect, not yet subject to scientific explanation, that has impelled both Eastern and Western psi researchers to engage in new ways of thinking. The same is true for the indisputable accomplishments of many so-called spiritual healers or healing mediums.[59,60] Spiritual cures can result from direct physical contact, but there is evidence of absent cures also.[59,60,179,295] We cannot entirely exclude a psychogenic component in most psi healing—and if the patient's faith increases the paranormal curative effect, it can only be to the good!

But in many instances the precondition of absolute faith is absent. In other cases that all scientists accept today, even the strongest faith cannot explain resulting bodily changes in the normal physiological way; the only way we can understand is to fundamentally revise our scientific assumptions and consider faith one of the strongest existing powers, which should be scientifically explored and described.

Experienced healers such as the American couple Ambrose and Olga Worral are convinced that the patients' attitude brings about not only psychogenic, but also psi cures which frequently occur quite independently of the patients' emotional attitudes, sometimes even among pronounced skeptics.[320]

During his life (he died in February 1972) Ambrose Worral cured a variety of disorders solely through laying hands on the affected area; in some cases this method even caused malignant growths to dissolve under his hands and the nidus of the disease to disappear entirely.[319,320] The same is true for his countryman Oral Roberts; for Harry Edwards, an Englishman; and for countless other healers the world over. They all believe that they transfer some kind of energy to their patients. They are as little in agreement on what constitutes this energy, however, as are the psi researchers who deal with this question.

The belief of ancient Indian and Chinese adepts in a mystical universal life-force or vital energy has such great significance for psi healing that we will devote a chapter to it. But allied manifestations can be

found in the animal magnetism discovered by Franz
Anton Mesmer, whose magnetic cures caused a great
uproar two hundred years ago.

Born in Weil, Mesmer earned his medical degree
and settled in Vienna in 1766, where he treated his
patients with steel magnets. He believed that he
had discovered a new natural agent which could be
transferred to many objects and could, as a universal fluid, be active in all living matter. He called it
animal magnetism, believing that it regulated the
development of diseases and their cure. Mesmer assumed that animal magnetism could be transmitted
from one person to another; for example, from physician or healer—the so-called magnetizer—to the
patient. He tried to transmit the magnetism by "stroking" the patient with his hands, both with and without
touching. Mesmer could show spectacular successes,
especially after he moved his practice to Paris. The
official medical establishment of his day, however,
would not accept the existence of animal magnetism
and—as it still does—minimized it as the result of
imagination.

Mesmer's practices have been maintained by
magnetizers or magnetopaths who attempt to transfer the life-force or magnetism to the patient by vertical strokes along his body to strengthen or cure him.
Many hypnotists still successfully make use of Mesmer's strokes—also called passes—with people resistant to hypnotic suggestion. This effect, too, the
opponents of mesmerism have tried to account for
psychologically.

Filipinos, some of whom are very sensitive, employ
a method similar to mesmerism for treatment. It is
probable that they did this long before any mi-
gration of ideas from Europe. It is astonishing and
inexplicable that many similar views and practices
have been preserved as traditional lore in so many
different parts of the world, where there can be no
possibility of contact until recently. Such "superstitious" practices may involve some concrete reality
which our sciences have not yet grasped but which

have been realized and utilized thanks to an extraordinary sensitivity or on the basis of natural senses or supersenses which have become largely vestigial in our civilization.[29]

In any case, the form of magnetic healing practiced in the Philippines—vertical stroking with the hands along the patient's diseased body—distinctly implies that more is involved than simple superstition.

Obviously Western and Philippine healers have this power to very different degrees. One American woman who was magnetized for phlebitis by the American chiropractor Nelson Decker, who happened to be in the Philippines at the time, reported that she experienced a sensation as if "thin threads" were being pulled out of her leg. This was followed by an improvement in her condition. Subsequently she consulted the Filipino healer Eleuterio Terte, who applied the same sort of treatment. But this time the patient had the sensation as if a "thick rope" were being pulled from her legs and an inexplicably rapid cure set in.[248]

In a similar case a complete cure was achieved even more abruptly. Whatever powers may have caused it were present in both healer and patient (the latter was herself a spiritual healer); though they varied in intensity from one to the other, they seem literally to add up. Toward the end of 1971 Sigrun Seutemann was investigating paranormal cures in the Far East. After overexertion she contracted a dangerous and painful case of phlebitis. When she arrived at Baguio Airport from Japan, she was dejected and did not know how to arrange her further stay. She had difficulty dragging herself to the taxi stand. She drove to her hotel and immediately sought out the native Philippine healer Tony Agpaoa. When he learned of her disorder, he simply laughed and told her there was no problem. He laid his hands on her legs, closed his eyes, and concentrated for several minutes. When he removed his hands, not only were the pains gone, but the inflammation seemed to have abated. After a quarter of an hour all discomfort and external signs of the inflammatory illness had disappeared, so that Sigrun Seutemann was able to walk completely normally. Nor did the condition recur.

This is an example of a typical paranormal cure, a cure through psi. Under ordinary conditions phlebitis cannot retreat completely in so short a time. Even if such a cure is brought about psychogenically, several hours would have to pass before the body's autonomous cure could take effect.

I have a report from Buenos Aires by Professor Federico Brosig about a patient with chronic sinusitis which resisted medical treatment. He heard of a "quack" Indian woman living in a miserable hut. A relative of Brosig's took the patient to see her. The entire treatment consisted of the Indian woman's laying her right hand on the patient's forehead and pressing on it and on the patient's nose for a considerable period. She then ordered the woman to go home and place damp, hot compresses on her forehead.

Only a few minutes after the first compress was applied, a quantity of evil-smelling pus began to flow from the patient's nose, ending finally in an outflow of solid substances. That finished the treatment; the illness, as it turned out, was permanently cured.

Healing through the laying on of hands has always been practiced among primitive peoples in the Americas, Africa, and Asia—but not only the laying on of *hands*, as the following example makes clear. Dr. G. L. Johnson of Durban, South Africa, was personally acquainted with the tribal chief Shembe from the nearby village of Ekupakameni. While Johnson, together with some Englishmen, was visiting Shembe, a native arrived with a message that a girl had been bitten by a poisonous snake and was at death's door. The whole group immediately proceeded to the wounded girl's hut. She still exhibited vital signs, but her arm was grossly swollen and infected. Shembe prayed fervently to his god in the shade of a nearby "holy tree," then returned to the girl and placed his foot on the paralyzed arm. To the great astonishment

of all the visitors, the youngster suddenly gave a start
and stood up. The onlookers saw the swelling and infection of the arm disappear as if by magic. At the
same time—so writes Dr. Johnson—they saw the
captured snake curl up and die.[29]

Anyone who rejects the assumption that an al-
mighty Being miraculously sent aid in answer to the
prayer under the holy tree will admit at least that absorption in prayer can be a means of collecting and
charging oneself with energy. Devout concentration
on a goal often awakens unsuspected powers, releasing effects that would not have been believed possible.

The following occurrence was reported by the late
Oscar Schellbach, a German psychologist and philosopher, midway through his life.

> When he was nine years old, my cousin Hans fell while
> playing and hit his shin against an iron scraper. Soon a
> swelling formed . . . and osteomyelitis set in. My uncle
> was beside himself, the doctors were insistent in their de-
> mand for an operation and possible amputation of the
> leg. During this time my uncle told his troubles to one
> of his fellow workers, a Baptist, who begged my uncle
> to come to a church service so that the whole congre-
> gation could pray for the boy. People will do anything
> for their children's health! So he went and prayed. From
> that very hour, all symptoms disappeared . . . the leg
> had healed without any outside help![226]

There is sufficient proof for the positive results of
praying someone back to health: documented cures
by adherents of Christian Science and other religious
congregations in North America and Europe, and in
Japan, the Seicho-Noe movement of Dr. Masaharu
Taniguchi, a form of psychic renewal which has reported sensational cures through group prayer.[271,272]
It is easy to explain such phenomena as the result of
suggestion or an "accidental cure." The easiest explanation, however, is not always the correct one. The

manifestations of animate nature do not cater to us by taking forms easily grasped by our reason.

In all probability absent cures without the patient's knowledge and a willingness to believe represent the greatest challenge to our reason. The Worrals and Harry Edwards have treated many patients on the basis of few or numerous brief contacts through letters with relatives of the patients. Air Force Major Günther E. Schwarz practices in Austria near Garmisch-Partenkirchen. Only a few patients seek him out in person; many only learned after their recovery that their families had written him. Among his outstanding successes is the cure of a young London secretary, Betty L., where he is said to have achieved—again without her knowledge—a spontaneous involution of a lymphatic cancerous tumor. Of every hundred follow-up letters that reach Major Schwarz, it is said, an average of fifteen thank him for a complete cure; over fifty report a definite improvement in the writer's condition; and about thirty claim no improvement.[179]

Absent cures automatically recall the mysterious remote effects of a contrasting kind as reported by ethnologists—"bewitching" in the context of black magic, voodoo, and similar arts. In these procedures healthy people are made ill, at times even killed. When I visited the Philippines, I was told there were witches in the little town of Rosales, on the island of Luzon. For an appropriate sum they will bewitch people whom the customer wishes ill. The affected persons, it is said, fall mysteriously ill and may even die. Such practices are not restricted to the Philippines; until the seventeenth century they occurred even in Europe. But today the centers of black magic are Java, Hawaii, the Philippines, Jamaica, and Brazil.

Without a doubt there are many impostors among black magicians, and the achievements of others can be accounted for by suggestion and hypnosis. For example, if someone knows he is being bewitched and

takes it seriously, he won't have to wait long for
symptoms to set in. Intensive autosuggestion can even
bring about a person's death.

The American dental surgeon Dr. Harry B. Wright
reports a case he witnessed in which a South American
medicine man exposed a member of his tribe as a
thief and sentenced him to eat a "death food." The
convicted person died even as he ate. But the food
was obviously not poisoned; for the medicine man
and other members of the tribe ate up the rest without any ill effects.[322]

Ethnologists and explorers report other cases which
cannot be subsumed under suggestion. There are
accounts of the "killing prayer" of the kahunas, or
tribal magicians, of Hawaii. Kahunas are traditionally
able to pray a person to death without his knowledge.
Max Freedom-Long, an American who studied the
kahunas on location after the First World War, reports the following authenticated experience of Dr.
William Tufts Brigham, curator of the Bishop Museum in Honolulu:

Brigham had spent years struggling to understand
kahuna magic and had befriended several genuine
kahunas. While Brigham was on a botanical expedition to the crater of Mauna Loa, one of the natives in
his crew, a strong young man about twenty years
old, suddenly fell ill. Quickly he became so weak that
he could not remain on his feet. Within a few hours
the patient's condition worsened without Brigham's
being able to determine the cause—until it occurred
to him that a killing prayer might be at work.

A kahuna killing prayer is said to result in initial
paralysis of the legs, which in a few hours spreads
upward until it reaches the heart and the victim dies.
In this case it was learned that the young man had
long ago forgotten that his tribal kahuna had in-
structed him never to have any dealings with white
men; he had left his home months before and had
assumed that the prohibition was not valid outside
his native village.

The doomed man's fellows demanded that Dr.

Brigham, whom they thought of as a big white kahuna, "send back" the killing prayer to the one who had enunciated it. Brigham was familiar with the practices and rituals of the kahunas; believing in the possibility of such effects, he decided to try. The exertion was terrible for him; sweat poured fom all his pores—but all at once he had the feeling of a monstrous tension being relieved. An hour later the patient was able to walk and eat. He recovered rapidly and the expedition could continue.

But the most interesting part came only when Dr. Brigham planned to visit the kahuna in question in his village. He found that on that very evening, at exactly the time when Dr. Brigham was sending back the killing prayer, the kahuna had jumped up from his sleep with a cry. Gasping and moaning he fell to the floor, lay there foaming at the mouth, and died that same night.[71]

This report has some common traits with the African tribal chief Shembe's healing of the snakebite. In that case too, the causal agent—the snake—was said to have died while the afflicted person was cured. Coincidence, slipshod reporting—or an actual event, though we are unable to interpret it?

A credible example from an entirely different culture comes from an article about shamans and medicine men by R. Koch. He recounts an eyewitness report from a Communist woman with a thoroughly materialist orientation who attended an incantation ceremony among North American Indians:

An Indian living far away had stolen all the traps belonging to a member of his tribe, which meant an irreplaceable loss for the victim. He sought out his tribes' medicine man and reported the matter. The following night—in the presence of the highly skeptical woman observer—the medicine man began his incantations.

What happened was downright uncanny. At first a number of voices, high above those in the tent, spoke and finally quarreled. The medicine man called on his animal spirits, the spirits answered in the same way.

And while horrible yowling, strong winds, and earth tremors rattled the tent, one could hear the growling of bears, the angry howling of wolves, and cries of other animals. Slowly the wild battle abated. The medicine man was totally exhausted.[112]

Hallucination, hypnosis, ventriloquist's tricks? Perhaps. But a short time later the wife of the thief arrived by sled and returned the stolen traps. Her husband had died—the very night of the ceremony.

3/FROM THOUGHT TRANSFERENCE TO ABSENT HEALING

Communication from one person to another without the use of the familiar five senses is generally accepted today, even by the sciences, in the form of telepathy. However, long before there was any scientific investigation of thought transference it was in practical use by primitives who employed it to transmit information over long distances.

Ethnologists have tried to explain the mysterious traffic in news among African primitives as a sort of Morse code using drums. Even before the Second World War, Professor Ernesto Bozzano of Genoa disputed this view through authenticated cases of telepathy among natives reported by European eyewitnesses.[29] The following account comes from Dr. G. B. Kirkland, government physician in Rhodesia when modern techniques of telecommunication were still unknown in that country.

A native was admitted to the hospital with a severely pierced liver; another native, under the influence of alcohol had knifed him. The wounded man asked Dr. Kirkland if he would live through the night.

The doctor answered openly and honestly that it was unlikely, whereupon the patient asserted that he wanted at least to see his family one more time. However, his relatives lived in a village fifty miles away. To reach it by uncleared jungle paths took a full nine hours.

There was no way to notify the family except by a messenger. The moribund man instead said that he

would "call upon" his kin. This was in the evening, at
sundown. The doctor guarantees that no drums were
used. Shortly before dawn the whole family, having
walked all night, arrived at their relative's deathbed.

The doctor who reported this incident should not
really have been so astonished, for by this time a number of "experimental investigations of mental suggestion" had already been carried out,[298] but "serious"
scientists had paid them little attention. One of the
first carefully documented experiments took place as
early as 1886, and the result can be considered sensational to this day. Pierre Janet, a highly regarded
French psychologist, and Dr. M. Gibert tried to hypnotize Léonie, a Breton farm woman, from distances
ranging from a quarter mile to a mile, without her
knowledge. Suspecting nothing, the farm woman was
at her home. Of twenty-five attempts nineteen were
totally successful; the others were partial successes or
gave inconclusive results. These experiments were
subsequently repeated and confirmed by a scientific
commission of respected authorities in Paris, with the
same subject and—as hypnotist—none other than
Charles Richet, a subsequent Nobel prizewinner in
medicine.

In the 1920s Russian scientists tackled these experiments anew. As soon became clear, the problem was
finding a suitable subject; not everyone can be hypnotized by just any hypnotist. In an investigation
of three hundred subjects it was found that only ten
or twelve were suited to telepathic hypnosis. Almost
all were hypersensitive and neurotic individuals.

Two Russian women, Ivanova and Fedorova, became famous for a number of significant experiments
conducted in the 1930s. The leader of the experimental series was the Leningrad physiologist Professor
Leonid Vasiliev, a pupil of the famous physiologist
Vladimir Bekhterev, who died in 1927.

The subject was placed outside the hypnotist's field
of vision, often in another room or even in a distant
village. At a moment not known to the subject, the
hypnotist began to suggest sleepiness by means ex-
cluding any communication by the normal five

senses. In doing so he tried with the greatest possible clarity to provoke sensations commonly experienced in the act of falling asleep and to combine these sensations with the image of Ivanova or Fedorova and then transmitted the order to fall asleep—all strongly reminiscent of the concentration exerted by absent healers on remote patients.

During Vasiliev's experiments a third person recorded the condition of the distant subjects. When the absent hypnosis had been effected, the hypnotist—again picking a moment unknown to the subject and the third person—began to suggest waking, proceeding in the same manner.

During 1933 and 1934, 260 attempts at telepathic hypnosis and waking were carried out.[298] Only 6 times was the hypnotist unable to put the subject to sleep, and only 21 times did hypnotic awakening fail. During the earlier attempts it took less than two minutes to put Fedorova to sleep, and she was awakened even more rapidly. For Ivanova the time spans were a little longer. Subsequently Federova's times worsened.

At the time nothing seemed more likely than a transfer directly from the hypnotist's brain to the brain of the subject, in the manner of radio waves; for technicians had recently developed the radio. During the 1920s, exposed dog brains were shown to contain various kinds of electrical potential, and in 1929 Hans Berger discovered the possibility of deflecting the brain's electric currents through the skull—a method that was further developed into electroencephalography (EEG).[298] If electrical currents of a vibratory nature can reach the surface of the skull, then it makes sense that electromagnetic waves and fields in the air around the human head can reach the brains of others.

No one doubted the Italian psychiatrist F. Cazzamalli when he "proved" the existence of mental radio waves with wavelengths from a decimeter to a meter.[38] In the years from 1923 to 1933 his work was seen as solid scientific confirmation of the electromagnetic theory of telepathic phenomena. Vasiliev

and his coworkers were also convinced that Cazzamalli was right, but they were disappointed when
they tried to reproduce Cazzamalli's experiments and
were unsuccessful with devices that would have indicated electromagnetic phenomena as carriers in the
telepathic process. They were forced to note that telepathic transference could not be interrupted by
physical screens which absorb electromagnetic waves.
For these experiments Vasiliev used cages with an
outer layer of steel and an inner layer of lead, the
joints being calked with mercury; their impenetrabili-
ty to electromagnetic waves had been tested by
means of electromagnetic generators and detectors.
One of two persons—either subject or hypnotist—was
placed in one of the cages; in other experiments hypnotist and subject were placed in different cages. If
the theory of "mental radio" was correct,[253] then
telepathic hypnosis would not work under these conditions. But Ivanova and Fedorova continued to respond to the mental suggestion of the hypnotist
through electromagnetic screening.

A further impressive phenomenon of telepathic
transference was its functioning over long distances.
The idea of direct conversation between a participant
in Berlin and another in New York by telephone was
utopian at the beginning of this century. Surely our
best physical detectors and the most complicated
combination of these devices are primitive compared
to more complicated biological systems,[4] especially
the human body.

On July 15, 1934, successful telepathic hypnosis
took place between Leningrad and Sevastopol on the
Black Sea, a distance of 1700 kilometers. At 10:10
p.m. Dr. L. A. Dubrovsky, in Sevastopol, began to concentrate on Ivanova, who was in Leningrad, and to
send her telepathic suggestions of sleepiness; at 10:11
p.m. the subject was noted to be in hypnotic sleep.
(Two days earlier, the Leningrad group had been
expecting a suggestion from Sevastopol between 5:00
and 7:00 p.m., but Ivanova gave no signs of sleepiness during this period. Subsequently it was learned

that, because of an indisposition, Dr. Dubrovsky had not carried out the mental transmission.)

Earlier researchers, decades before, had claimed to have observed cases of spontaneous telepathy across long distances. The British Society for Psychic Research had documented many such cases, among them one in which telepathic communication had taken place between one person in England and another in Australia.[298]

Such authenticated occurrences speak against the theory of electromagnetic transmission; normal electromagnetic effects decrease in intensity with the square of the distance. It follows that the intensity of a supposed electrical brain wave leaving a human brain in Leningrad must become unimaginably diminished on arrival in Sevastopol.

During the Apollo 14 mission to the moon, Captain Edgar Mitchell telepathically communicated card symbols to four people in the United States, one of whom was Olof Jonsson, a sensitive.[259] Many interesting and unexpected results were noted; further experiments of this sort need to be carried out. Mitchell carried out his in-flight experiments on his own initiative, alongside his official mission. According to Mitchell, as late as the fall of 1971 NASA was not interested in investigating psi phenomena, although such research would have required no significant additional expenditure. NASA is said to have rejected a telepathy program in the framework of the manned spaceflights, suggested by the American Society for Psychic Research.[300] The Soviet sector seems much more open-minded about these problems.

Many factors seem to indicate that telepathy and mental suggestion involve an entirely different principle, unknown to our rigorous sciences. The celebrated physicist Pascual Jordan, a hundred years ago, pointed out that parapsychology must renounce attempts at physical explanations of telepathy.

Apparently there really is such a thing as the influence of one person on the psyche of a recipient or percipient who is far away—without any of the scientifically acknowledged carriers, such as sound or light waves or radio waves.

In an experiment in a private group I attempted telepathically to transmit a headache to eight people. The subjects were expecting a mental suggestion but did not know what it would be. The test was carried out in the dark so as to exclude conclusions based on unconscious gestures and facial expressions. Within two or three minutes four or five people felt the onset of a headache; one, who was somewhat gifted psychically, experienced such an intense headache that a psychologist and psychotherapist who was present could make it recede only through counter-suggestion.

It is likely that sensitive people, having telepathically received such a negative sensation, autosuggestively continue it. And since the greatest effects are possible through autosuggestion, no basic obstacles remain in the way of so-called black magic. We do not know the limits of normal suggestion or autosuggestion—cases of death by autosuggestion have even been reported[225]—nor do we know the limits of mental suggestion. If it is possible to transmit negative suggestions in extrasensory ways, the same process should be possible for healing.

Healers claim that, confronted by a picture of an unknown patient, they can "adjust psychically" and take up psychic contact with him without knowing where he is. Absent healers allege that once the connection has been made, they often experience the situation of the ailing person, sometimes down to the smallest detail, and feel the disorders as if in their own bodies—for example, the Swiss healer Ludwig Rizzoli and the German healers Franz Luner and the late Dr. Kurt Trampler.[179,267]

Results of attempts at telepathy by Soviet researchers seem to confirm this. Their experiments with mental suggestion sought to determine if it is necessary for the hypnotist to know in what direction his subject is located if the latter is a considerable distance away. Anyone who believes in a physical ex-

planation of the phenomenon will assume that the
sender must direct his psychic power, like a directional antenna, to the proper cardinal point. However,
the experiments showed that it made no difference
whether the sender knew the whereabouts of the receiver; nor did the hypnotist need to have seen the
place in question.

On the other hand, there was a crucial necessity
for a "psychological directional orientation"; that is,
the hypnotist had to know *who* the subject was in any
particular experiment—which person was sitting in
the screening cage: Ivanova, Fedorova, or someone
else. If two receivers were present in the same place,
the mental suggestion worked only on the one on whom
the hypnotist had focused. Another person in the
same place never fell prey to the sender's mental suggestion. "The content of the suggestion to be transmitted," Vasiliev noted, "must be accompanied by
the *mental picture* of the person to whom the suggestion is to be transmitted."

It is for this reason that healers—if they do not
personally know the patient—normally require some
information about him, or a photograph, sometimes
also an object normally carried on his body. Often a
letter written by the patient is sufficient; but almost
always a picture is more effective.

In 1923–25 experiments in telepathy were carried
out between Paris and New York. Of twenty experiments, the successful five were ones in which the
sender and the receiver knew each other.[298] Now
and again, however, a sender "finds" a person entirely unknown to him, without a picture, on the
basis of his name and address. In such cases, however, the senders are exceptionally qualified sensitives.[71,72,258]

Quite often a healer engaged in absent healing
(or, quite generally, a sender engaged in any form of
telepathic communication) becomes aware of the moment when contact is made or when his purpose has
been achieved. This generally occurs after very ex-
hausting concentration and manifests itself as a sudden indefinable feeling of total, pleasurable relaxation,

combined with an inner certainty that a positive result has been attained or that the matter will take care of itself. Any anxiety, fear, or uncertainty disappears. The healer "knows," without knowing exactly how he knows, that the mental suggestion emanating from him has arrived. Anyone who has ever experienced this knows the feeling clearly and knows too that it has no equivalent in everyday feelings and ideas.

Just as the sender or healer often knows whether he has found his subject, the receiver or patient often becomes aware that a contact has been established. For example, Ivanova and Fedorova were able to identify who had sent them mental suggestions during tests involving more than one hypnotist.

Both the skills of the sender (healer) and the sensitivity of the receiver (patient) are crucial to a successful outcome. This probably accounts for the unusually uncertain prognosis in psychic healings, which depend not only on the healer but also on the psychic and parapsychic structure of the patient. There are many cases of patients suffering from the same disease who get different results from the same healer.

Generally speaking, the disposition for psi phenomena appears in varying degrees. If we do not notice certain phenomena or cannot produce them on demand, that is not to say that they do not exist. Western man's strength lies in the area of reason. The deeper, irrational layers of the subconscious are often largely atrophied among highly civilized peoples. Among cultures not yet so strongly intellectualized, however, these psychic areas are still active. Therefore, a good medicine man or kahuna with long years of training in magic can produce effects a Western scientist can neither replicate nor explain, but not in any way based on trickery.[71,72]

During the 1960s the Japanese scientist Dr. Hiroshi Motoyama investigated the "direct influence of the spirit" on the body of another person—eliminating all physical means and any inclusion of the known senses. In some ways his work represents a continuation of Leonid Vasiliev's experiments. Motoyama followed the usual course by placing two people in separate cages; one functioned as the receiver, the other as the sender. During one set of experiments the receiver was shielded from radio waves or similar electromagnetic rays by a Faraday cage. During the tests, highly sensitive apparatus was used to measure such physiological functions as breathing, cardiac activity, circulation, and the autonomic nervous system (especially the interplay between sympathetic and parasympathetic functions) in the receiver, as well as occasionally in the sender. Brain waves were recorded by encephalography. Heart and circulatory functions were monitored by plethysmography—that is, by measuring the volume of blood in the peripheral veins—and occasionally by electrocardiography. The sympathetic and parasympathetic functions of the internal organs were determined by measuring electrical skin waves. (There is no room here to go into technical details of research carried out over a period of several years.[161,162])

The subjects were all paranormally gifted: Indian yogis and the Philippine healer Antonio Agpaoa, as well as so-called normal people, mostly students from Japan and India. All were lying down in relaxed positions or adopted yoga positions of rest. The sender was given a signal by Motoyama to concentrate on the person stationed in the other room and to direct "psychic force" at him.

As soon as the gifted sender concentrated on the receiver, significant, sometimes very intense changes generally began to occur in the measurements of the receiver's bodily functions—for example, in the breathing rhythm, which returned to normal only when the sender ceased his concentration. Further, an excitation of the recipient's sympathetic nervous system was noted, which subsided twenty to thirty seconds after the sender ceased concentrating. The plethysmographic findings during concentration made it clear that the receiver's heart began to beat more quickly and more shallowly, with lessened amplitude.

Other functions also showed significant alterations. Of course their severity depended on the particular training of the subject and on his paranormal
capabilities. Thus, when Agpaoa concentrated on the
recipient, the recipient's breathing became more rapid; but when a highly gifted yogi did the same, the
recipient's breathing slowed. Parallels in the enceph-
alographic recordings between the sender's concentration and the receiver's reaction were also noted.

The influence of the sender on the physiological
functions of the receiver was strongest in the breathing process, followed by changes in cardiac and
circulatory activity; in third place was the effect on
the sympathetic nervous system.

Similar experiments were made at approximately
the same time by Russian scientists. One Soviet experiment is very interesting in this context: a mother
rabbit was deprived of her newborn offspring, and
the young rabbits were placed in a submarine far below the surface of the ocean, beyond any possibility
of radio contact. The mother rabbit was on land, in a
laboratory, where her brain waves were monitored by
electrodes implanted in her skull. The young rabbits
on the submarine were killed one by one; each time
one of the rabbits was killed, changes in the mother's
encephalograph were clearly observed. The instruments precisely registered the instant of death of each
of her young.[184] (It is impossible not to be reminded of
reports from periods of war of mothers sympathetical-
ly experiencing the deaths of their sons at the front.)

As was to be expected, Dr. Motoyama also determined that, the quality of the sender being equal,
the effect of any paranormal transmission on the receiver was strongest when the receiver was not a
"normal" but a paranormally gifted individual.[162] The
extent of this latent talent varies widely. Therefore
individuals with psychic tendencies will ordinarily respond much more strongly to paranormal methods of
therapy and surgery than individuals without psi
talent.[161,162]

Dr. Motoyama has proved that the physiological
effects described above are particularly strong when

the recipient's autonomic nervous system is such that the sympathetic and parasympathetic nerves are in balance, but the parasympathetic system wields a slightly stronger influence. Presumably these conditions are favorable to the emergence of psi phenomena. Further, Motoyama investigated the physiological characteristics of paranormally gifted people as compared to those of "normal" people and those of the mentally ill. Without going into detail, within the autonomic nervous system the neural functions of the various internal organs—such as the heart, lungs, and kidneys—have a greater autonomy and independence from each other in strongly paranormally gifted people.

During many of his feats the Brazilian Carlos Mirabelli,[82] probably one of the most powerful mediums of this century, increased the frequency of his heartbeat to 150 to 200 per minute and more, after which his pulse fell to 40 per minute and below. That is, he behaved in a manner which a physician would have to call pathological, but no harmful effects set in. *Genuine paranormal feats thus have nothing to do with pathological states*—a realization that, unhappily, is still not very widely adopted.

It is interesting that the original Indian yoga training includes exercises that lead to an increase in several physiological functions. Hatha-yoga begins with breathing exercises which often aim at an extremely long holding of the breath, which can result in physical damage if certain rules are not observed. Dr. Motoyama tells of one Indian yogi who was able to "stop" his heart voluntarily for as long as six seconds. His electrocardiogram, taken at the University of Rajasthan in northwestern India, clearly showed the abnormal slowing of the heartbeat. In a normal individual, a heart stoppage of this duration could be fatal.[163]

Dr. Motoyama first observed the psychic healers in the Philippines in 1966. He brought along his instruments for recording encephalograms, plethysmograms, the breathing process, and galvanic skin waves. He was especially eager to test Agpaoa. It took Motoyama a full hour before the Filipino, lying on a couch, was properly connected up to the instruments. After Agpaoa's physiological functions in a state of relaxation had been recorded, he was asked to concentrate on his healing powers. Immediately the apparatus broke down and could not be repaired. The experiment had to be stopped.

Agpaoa laughed, not without malice, and said, "I'm sorry your equipment broke." Then he pointed to his hands and added, "Mine never breaks."

To this day Motoyama is not sure whether the equipment failed because of a sudden overload from Agpaoa's extraordinary concentration or because of a direct psi effect on the machinery—as has sometimes been observed in paranormal situations[21]—or whether an ordinary short circuit coincidentally set in just at the moment when Agpaoa concentrated most strongly. A similar case was reported to the author concerning an American healer. A subsequent repetition of the experiment in Tokyo persuaded the Japanese researcher of the healer's enormous power of concentration and proved that his physiological functions ran their course quite differently from those of "normal" people.[159,163] The unusual physiological functions of the paranormally gifted are only one aspect of the problem, and perhaps only the periphery of more wide-ranging changes which cannot be measured, since we still lack the proper detectors.

Telepathic rapport probably influences our interpersonal relations to a degree that we do not consider possible today. Probably telepathic waves are in constant flow among individuals, even when the contents do not become conscious. They are nevertheless somehow caught physiologically and brought into play for the work of the unconscious in forming judgments and generating feelings. However, extrasensory awareness or the telepathic rapport between people ordinarily represents only a tiny fraction of the communication established by way of the normal senses; under special conditions, on the other hand, extraordinary effects can appear which we regard as "miracles"—or shrug off and ignore as "fraudulent."

Extrasensory contact in normal life is likely to be inextricably interwoven with the five senses; especially among individuals who have a strong spiritual bond, such contact is often very intense.

It may also appear strongly between doctor and patient. It probably represents a considerable factor in the practice of every good physician. This recalls the experiments with placebos. Pseudomedications very often produce strong effects if the patient takes them in the belief that he is being given genuine and effective medication, but the placebo effect is especially strong if the doctor or nurse administering the placebo is unaware of the medication's true nature. (We call such tests double-blind experiments.) This suggests strongly that the parapsychic component in the rapport between doctor and patient varies from case to case, and that a good physician must be able to employ more than solid medical expertise.

It is probable that telepathy plays a much greater role than most psychotherapists are aware of. Hans Naegeli-Osjord, a Swiss doctor, told me about one interesting case that happened to him during a psychoanalytic session with a patient.

During psychoanalysis[30,47] the patient lies on a couch; the analyst generally sits out of sight, at the head of the couch. One day Dr. Naegeli-Osjord, suffering from hay fever, had taken some antihistaminic medication, and during the session he had to fight a sudden attack of drowsiness. Having nevertheless dozed off for a split second, he sought to bridge the gap by asking about the dream the patient was reporting to him; he asked what the lady in the blue coat had done. The analysand was extremely surprised by the question, since he had not yet mentioned this "dream figure." The unmentioned dream element had been telepathically perceived when the doctor sank into his own unconscious for a short moment.

It can be assumed that such psychic transmissions

represent curious exceptional manifestations, with no practical significance. Some university parapsychologists believe that telepathy represents only an infinitesimal, more or less ineffectual element. This view has perhaps been reinforced by the Zener card tests practiced in the West for decades to investigate telepathy. These tests have shown that some people have scores above what the laws of probability dictate; for example, of twenty-five cards, with an expected result of five correct guesses, they correctly guess seven or eight over a long run. In comparison to the theoretical potential of twenty-five "corrects," this seems very little, and it is easy to conclude that telepathy is only a marginal manifestation.

However, it is questionable whether the usual telepathic card tests result in a reliable quantitative picture of the subject's extrasensory gifts. Many people with outstanding paranormal talents have achieved only relatively meager results in card tests. Experimental conditions differ markedly from situations that allow telepathic manifestations to appear spontaneously in daily life.

In 1973 Harold Sherman, president of the ESP Research Associates Foundation in Little Rock, Arkansas, participated in telepathic experiments with the North Pole explorer Sir Hubert Wilkins, supervised by the renowned Professor Gardner Murphy of Harvard. Sherman successfully received telepathic messages in New York which Wilkins was sending him from the North Pole purely in the form of thought messages. But Sherman's scores in card tests fell far short of what might be expected—because, in his words, he could not take such sober scientific tests very seriously. In his daily life, on the other hand, extrasensory perception has saved his life on at least two occasions.[244]

Extrasensory rapport seems to appear especially strongly in groups. In such situations an enormous reinforcement of telepathic transmission may take place. A group in harmony with each other is something like a new unit, a new individuality. A person behaves quite differently in a group; he has feelings which, left alone, he was not aware of, and he takes actions he would not have taken as an individual.

Every psychologist accepts the fact that man in the mass is much more suggestible than the individual. Rabble-rousers and demagogues know all about the value of psychic transmission in the mass, which proliferates almost like a psychic infection—sometimes more quickly than would be possible through the five senses. Many a person who has gone to a political rally with a strongly antagonistic attitude has—in spite of his logical arguments to the contrary—felt an irresistible force which threatens to carry him along. Perhaps parapsychology will one day be able to explain why mass psychology cannot be derived from the psychology of the individual. Just as actors are capable of far better performances in front of enthusiastic audiences than when they perform to apathetic ones, the paranormal abilities of mediums often come to the fore much more strongly in sympathetic groups than in the sanctum sanctorum of a laboratory. Kathryn Kuhlman has held religious mass meetings in Los Angeles with spectacular demonstrations of healing. She often calls up a stranger from the crowd, makes a correct diagnosis, and then calls out to the sick person: "You are healed! You are healed!" Such sensational cures occur that it is difficult to account for all of them by autosuggestion.[122,251,257] On the other hand, a harmonious group can be disrupted by a single individual who does not fit in. This person may disturb the group image as a whole, as can be objectively proven by measurements of the physiological functions of the group's members.[184]

Investigations by Soviet researchers proved that their mediums' effects diminished sharply or were totally absent when persons skeptical or hostile to the medium attended the demonstrations. The prize Soviet medium, Nina Kulagina, has developed the power to psychically "freeze" overly suspicious observers. In a Moscow medical institute, in the presence of six physicians, she speeded up the heartbeat

of one doctor, the most skeptical among them, to
such an extent that he fainted.[98]

This remains an exceptional achievement. The psychic force fields of everyone present affect the medium's subconscious like the strongest mental suggestion
—and after all, it is the medium's subconscious that
stimulates paranormal activity.[163] If dyed-in-the-wool
skeptics are present, they may totally block the emergence of the paraphenomenon, always influencing it
to a greater or lesser degree.

Mediums holding private séances with sympathetic
participants or under the control of understanding
scientists have achieved stupendous results, whereas
the same mediums had only poor results or none
when monitored by "strictly scientific" and negatively
prejudiced examiners prepared only to discover the
"trick." It is not even very important what the observers are thinking; the convictions stored in their
subconscious work on the medium, for people think,
feel, experience, and live out of the totality of their
subconscious and not on the basis of a passing conscious thought.[223]

We are only on the threshold of exploring the many
methods of communication among living beings, but
as early as the 1920s Vladimir Bekhterev, working
with the famous animal trainer Vladimir Durov, investigated the phenomenon of telepathy between
man and animal. Durov mentally suggested certain
motions to his dogs. His constant dealings with animals of every kind had persuaded him that trained
animals often carry out tasks about which the trainer
has only been thinking.[184,298]

Spiritual contact between man and animal can
arise in ways that are more human than animal—even
on the animal's part. Many dogs spend hours or days
whimpering after the death of their master, though
there was no way for anyone to tell them of the event.
The bottle-nosed dolphin exhibits traits and characteristics we tend to view as typically human: affec-
tion, friendship, helpfulness. Dolphins are known to
rise from the depths of the ocean and invite humans

to play. A two-thousand-year-old legend seems to be hard fact now: dolphins have saved shipwrecked individuals from death by drowning.[86] It seems likely that communication between man and animal involves much more psi than had heretofore been supposed.

In 1968–69 Cleve Backster reported some singular discoveries, which he had made some time earlier, about plants. It was part of Backster's professional duties to instruct members of government agencies in the use of electronic lie detectors (polygraphs). One day it occurred to him to use such an instrument for experiments with plants. More specifically, he wanted to know how long it takes water to rise from the roots to the leaves in one of his plants, a species of agave. Since the lie detector, among other things, measures electrical conductivity in the human body, Backster connected two of the detector's electrodes to a plant leaf and expected a rise in electrical conductivity with the rising of the water in the plant. The polygraph showed peculiar reactions; in a human being they would indicate violent emotional swings.

When people are threatened, the polygraph generally shows a strong reaction. For this reason Backster arrived at the idea of threatening his plants. He dipped a leaf in a cup of coffee—no reaction. He played loud music—no reaction. Finally he thought, "I'll burn the damn thing." At that instant the polygraph attached to the plant registered a very violent reaction. Running a burning match along the plant also led to "extreme agitation." Further, the polygraph registered a strong reaction when Backster's dog came into the room.

Backster killed some shrimps near the plants, and the polygraph needle jumped. It really looked as if plants have emotional faculties and memory; for, according to Backster, he was able to condition them with Pavlovian reflexes. The Russian biophysicist Viktor Adamenko apparently goes so far as to consider that plants which have "witnessed" a killing will be able to "recognize" the murderer among other persons.[4]

Backster cultivated the psychic rapport between himself and his plants over a period of time through loving care; like telepathy, this rapport is said to have worked across considerable distances. Judging from the polygraph records, events in Backster's daily life appeared to affect the plants' feelings.

Cleve Backster was well known to be a professional skeptic, a specialist in lie detection who could not be fooled; nevertheless, his first accounts of communication with sensible plants were met with ridicule. But the scornful voices were stilled soon thereafter, when American and Soviet researchers began to look into the Backster effect. Since then more than a thousand laboratory experiments have shown, among other findings, that plants react when a fertilized egg is broken in their vicinity or when a wound on a human body is treated with an antiseptic. The polygraphs register the fact that plants "call out," "faint," are "pleased," and so forth.

We should also mention experiments carried out in the late 1960s involving Ambrose and Olga Worral and conducted by Dr. Robert H. Miller, a chemist. In a laboratory in Atlanta, Georgia, the standard growth rate of leaves of rye grass was established with a mechanism devised by Dr. H. H. Kleuter of the U.S. Department of Agriculture. Roughly six hundred miles away, in Baltimore, Maryland, the Worrals concentrated on the plants at an agreed-upon time —9:00 p.m.—calling up a mental image of luxuriant growth. At the same time the plants' growth rate began to increase by more than 800 percent, the acceleration lasting for several hours.[149] Previously other investigators had made similar experiments using other groups of healers. They had achieved increases, but not of this magnitude. Nor did their experiments have the same scientific rigor as Miller's.

To sum up, everything points to a relationship connecting all animate matter, and the existence of an information-transmitting energy which may prove to be identical with or related to the energy from which psychic healers and surgeons draw their strength.

4/PSYCHIC DIAGNOSIS

Just as in established medicine, psi diagnosis precedes psi healing. One of the methods of diagnosis is telepathic sounding of the patient's bodily functions and disorders. In contrast to mental suggestion, the healer plays the role of the active recipient. The term here is "telemnesis."[29] A highly gifted healer will be the active receiver in paranormal diagnosis, while in healing procedures he will be the active sender. Telemnesis allows not only the reception of the transitory content of the conscious—that is, whatever the other person happens to be thinking—but also the telepathic grasp of whatever information is stored in the subject. The informational content of the subconscious can—or so it seems—be tapped by telemnesis.

In the view of many researchers, the subconscious is not a strictly scientific reality, but a purely psychological construct.[218] But as a practical working concept the subconscious has proved extraordinarily serviceable. Activating the subconscious can release unsuspected powers in an individual, suggesting that this psychological construct must be supported by reality, even if we cannot give it a scientific definition yet. But in strictly scientific terms, we are not yet able to understand even the conscious mind.

Man's psychic life has often been compared to an iceberg, of which only the tip is visible. The greater part of our psychic life runs its course in areas which lie *outside* our consciousness, in areas still unplumbed whose possibilities are still unsuspected.[170,171,225,226]

The subconscious is the storehouse of information and memory for all our experiences, emotions, and perceptions. Events that occurred years ago are by no means totally forgotten; given the right circumstances, they may be brought back to the surface of consciousness in association with some new event.

The habits, the many little acts we carry out automatically and without reflection, are brought about by the activities of the subconscious. Everything that we have learned and that seems to proceed automatically is guided by the subconscious. Even the simplest procedures, such as standing or walking, are ordered by the subconscious before they run their automatic course. All learning is, at bottom, training by the subconscious. Even the processes psychologists call conditioned reflexes are the automation of an unconscious process that cannot be directly influenced by the will.

But it also often seems that the subconscious contains a kind of knowledge beyond what we have absorbed in this life, that was already extensively present at birth. The subconscious largely directs the functions of the internal organs, such as the activities of the stomach or the secretions of the salivary glands. We are not dealing with purely mechanical-physiological functions, since these processes are so easily influenced by psychic-spiritual factors—that is, by ideas and thoughts. The sight of a hair in the soup can instantly block the secretion of the salivary and abdominal glands; in particularly sensitive people it can even produce nausea.

We are still not sure how the relationship between psychic-spiritual and physiological body reactions works. But there are numerous signs that every subconscious contains a powerful intelligence center that controls the body's biological processes, an organic unconscious that is informed about every detail of one's own body, including latent diseases that go unnoticed by the conscious awareness. This knowledge does not reach the conscious self—at least *not yet*.

A search has been made for techniques to reach the information stored in the deep layers of the psyche—with varying results. One way to appeal to one's own subconscious is the pendulum.[129] To a

thread 4–8 inches long is attached an object generally made of metal; brass is most often used. The
subject takes the thread between his thumb and index
finger and rests his elbow on a firm surface so that
the pendulum can swing freely. Various meanings—
such as yes and no—are assigned to the different directions of swing. Then questions are put to the
subconscious, and the person waits without consciously affecting the movement of the pendulum.

In general the subconscious announces itself un-
aided. The pendulum begins to swing in a particular
direction. The movement of the pendulum ordinarily
comes about through unconscious muscular movements called ideomotor movements; they may well be
the expression of the subconscious as it tries to bring
itself to the attention of the conscious self by way of
minute muscular motions. This is neither magic nor
superstition; it only shows that the subconscious
"thinks" and judges and wants to answer the questions of the conscious self. That does not mean that
the answers must invariably be correct. Lack of training in this technique of questioning, wishful thinking
on the part of the operator, insufficient elimination of
the conscious self, and a series of other factors can
distort the outcome. But with increased training, increasingly better results can be achieved.

The American expert on hypnosis Leslie LeCron
has described an interesting pendulum experiment.
Given the unconscious's presumably enormous capacity for knowledge, the experiment set out to determine whether a pregnant woman's subconscious
knows the sex of her unborn child. For the experiment, 402 women were introduced to the technique
of consulting the subconscious through the use of the
pendulum, and they "swayed" for the sex of the unborn child. In 360 cases the sex was correctly predicted. This is unusually convincing, for it amounts to
90 percent accuracy, where only 50 percent correctness is expected. Incorrect results were probably
brought about by the women's wishful thinking. In
three cases twins were said to have been correctly
predicted, even as to sex.[129]

Some diagnostic psychics are able to establish telepathic contact with the organic unconscious of others
and to elicit information from it—a frequent form of
paranormal diagnosis. The healer directs his thoughts
to the patient. The patient may be there or at a considerable distance. The German healer Dr. Kurt
Trampler[136,267] has stated: "I think about the patient and try to feel myself completely into him. Soon
after I adopt this mental attitude, I start to feel the
patient's disturbances in my organism. I feel his
pain, his ailments. I know the seat of the causes of
his illness."[179]

This phase of telepathic reception is immediately
followed by the phase of influencing the patient,
reminiscent of mental suggestion. Dr. Trampler continues: "The healing process in the patient begins at
once, and I can feel it as well."

In establishing the first contact between healer and
patient, sympathy and antipathy are crucial. Agpaoa
stresses again and again the importance of the patient's full trust in the healer. Whenever he had
difficulty in establishing nonverbal informational contact, he held a medallion between thumb and
forefinger and stared at it while pondering specific
questions. The answers were given to him by his
subconscious in the form of a visual impression: his
thumb, pressed against the medallion, changed color
for him. Different colors held different meanings. In
principle this is a variant of the pendulum method,
except that the subconscious selected other ways and
symbols to make itself understood.

More recently Agpaoa has taken his bearings from
auralike colorations of the patient, which he claims to
perceive, in combination with colors that appear
around his own fingers when he brings them close to
the diseased parts of the patient's body. But his subconscious communicates with him not only through
optical impressions, but also by a sensation in his
fingertips. He claims that when he passes his hands
over the patient's body at a distance of an inch or so,
he "feels" the diseased area and "knows" what the
trouble is. Manila healer Juan Blance goes so far as

to "see" the diseased organ. The capacity to utilize visual imagination is a regular part of the training for psychics and healers in the Philippine Spiritist churches.

Professor Hans Bender discusses the case of Mrs. S., who also identified diseases by paranormal methods. "At the beginning of her activities, before she possessed any kind of medical knowledge, she diagnosed a patient in whose case there was absolutely no reason to expect a positive reaction to the Wassermann test (though such a reaction was later confirmed); she reported that she could detect small, waxy, glassy, corkscrew-shaped formations in his spinal fluid."[18]

Considerable telemnesic skill is also possessed by Helga Kramer. Whenever a new patient comes to her, she takes his hands in hers and concentrates. In a short time she experiences the manifest disorders as well as latent diseases of the patient in her own body. These may range all the way from headaches through chest pains, heartburn, and rheumatism to cold feet. In many cases, she can sense special drugs and medications that have been absorbed by the patient in noticeable quantitites (such as penicillin), as well as poisons (nicotine among them). From the way she experiences the complaints in herself, she believes herself capable of deducing useful hints concerning therapy. When the consultation is finished, she must, as she puts it, "shake off" the empathized complaints, at which she always succeeds with ease. We cannot make any statements on the reliability of her diagnoses, since scientific data are not available. But the healer naturally verifies her paranormally received findings by consultations of a conventional nature.

Another interesting facet is Kramer's music test, as she calls it. She sits down at the piano. A subject—a person not previously known to her—puts his hand on her medulla oblongata. After a short time she plays an improvised melody that musically expresses the temperament and mood of the person in question. The procedure further allows some very surprising but generally applicable assertions to come out. One

may disagree on whether we are dealing with telepathic tapping of the organic unconscious or with
clairvoyance—but we know even less about what
clairvoyance is all about than we do about telepathy.

Perhaps the greatest master of psychic diagnosis
was the American Edgar Cayce, who died in 1945.
In order to diagnose, he put himself to sleep. In this
condition his subconscious seemed capable of establishing a psychic connection with anyone and of draw-
ing information from the organic unconscious of others.
His subconscious generally expressed itself directly, and he spoke in his trance. He made accurate
diagnoses for his patients, most of whom were not
present but had asked his advice by letter—often
from other continents—just as most absent healers only rarely encounter their patients face to face.

After awakening, Cayce knew nothing of what he
had said in his sleep. In a waking state he was unable
to diagnose or make predictions—that is, there was
no contact between his subconscious and his conscious
self. He had absolutely no medical training and no
understanding of the technical terms he used in his
trance. Often he uncovered causal connections among
various disorders that had gone unrecognized by physicians in spite of the most thorough examinations but
which were subsequently confirmed.[258] Many books,
articles, and doctoral dissertations have been written
on the "sleeping prophet," but Dr. Harmon Hartzell
Bro has given a thorough and generally readable analysis of the principle of Cayce's readings:

A typical medical reading began with an evaluation of the
severity of the disorder which had caused the patient
to consult him. Then the reading passed on to the critical point of the body's malfunction—an infection,
injury, or some other abnormality. Sometimes this point
was quite different from what the patient or physician
had expected; thus Cayce localized the critical site of
epilepsy in the lower abdomen and only secondarily
in the brain. He sought out the fundamental diseases
of the body as if he were studying a whole stack of

X rays and laboratory reports and not as if he were lying asleep on a couch, often hundreds of miles away from the patient . . . .

Commonly he continued by going through the most important bodily systems, mentioning their history for the patient in question, in addition to their current functions and even the specific symptoms, as well as the feelings they communicated to the patient at a particular time of day or night. He made it a principle to describe how each system contributed to the malfunction or disturbance of another, and he often declared emphatically that it was necessary to treat the whole person, not simply a given set of symptoms with some arbitrary medical name.

First he examined the circulatory system—the circulation of the blood and the lymph glands. He seemed to have no difficulty in furnishing statistics of blood counts, toxins in the bloodstream, blood pressure, focuses of infection, or constrictions in the arterial system. He examined the function of endocrine glands and their effect on the blood, blood sugar, and microorganisms. (He could even describe how such a microorganism looked under the microscope.)

Then he went on to the nervous system, first the cerebrospinal and then the autonomic, and described any damage or irregularities. If any sense was functioning abnormally, he explained how and why. He also mentioned reaction times, patterns of pain, and excessive or insufficient stimulation of any bodily part. When desirable, he isolated specific nerves and ganglia and demonstrated their precise position and function in the body.

Next Cayce addressed himself to the most important organic systems. He examined the condition of the brain, followed by the breathing mechanisms, from nose to lungs, registering typical patterns of congestion, alluding to any history of tuberculosis; when appropriate, he indicated the results of X-ray examinations. He continued with the heart, its circulatory system, and the oxygen content of the blood. Cayce effortlessly made statements about the pulse, the functions of the cardiac valves, deposits in the heart and the cardiac region,

and any history of heart disease. Next he investigated
the complete digestive system, from mouth to elimina-
tory organs. He often examined the acid-alkaline
balance, peristalsis, liver and pancreatic secretions,
elimination, and renal function. The sexual organs as
well as the uterine apparatus were examined when
advisable, and special attention was given to the functions of the endocrine glands as well as the allied
questions of metabolism and the body's capacity for
growth and recuperation.

At this stage Cayce had generally been speaking for
half an hour or longer in an unconscious state. It was
time for him to move on to complicated questions of
treatment, to which he devoted himself with the same
thoroughness, for he insisted on structuring a program
for the patient's cure that would remove the causes of
the disease, not just the symptoms.[31]

Compared with the activities of Edgar Cayce, the
radiesthetic method of paranormal diagnostics seems
altogether conventional. Healers all over the world
have always attempted to locate the nidus of a disease by letting their outstretched hands glide over
the body at a distance of an inch or so and concentrating on the "vibrations." On occasion they will
make use of the pendulum—like the celebrated
French healer Maurice Mességué[140]—or of a divining
rod, like the German practitioner Jósef Angerer.
Though such aids are not essential if the healer is
sufficiently sensitive, they do seem to increase the
effect. Some healers use this method to detect irregularities in the force fields of the body, enabling them
to locate a nidus. Even when the site of the infection
is obvious, as in the case of an external growth, the
method may facilitate a judgment of whether it is
benign or not. Among the Philippine healers this is
the most commonly used form of diagnosis.

Often there is no way to compare the diagnoses of
healers and established physicians, since paranormal
healers often do not give the kind of diagnosis that
satisfies a conventional physician. They simply locate the sites of the disturbance and recognize their

connection with other bodily areas—especially with
the psychospiritual realm.

We must consider that mental suggestion and telemnesis really exist; but this is not to say that we
understand them or can explain them scientifically.
Paranormal healing phenomena cannot be compre-
hended on the basis of our established scientific concepts. Radically new assumptions are required before
we can explore a form of energy which may play a
decisive role in every part of the animate world.

5 / ACUPUNCTURE:
A PSI PHENOMENON?

The presence of a new biological energy not yet accounted for by Western science has often been postulated.[71,72,318] Eastern, especially Far Eastern, cultures believe in such a life energy. However, note that until 1896 scientists knew nothing of radioactivity although it has existed since long before there was terrestrial life.[73]

Ancient Chinese doctors believed in a life energy or vital energy coursing through the body—*ch'i*; its flow was said to keep the body alive, and it manifested itself in two forms: yin and yang.[55] Disruptions in the flow of this all-motivating force were said to cause disease and pain. As long as five thousand years ago, Chinese sages are said to have developed a form of medical treatment based on this cosmological philosophical system: acupuncture.

According to Chinese tradition, the vital energy flows vertically through the body in twelve or more main channels, or meridians, which are in no way identical with the nerve trunks traversing the body.[23,24] Along these meridians lie a great many points; Chinese acupuncturists are familiar with about eight hundred. On each point the stream of vital energy can be influenced through puncture, pressure, or moxibustion; when disturbances are present, the energy stream's balance can be restored—causing the disease to disappear. (In moxibustion certain dried herbs are heaped around the inserted needle and burned on particular acupuncture points; in the process the needle becomes red-hot without the skin's being burned.[192])

The insertion of thin needles at particular points of

the body's surface can influence diseased organs in distant parts of the body. The most astonishing aspect of acupuncture—the reason why it has aroused so much attention in the West—is its ability to completely alleviate pain, often for several hours, simply by the insertion of two or four needles (sometimes only one) at a point on the skin generally far away from the locus of pain. Even the most difficult operations can be carried out with acupuncture anesthesia. The patients retain full consciousness. Sometimes they get up right after the operation and walk out of the operating theater unassisted.

"I have seen more acupuncture than I can logically deal with. While watching these procedures, scientific reason steadily tells me, 'My God, that can't be true.' But you go on standing there and watching. I'm still not clear in my mind how acupuncture works, but I have to admit that there's something real about it." So declared world-renowned heart specialist Professor E. Gray Dimond after his return from the People's Republic of China in October 1971. Together with another heart specialist, Dr. Victor Sidel; Dr. Paul Dudley White, at one time personal physician to President Eisenhower; and Dr. Samuel Rosen, an authority in the field of otology, Dimond was a guest of the Chinese medical society. What interested him most were operations that relied exclusively on acupuncture anesthesia.

He was present at ten such operations. One was performed on a Chinese surgeon suffering from tuberculosis. In front of Dimond's eyes, a 1½-inch needle was inserted into the patient's left arm. No other anesthesia was administered. While the patient was lying on the table, clearly fully conscious and free of pain, the surgeons removed the upper half of his left lung. "The patient's thorax gaped wide open," Dr. Dimond reported. "I could see his heart beating, and all the time the man was chatting cheerfully and quite coherently. When the procedure was about halfway finished, the patient declared that he was hungry; the surgeons called a pause and gave him a jar of stewed fruit to eat."[55]

Is it conceivable that the patient had earlier been administered a different, conventional analgesic? Dr. Sidel, professor of public health at Albert Einstein Medical College in New York, answered this question in an interview. "I stake my reputation on the fact that these patients were prepped only by acupuncture. . . . My conviction is firm; I have no doubt that the pain was eliminated by these means. . . . The people were wide awake."[55]

In another operation witnessed by the American physicians, a thoracic tumor was removed. A single needle inserted laterally in the nape of the patient's neck eliminated the pain that would have been caused by the incision, removal of the tumor, and suturing. "The patient sat up, smiling. He reached for a little red book with the sayings of Chairman Mao, waved it about, and said, 'Long live Chairman Mao. We welcome our American friends.' Then he buttoned up his pajama jacket, climbed off the operating table, and as if nothing had happened, wandered down the hall to his room."[55]

Austrian surgeon Dr. Johannes Bischko, who has been practicing acupuncture for the past twenty years, was in China in the latter part of 1972 and witnessed operations using acupuncture anesthesia. His movies of what he had observed were presented on German television. They showed a Caesarian section, removal of an adenoma (benign glandular tumor), dental extraction, removal of a lobe on the right lung, and removal of a large ovarian cyst.

All the patients were fully conscious; some had a snack during the operation. The inserted needles were vibrated manually or stimulated electrically. No artificial respiration was used in the lung operation; rather, the wide-awake patient was given controlled breathing therapy. After the operation he was in the best of spirits and chatted in English with the foreign observers.

In the same year Dr. Mildred Scheel (wife of the West German foreign minister) witnessed acupuncture surgery in Peking. Dr. Scheel, a specialist in radiology and radiotherapy, made the following report on a Caesarian section on a young woman.

> The patient was already on the table. My question if the woman had received any kind of medication was answered in the negative. I was told that it was not necessary. . . . The patient told me that she had had her first child by Caesarian also—quite painlessly, with acupuncture anesthesia. . . .
>
> Two women physicians inserted 2-inch hairline needles into the woman's calves, a hand's breadth above the ankles. Two more needles were inserted under the knee joint on the inner side of the calves, and two more, about 4 inches long, around the navel, also very deeply. All the needles were connected to a power source which applied 2400 vibrations per minute to the needles on the abdominal wall and 140 to those on the legs.
>
> There was a wait of about twenty minutes. Then the standard vertical incision was made, beginning below the navel; the knife penetrated the skin and fatty layer. A second deeper cut opened the center line of the fasciae; after that, the uterus was opened up. . . .
>
> The procedure caused astonishingly little bleeding, and the patient followed the operation with wide-open eyes. Both surgeons even chatted with her. One of the acupuncture technicians, who monitored pulse and blood pressure, put bits of apple on a fork and put them in the patient's mouth. It was simply incredible.
>
> After the delivery a tubal ligation was performed at the patient's request (that is, her fallopian tubes were tied), since she did not wish to have any more children.[55]

According to Chinese reports, hardly any disease has not been treated—successfully—with acupuncture. This assertion need not be taken as Maoist propaganda. Even in Western Europe we have precise statistical material on acupuncture treatment of several hundred illnesses. The French physician Dr. J. Mauries has treated 108 different ailments exclusively with acupuncture needles, each time under the control of two other physicians. An English doctor, Felix Mann,[142,143] has employed the acupuncture method in 1200 cases of illness and debility. In March 1972 a surgical team led by Professor Eduard H. Majer, at the Viennese University Polyclinic, removed the tonsils of a thirty-five-year-old woman without local anesthesia. Before the operation, two acupuncture needles with diameters of about 1/10 millimeter were inserted in one arm; according to the ancient Chinese teaching, the corresponding points are connected with the throat. The operation took eight minutes. The patient experienced no pain whatever and was able to go home two days later.

Two months later the first surgery with acupuncture anesthesia in the United States was done at Albert Einstein Medical College for a skin graft on a sixty-five-year-old patient. The transplant, from the right thigh to the left foot, was carried out without any difficulty.

Although successful acupuncture anesthesia has long since ceased to be an exception even in the West. it has not gained a secure footing in Western medicine. There are three reasons for this omission. First, established medicine is basically skeptical about "innovations" from areas other than the conventional fields of medical research and discovery—and particularly skeptical about a method said to be handed down by Chinese sages of ancient times. Second, the basic concept of acupuncture seems doubtful because of its lack of scientific basis; the cause of the results produced by acupuncture is not yet understood. Lastly, not all acupuncture treatments are successful, and the reasons for failure are just as hard to fathom as those for success. In any practice, therapeutic failures, explicable and inexplicable, are probably not unusual, but acupuncturists do "operate" with a power they cannot explain. They know *that* it works, but not *how*.

For a time the West attempted to account for acupuncture by relating it to hypnosis. Professor Rudolf Frey of the University of Mainz considers acupuncture anesthesia a special form of hypnonarcosis. The fact that 20 percent of patients allegedly do not respond to acupuncture anesthesia seems to confirm his hypothesis. On the other hand, the fact that animals can also respond to acupuncture casts doubt on the theory of suggestion. Experienced acupuncturists, such as Dr. Motoyama and Dr. Bischko, defend the view that acupuncture is not related to hypnosis.[23,158]

As early as the nineteenth century the English physician Henry Head connected diseases of the internal organs with an excessive sensitivity of particular places on the skin. The heart, abdomen, kidneys, and other organs are served by the spinal cord just as the skin is. The various areas of the body are assigned to specific segments of the spinal cord; a given spinal segment is discernibly connected with a particular internal organ and with a sharply delineated area of the skin surface, providing a neural connection.[27]

When an organ becomes diseased its state is reflected in the related spinal segment, and some debility also becomes manifest in the skin whose nerve fibers emanate from the segment. The connection is pertinent not only for diagnosis but also for therapy. Now and again it is possible to influence the internal organs retrogressively from the corresponding skin areas (dermatomes) by applying various stimuli. This procedure is called segment therapy.

Some Western scientists see in this relationship a clue to the effects of the acupuncture needle. Though it may apply in some cases, the entire scale of possible effects of acupuncture can hardly be accounted for by segment therapy. For example, it is hardly likely that a neural connection exists between the toes and a painful dental root. Dr. Motoyama has shown that acupuncture points and dermatomes often do not coincide, no matter how we look at it.[158] For example, one acupuncture point of the Sansho Ke meridian is located in the tip of the index finger. The spinal and sympathetic nerves distributed over the tip of the index finger and the arm belong to certain segments of the spinal cord. The acupuncture points responding to the index finger acupuncture are Sanshoboketsu and Sanshoyuketsu, which from the standpoint of Western neurology belong to quite different segments.

The spinal cord also includes vertical connectors, as between spinal vasomotor centers in the lateral horn cells of the segments, which connect the levels of various cross sections with each other. For this connection the expression "intercom" has been used.[51] To use this to completely explain all the effects of acupuncture, however, seems somewhat forced and unlikely.

Further, Dr. Motoyama refers to experiments by a physician, Dr. Nagahama.[55] This professor at a leading Japanese university treated a patient who had at some earlier time been struck by lightning, had survived the shock, but had retained an extreme sensitivity in his skin-sensory apparatus. This patient felt the "needle echo" of the inserted acupuncture needles—that is, after the needles had been inserted at the beginning point of a meridian (Genketsu), he felt the transmission of the impulse and could accurately describe the route. The localized trail of the stimulus conduction precisely coincided with the acupuncture meridians specified by ancient Chinese doctors and did not lie along the neural paths as we know them.

Dr. Nagahama set out to determine the speed of the impulse transmission in the meridians; he discovered that these were very much slower (4–12 inches per second) than the speed of an impulse in the spinal and autonomic nerves (several yards per second). Dr. Nagahama conducted further interesting experiments, including some concerning the interconnections of various meridians, which will not be detailed here but which also confirm traditional Chinese beliefs.

The anatomic and physiological bases of the points and meridians allow of no connection with blood, lymph, or neural paths of Western medicine. Can it be that a principle still unknown to our sciences is at work here?

Western medicine has looked at the human being

more or less as an aggregate of organs, tissues, and cells, so that man is seen as the result of chemical and, perforce, physical processes. Biochemistry and physiochemistry have therefore come to play an increasingly larger part in the training of Western medical students. Although during the last few hundred years physiologists have diligently amassed a quantity of factual material concerning the electrical processes in the human body, the physical force fields of the human body are still seen as more or less marginal apparitions of the body's chemical and physiological processes.

During the nineteenth century bioelectrical currents were discovered in the brains of animals. We mentioned in discussing telepathy[298] that in 1929 Hans Berger proved that electrical brain currents could pass out through the scalp. The fact that electric currents flow in man is, in the words of the American surgeon Dr. Stanton E. Maxey, "a fact widely recognized today but far too little contemplated as far as its effects are concerned."[145]

In 1934 Dr. George W. Crile, founder of the Cleveland Clinic, asserted that each human cell represents a tiny battery which produces its own current. He was held up to ridicule at the time, but NASA scientists have confirmed and extended his theory. Since that time many other discoveries in the field of electrophysiology have been made, though we cannot go into detail here.

The acupuncture points are sites of extraordinary electrical skin properties.[5,8] Not only are the electric potentials or conductivities at the acupuncture points distinguished from those of the surrounding skin areas, but the various acupuncture points also differ in their electrical properties from one another. These points are said to be perceptible as pale yellow coloring for people with a highly developed optical capacity for differentiation, and they are said to possess good conductivity for sound waves and excellent electrical conductivity, whereas the actual skin structure does not seem to show any difference. But by means of suitable detectors the acupuncture points can be clearly located on the basis of their different characteristics from the surrounding skin.[5,8] Years ago Soviet researchers developed the tobiscope, a small transistorized electronic gadget. When the probe is passed slowly across a person's skin, a light flashes whenever it moves over an acupuncture point. A bright flash is said to indicate good health, while a weak glow, it is claimed, points to present or potential disorders.

We are probably far from recognizing the skin's full range of perceptions; at present we consider it largely restricted to perception of touch and temperature. On the lower levels of development, nerve cells as receptors for light, sound, and smell are distributed over the entire surface of living organisms. Earthworms, which are eyeless, perceive light through the skin. (Soviet biophysicist Viktor Adamenko assumes that the human skin can react to certain electromagnetic waves.) The acupuncture points of our skin react to various external influences. In some people, acupuncture potential or conductivity alters before the coming of a storm—long before meteorological instruments can register it.

The healthy body demands a complicated and sensitive balance; the electrical relationships among acupuncture points may well have a profound influence. Disturbances may, therefore, be redressed through controlled stimulation of the energy centers of these "life-force currents" in the body by acupuncture so that the potential relationships of the energy points are newly engaged. The alteration of an acupuncture potential through the insertion of a metal needle may have several causes; but after all, acupuncture has been a purely empirical form of therapy up to now.

Interestingly, emotions also bring about changes in the electrical properties of the acupuncture points. According to Adamenko, other areas of the skin show no change in electrical conductivity even under the strongest emotions, provided that the skin is dry.[5] Thus the patient's mental attitude is not without influence on the results of acupuncture. Perhaps a patient's extremely negative emotional attitude can block a harmonization of his acupuncture potential. However, we should not conclude that the result is merely a placebo effect; for the measurable electrical data at the acupuncture points have nothing to do with superstition. The fact that "only" 80 percent of patients respond positively to acupuncture anesthesia cannot lead to the conviction that all of them are acting solely on suggestion. Further, the effects of some powerful drugs used in Western medicine may be enhanced by strong suggestion on particular patients; these remedies cannot therefore simply be considered placebos.

Changes in the electrical relationships of acupuncture points may also be brought about through hypnosis; even the depth of a hypnotic trance can be controlled in this way. Adamenko and his coworkers were able to differentiate among three groups of hypnotic subjects: nonsuggestible people who remained in a normal state; persons who, under hypnosis, slept with their eyes closed; and finally those who, in the deepest hypnotic trance, were able to open their eyes without waking. The subjects were given a wide variety of suggestions—that they were smelling particular flowers, that they were famous composers, and the like. The first group exhibited no changes of any kind in acupuncture conductivity; the second showed changes of medium intensity; and the last group experienced quite extraordinary changes in conductivity.

Autosuggestion and autogenic training can also produce changes in acupuncture point conductivity. There are people who train themselves to achieve voluntary changes in the acupuncture conditions so that they can turn on a light by applying electrodes to suitable points on the skin in combination with corresponding mental concentration.[8]

The condition of the inner organs and functions of the body as a whole seems to stand in close relation to acupuncture conductivities. Some years ago Dr. Motoyama determined that if the differences between the corresponding acupuncture points on the right and left side of the patient reached a certain level, they pointed to overt or incipient disorders of the internal organs.[158] Dr. Adamenko further pointed to the appearance of semiconductor properties in the corresponding acupuncture channels when diseases of the internal organs became manifest, the conductivity varying between the forward and backward direction. The ancient Chinese concept that illness represents an imbalance in the life force seems aptly to characterize the electrical relationships now being discovered by science. These relationships are, of course, even more important to acupuncture therapy. The alteration of the electrical conditions at the acupuncture points seems to arouse reactions in the internal organs and the body as a whole.

We may be dealing with an important intermediary station between body and psyche. We know that a depressive emotional state has a deleterious effect on bodily functions and health, though we are not able specifically to define the linkages of this connection. Perhaps the acupuncture points represent an important element in the body-mind relationship; they may also be related to psi functions.

All chemical processes—even those in the body—are related to electrical forces. An electrical field forms around every nerve whenever there is the slightest activity of the muscular fibers. Any change in an electrical field is always accompanied by a magnetic field; conversely, every change in a magnetic field leads to the emergence of an electrical field. Such fields, which can be transformed into each other, are called electromagnetic fields. The human body is saturated with innumerable, infinitesimal electromagnetic fields which combine into one large electromagnetic biofield. The acupuncture points may well be crucial nodes in this biofield.

Professor H. S. Burr, a longtime member of the School of Medicine at Yale University and the author of nearly a hundred scientific publications, believes that the entire universe is organized by an electromagnetic field which determines the condition of matter.[33] Man, as part of nature, is influenced by these fields—even guided by them. Each person has his own energy field, or, as it might be called, his own energy body, but so has every animal, plant, and egg, every cell, molecule, and atom. According to Burr, the energy body prescribes how the crystal, cell, animal, person, and so on, will look, from the day of their creation to the end of their existence.

A significant aspect of Burr's work is the hypothesis that the biofield allows statements about diseases as soon as they can be recorded, as well as about diseases that will become manifest only later. Burr proved that the measurement of the electromagnetic biofield of an ovary facilitates a prediction about the formation of tumors and their possible malignancy.[33,145] Soviet researchers claim to have determined far-reaching changes in the electromagnetic biofield of affected tissue before clinical proof of cancer can be established. If the human biofield or energy body is primary and causative, affecting the physical body in aggravating ways, and if the acupuncture points are important sites in this energy system—then no fundamental obstacles prevent our understanding acupuncture therapy.

Some disturbances in the body's biofield appear to be evoked by old, often forgotten scars or other changes in normal tissue structure. Such disturbances can in turn affect organic and physiological functions. Neural therapists attempt to remove the cause of the disorder—which probably lies in the discontinuity of the scarred tissue structure—by injecting the trouble spot with Impletol or other neurological drugs; this treatment seems to alter the nature of the scar in such a way as to restore the harmony of the biofield at the injected site.[53,54]

The following case is one of the numerous examples recorded by the physician and neural therapist Dr. Peter Dosch:

Dr. H.S., a thirty-one-year-old veterinarian, was paralyzed in both legs for two years. He had been treated at a municipal hospital and at two noted universities; numerous medications and methods of treatment had been tried, but finally he had been dismissed as incurable. His history revealed many attacks of tonsilitis, twenty scars from grenade splinters, and the statement that the first paralytic manifestations had set in eight days after he had accidentally punctured his finger with an infected needle.

A professor had rendered the expert opinion that this ordinary injury could not have caused the paralysis. The case had therefore been turned down for workmen's compensation.

As for the neural therapeutic treatment:

An exploratory injection into the patient's chronically infected tonsils produced no reaction. But a few drops of procaine injected into the tip of the finger in question (which gave no external evidence of any injury) caused the paralysis to disappear completely and permanently within a few minutes. If the patient had not mentioned the puncture, he would certainly have remained chained to his wheelchair for the rest of his life. The veterinarian has now been professionally active for fourteen years without a relapse. Naturally now he employs procaine in his treatment of animals. He, too, has achieved perfect Huneke phenomena, thus refuting a frequent objection by our opponents that we cure purely by suggestion—that is, that our therapy is a kind of hypnosis.[54]

In both acupuncture and neural therapy, seemingly insignificant causes can produce the most severe effects; for example, a needle inserted in a toe facilitates painless dental extraction; or an injection of Impletol into a forgotten scar in the armpit immediately cures chronic renal colitis.[179] The discrepancy between the insignificance of the cause and the extent of the effect will appear suspect on principle to the established physician. The general belief is that a severe therapeutic effect must have an obvious cause; that any medication must be given in large quantities to be effective. Much scorn used to be heaped on homeopathy because its practitioners prescribe relatively harmless medications in highly diluted doses. At best allopathic doctors grant a placebo effect to account for cures obtained in this way.[196] But this aspect may present a certain analogy with acupuncture, when the proper gentle stimulus is applied to the proper site.

Homeopathy too can be effective with at times the weakest of stimuli, properly chosen.[74,201] Opponents of homeopathy argue that some children in play have ingested the entire contents of homeopathic medicine chests without any effect, except perhaps getting drunk on the alcohol contained in the medications. Therefore, they argue, no significant cures can be expected from such drugs. One could just as easily argue, because children have often stuck themselves with needles without coming to any harm, that acupuncture could also be expected to yield no remedial results.

Biological systems are highly sensitive to various kinds of electromagnetic rays. Some of these are of such minimal intensity that they evoke no measurable physical effect in "man, the molecular aggregate," but are nevertheless perceived by the sensory faculties or the biological organism.[195]

One is tempted to make comparisons with the results of modern information theory: it is a matter not so much of the amount of transferred *energy* but of the amount of *information*. The application of information theory to biology has shown that biological effects do not depend solely on the amount of energy introduced into a particular biological system, but also on the amount of information. Information-carrying signals only cause a suitable distribution of the energy present in the system and regulate the processes taking place. If the sensitivity of the system is sufficiently high, little energy is needed to transfer information.

Allopathy typically transfers concrete chemical matter and thus a large amount of energy. Homeopathy, and probably acupuncture as well, transfer "information" of relatively slight energy content; energies for the healing process must be supplied by

the biological system itself. The energies inherent in
the biological system are simply directed into new
paths by the transferred "information." It is entirely
possible that bioinformation research may help
homeopathy win ultimate recognition.

6/THE UNDERRATED FORCE FIELDS IN MAN

The theory of a biofield in and around man seems to support an ancient assertion which originated with Indian and Far Eastern philosophers, was taken up by theosophists[25] and mystics in the West, and is presently represented by anthroposophy: the assumption that man and every other living being possesses, besides the ordinary physical body, a so-called astral body. Some authors designate it as the "etheric body," "phantom body," "soul body," or "subtle double."

This concept, subject of heated controversy to this day, is strongly reminiscent of the theory of a vital current held by the old Chinese acupuncturists. It coincides with the basic yoga teaching that, besides his physical body, man has a "subtle body" in which flows the universal life energy the Indians call prana.[158]

The concept of a second, "subtle" body in man can also be found among the Egyptians of five thousand years ago, among Tibetan monks, and among almost all shamans and medicine men on all continents.[29] The astral body is said to produce an emanation, and this is said to form an aura surrounding all living beings and plants.

Moses, prophets, and Christian saints have always been depicted with a circle of light surrounding their heads; it is claimed that this ring was especially noticeable during states of ecstasy. Christ was frequently depicted in a glowing cloud surrounding his whole body.

Two hundred years ago, Franz Anton Mesmer claimed that a glowing ether emanated from all living things, and he connected this phenomenon with animal magnetism.[287] The scientific world disputed Mes-

mer's claim, on the basis of an investigation toward
the end of the eighteenth century by the Paris Academy of the Sciences—the same academy which,
faced some years later with the question of meteors,
stated that "stones cannot fall from the sky."

In the nineteenth century Karl Freiherr von Reichenbach, a German naturalist, thoroughly dealt with
the phenomenon of rays emanating from the human
body.[206,207] Until then Reichenbach's life had been
rich in scientific successes, and he possessed a
knowledge of natural science outstanding for his day.
For twenty years he experimented with about five
hundred sensitives. For lengthy periods—at times for
several hours—he kept his subjects in complete darkness in the cellars of his castle Reisenberg near Vienna. Their eyes adapted to the darkness to such an
extent that they were able to perceive the slightest
appearance of light. The sensitives allegedly began to
perceive a glow radiating from the others in the
cellar. Reichenbach called this emanation Odic force.
According to Reichenbach's subjects, every exposed
skin area was surrounded by a whitish glow. The col-
or merged into a reddish or red tint if the person was
or was about to fall ill. Among the highly sensitive
a still greater ability to differentiate colors was alleged. Green, red, orange, and purple lights glowed
against a background of blue and yellowish red.

Thoroughly agreeing with Mesmer, Reichenbach believed that he had proved that Odic force could be
transferred to other bodies without always necessitat-
ing an immediate contact. These assertions are supported by numerous psychic healers, contemporary
psychics, and the most recent research results of Soviet
and Czech parapsychologists.[100,101,139,184]

In the United States, Dr. Shafica Karagulla, among
others, addressed herself specifically to Reichenbach's
experiments. This physician, born in Turkey, has
worked in the field of neuropsychiatry in four countries and was named to the presidency of the Higher
Sense Perception Research Foundation in Beverly
Hills, California, which concerns itself with psi research and the problems of creativity. Dr. Karagulla

works with a sensitive who perceives the aura and sees the energy body which, in her experience, penetrates the normal physical body like a glittering web of bright flashes of light and steady rays. Many strictly controlled experiments have confirmed a series of the experiments carried out by Reichenbach.

A hundred and thirty years ago, however, his scientific colleagues considered Reichenbach less than mentally competent. Emil Du Bois-Reymond, a highly regarded Berlin physiologist, described Reichenbach's Odic force researches as a "tissue of the sorriest errors ever brought forth by the human spirit, fables good only for burning, outdated fiction, witches' tricks." And Karl Vogt, a Swiss zoologist and anatomist, called Reichenbach's Odic force "nonsense based on an aggravated nervous excitability."[100]

In all parts of the world there have been stories about especially sensitive persons who were able to directly perceive the aura of living matter. The independent testimony of many sensitives who never had direct or indirect contact with each other is in agreement on important basic points. It is quite opposed to the laws of probability that hallucinations could accidentally have brought about such massive coincidences among people of quite different temperaments and entirely different cultures.

The aura often plays a significant part in psi healing and paranormal surgery. Olga Worral and Sigrun Seutemann, both diagnostic psychics, recognize many diseases directly, using no mechanical tools, simply by examining the aura. All it requires of them is a certain amount of concentration and a switch-over in their perceptual functions. They do not believe they take in the auralike emanations with their physical eyes—although their normal sight is an integral part at the beginning—but rather that this perception is brought about directly through the biofield. After a time Olga Worral can close her eyes and continue to "see" the aura as well as its alterations down to the smallest detail.

The English healer Gordon Turner has made in-

teresting statements about further information that can
be derived from the aura.[295] He believes the aura is a
dynamic manifestation in constant motion, reacting to
influences from the environment, emotions, and diseases of the body with changes in color, intensity,
shape, and size.

Further, according to Turner, age and experience
increase the differentiation of the aura. The aura of a
little child is simpler and visible only very near the
body. The aura of an unborn child is said to be visible
as early as six months before birth within the mother's
aura. Animals allegedly have an aura similar to that of
humans, but less complex and more undifferentiated,
similar to that of a small child. The lower the animal
stands on the ladder of phylogenetic development,
the simpler its aura. Nevertheless, there are occasional
differences even among animals of the same species.
The aura of herd animals seems to reflect the herd instinct; individual fields order themselves into a large
aural field surrounding the group as a whole. It might
properly be called a group aura.

Among low forms of life the aura of all the individuals is identical, not showing any individual traits dis-
cernible to sensitives. Exceptions occur only when an
animal falls ill—when, according to Turner, "the aura
turns a muddy brown and clings to the body." Such
animals frequently separate themselves from the group
or are chased away by their fellows, perhaps as a
result of a sort of group intelligence aimed at pro-
tecting against transmission of the illness, like the behavior of the healthy populace toward lepers in the
Middle Ages.

Among the more highly developed animals, some
are more intelligent than the rest of their kind, and
this difference is expressed in their aura. Here the influence of environment also plays an important part.
According to Gordon Turner, one can find more individual traits in the aura of household pets than in
those of wild animals. He cites as an example his
observations of a parakeet which had been confined
alone in a narrow cage and had a very weak, gray
aura. As soon as he was put in a communal cage, his

aura turned bluer and expanded; this change can be interpreted as a sign of heightened spiritual activity and greater well-being. The spoiled darling of a particularly animal-loving family had a hearty blue, extremely wide aura. Still another showed an aura very differentiated in color. This animal developed unusual intelligence.[295]

These determinations are directly in line with the empirical results of modern group psychology. Applied to the human psyche, the findings indicate the variety of ways a child may develop, depending on whether he is growing up in a happy home, an asocial environment, or an institution.

When discussing telepathy, we pointed out that man as a herd animal is psychically different in the group than as an isolated individual. Whenever a number of people come together, moved by similar emotions, the sensitive is said to be able to perceive one aura around the whole group—for example, at concerts, religious ceremonies, mass meetings of young hippies, or political demonstrations of fanatical extremists. Telepathic communication in a group becomes plausible when we assume the presence of the aura field. The coordinated behavior of swarms of insects, flocks of birds, and schools of fish is also illuminated by this point of view.

Psychic healing seems to be reflected in the aura— that is, the process of psychic healing can sometimes be seen by a sensitive. Gordon Turner claims that as soon as a healer lays his hands on the patient, a merging of their two auras takes place. Within a few minutes all the colors previously present subordinate themselves into a predominant blue, extending far beyond the normal limits of the aura. After treatment, the sensitive still sees the aural signs and colors that had earlier indicated the disease, but they fade out very rapidly or seem to rush away from the patient's body. When healing is spontaneous and complete, the aura returns to its normal coloration after five minutes. In other cases it is possible to detect tiny points or scars in the aural field for weeks, months, or years, depending on the severity of the ailment.

The statements of sensitives concerning human auras differ, especially about the colors they observe. This discrepancy is understandable when we realize that the psychic's subconscious must translate a paranormal experience into familiar optical concepts of color and shape. A subjective factor must enter into any association of abstract concepts with concrete impressions.

Scientists generally consider statements on extrasensory perception by sensitives irrelevant. Indeed, there is some lack of reliability of even the normal senses—not to mention such possibilities as hallucination and suggestion; and the statements of physical detectors are generally more reliable. It would be ideal if we could use physical detectors for all these processes, but unfortunately such devices have not yet been invented. A highly gifted sensitive's perception is still considerably larger than all the technical instruments at our disposal, so we should not ignore the testimony of good psychics, especially since scientists in some special fields rely more and more on other "biological detectors" in the form of generally simpler life forms.[91] As the French physician and Nobel prize-winner Alexis Carrel put it, "The importance of a subject for investigation is never based on whether, given the appropriate status of techniques of physical proof, it is or is not easily accessible."[35]

It has been shown that "man the detector" is less unreliable than many scientists assume; a large number of paraphenomena have been observed from earliest times, then decried by the exact sciences, and are now being accepted after all. Even if many mediums' statements cannot be corroborated scientifically, they nevertheless furnish valuable clues. One statement by Turner on the phenomenon of death seems to point the way.[295] Three times he observed a person's death, and each time he had the same perception. The aura of the dying person lost its color, became a dull gray, and retreated back into the body. At the same time, an indistinct form, of approximately the same shape as but somewhat larger than the physical body, detached itself from the body, moved away, and hovered about a yard above it. Turner took this shape to be the astral body or what many researchers today call the energy body. After an unusual play of colors which seemed to fill the entire room, the aura and the supposed energy body disappeared. These phenomena lasted anywhere from fifteen minutes to three hours.

The prehistoric concept of spiritual survival after physical death is still ridiculed by many in our culture, who are not aware of the large body of reliable data amassed in the course of the last hundred years to support the theory,[187] in part by very skeptical researchers. The American Arthur Ford—theologian, psychologist, and medium—created a sensation with the description and analysis of his psychic "contact with the beyond," in his *Report of Life After Death.*[70] Wernher von Braun notes: "Science has determined that nothing can disappear without a trace. Nature does not know destruction, only transformation. Everything science has taught me and is teaching me still strengthens my belief in a continuation of our spiritual existence beyond death."[70] The father of the idea of space travel in Germany, Hermann Oberth, expressed himself similarly.[187]

Some psychics are convinced that the astral body, under particular conditions, can temporarily detach itself from the physical body even during life. Imaginative people tell the most fantastic stories about so-called astral wandering, often discredited by people who may uncritically jumble together genuine phenomena and fraudulent accounts.

There are many corroborated reports, in agreement on crucial points, about serious and completely lucid people who, for example, during serious illnesses or surgery, found themselves fully conscious, hovering outside their own bodies. Subsequently they insisted that they could clearly see their own body lying on the operating table; in proof they cited details which they could not possibly have known from the position of their physical body; in some cases these could all be verified.[171,244]

Indian yogis and Tibetan lamas have always been reputed to be able to will the temporary separation of their astral bodies and to consciously experience this wandering. Reports of this sort are generally regarded in the West as the superstitions of a low cultural level and are not seriously investigated. Lately, however, such talents seem to be turning up in the West as well, though infrequently. The American electronics engineer Robert Monroe[152] seems able to transfer his consciousness to faraway places in such a way that he can clearly see events and people there. "Normal" people cannot see him, but he is perceived by clairvoyants. Scientific experiments under test conditions are said to have had positive results.

A further case concerns the American artist Ingo Swann. A representative of the American Society of Psychical Research tested his unusual paranormal faculties. Swann sat in a darkened room, connected to electrophysiological instruments, and was given the task of "leaving his body" and observing objects which he could not see from where he was sitting. After these "excursions," Swann was asked to describe the objects precisely in the perspective from which he claimed to have seen them in his out-of-body state. He made sketches which were evaluated by a psychologist through "blind judging." All tests came out positive. The probability that the same results could have been obtained by chance was on the order of 1:40,000.[245] Equally incredible is Swann's alleged ability to observe a subterranean electronics installation while in his out-of-body state and afterward to sketch the mechanism correctly. Such reports arouse dangerous speculations. We think of secrets supposedly safely guarded in vaults and out of reach of the unauthorized. Perhaps paranormal achievements of this sort are reserved for a more mature humanity; misuse of these powers could have catastrophic consequences.

At present, pararesearchers still hold conflicting views. Whether Swann's spiritual force and perception fields can externalize themselves—or whether it is "only" a matter of clairvoyance, as some investigators believe—is a pretty fruitless argument as long as we do not know the nature of clairvoyance. At the 1972 Parapsychology Congress in Hot Springs, Arkansas, American physicians told me much evidence suggests that the biofield of the human body or parts of it temporarily leave the physical body and are able to survive at death at least for a time; that the real seat of our feelings is not the brain and nervous system, but the energy body, to which the physical body is subordinate.

An extreme form of this alleged separation, during which the separated part is perceived by others, is bilocation, reported in combination with inexplicable healing results by the Capuchin monk Father Pio in the monastery Giovanni Rotondo near the southern Italian city of Foggia. Pio was frequently said to have been seen in two widely separated places at once. Here is a short precis of the case of Mario D. from Viareggio:

In 1940 Mario, at that time twenty-four years old, had a work-connected accident—injury to the lumbar vertebrae, with consequent atrophy of the sacrum. Wearing a plaster corset, he was able to perform limited work, until in 1950 he collapsed from physical exertion. After that time he experienced complete paralysis and anesthesia of both legs. The patient was tied to the bed. Specialists could neither make a diagnosis nor alleviate the condition. On March 17, 1951, he faced final separation from his job on the grounds of illness exceeding one calendar year.

On the afternoon of that day his wife brought home a book about Father Pio and begged her husband to ask for the monk's help. The patient had a distaste for religion in general and clerics in particular, and after laying the book aside, he said without conviction, "If you've already performed so many miracles, why don't you help me too?"

At that moment he saw the door to his room opening. A hooded Capuchin monk entered, came toward him, and said, "Get up, there is nothing wrong with you anymore."

At the same moment he felt eight arms raising him

from the bed and laying him gently back down. Immediately thereafter the monk went out the door, while a smell of lilies remained in the room. Mario's wife, who was also present, had noticed nothing beyond her husband's strange behavior and feared for his reason when he suddenly got out of bed. The following day he reported for work and was obviously cured.

When, a year later, Mario traveled five hundred miles to visit Father Pio and thank him for his help, the monk seemed fully acquainted with him and his situation. Mario's doctor declared in writing that he had treated the patient for a long time for primary chronic arthritis with severe structural alterations in the lumbosacral region, but that treatment had not brought any improvement. The patient's complaints had ceased suddenly and had never returned. Such a remission as appears to have set in for this patient is not subject to medical explanation.[18]

Professor Hans Bender believes the case can be largely explained as wish fulfillment, hallucination, and telepathy, but he does not entirely exclude the "theory of soul travel."[18] This paraphenomenon or a similar form of it was frequently associated with Father Pio.

A great many phenomena do not fit our scientific concepts of the cerebrospinal nervous system as the sole perceptual instrument. These include the phenomena of so-called sense transfer.[100,254,268] This relatively rare occurrence has been reported and confirmed many times. As early as the beginning of the nineteenth century the French physician Petetin noted that some of his patients' sense—such as sight, hearing, and smell—were transferred to other sites of the body.[254]

The world-famous Italian doctor and psychologist Cesare Lombroso had a patient whose sense of smell wandered. If Lombroso held ammonia under her nose she evinced not the slightest reaction. But an even faintly odorous substance held under her chin produced a strong reaction. In the course of time the seat of the sense of smell shifted down to her feet. During the nineteenth century Dr. Angona treated a young Italian girl in Carmagnola who, in a sleepwalking state, recognized coins held to the nape of her neck and experienced smells on the backs of her hands. Subsequently her sight and hearing are said to have gradually shifted to the abdominal wall.[254]

Phenomena of this sort obviously confuse our ideas about sensory perceptions, for seeing is normally done by the eyes. But if there is some truth to the view of the ancient occultists that experience takes place in the astral body—in a sense, "behind" the brain—the signal reaching the brain would be passed on to the astral or energy body in order to be experienced. Alongside this normal course might be another, para-normal, way by which the energy body, as perceiving body, would use other contact points.

The connection between the energy and physical bodies is probably very complicated. There does not seem to be a single link by way of the brain; rather, several facts indicate that communication between both systems extends over the whole body by way of the acupuncture points.

If this point of departure seems nonsensical to any-one, let him offer a better one. But these problems cannot be solved by ignoring them. Many Soviet scien-tists do not suppress uncomfortable phenomena but in-vestigate them with special interest. In 1962 they concluded that Rosa Kuleshova, aged twenty, could distinguish color with her fingertips. A six-week in-vestigation in the psychiatric hospital at Sverdlovsk revealed that she could feel color even behind a card-board layer and that her fingertips could "recognize" colors covered with glass, cellophane, and other ma-terials. These findings eliminated the possibility of slight structural or temperature differences in the col-ors themselves which might be perceived by an un-usual sense of touch.[156,184] The objection that this "eyeless sight" is enormously rare does not bring us any closer to solving the problem of where our expe-rience of things originates. The only thing that seems certain is that in resolving all these questions, we must focus on the energy body or biofield. Such parapsychological expressions as "making contact with the subconscious of another person" are surely valuable as philosophical-psychological concepts, but they do not satisfy the scientific thinker. On the other hand, "transfer from one biofield to another" is a concept that can be scientifically illuminating.

Some parapsychologists believe that though strong evidence supports the existence of something like the energy body, science can proceed without this assumption.[222] It is doubtful that such an attitude is fruitful for scientific progress, for in the final analysis we are dealing with the question of whether or not there is such a thing as the energy body. The French philosopher Henri Bergson noted in 1913 that one need not be surprised when a scientist clings to his method like a workman to his tools. He loves it for its own sake, independent of its achievements.[19] The scientist must still guard against elevating his scientific methods and modes of thought to ends in themselves.

If the energy body or biofield represents an entity that can be separated from the body, then it seems we are dealing with more than a secondary manifestation of biological processes. Many Soviet and Czech researchers seem inclined to the view that the energy body is the superordinate, organizing part of man.[105,106,184] Illnesses, they claim, first manifest themselves as imbalances of the energy body. The material body represents the active, not the causative level, as the majority of scientists continue to assume.

From this it follows that in any medical treatment the disorder must be attacked in the energy body; otherwise the cure will not be permanent. The majority of remedies in use today are attacks on gross symptoms and effects in the end stage—which is not to say that they are not justified. But the ideal method would be one that attacks the illness on the causative level. The masters and founders of Indian yoga recognized the energy body as more central to treatment, and the Chinese acupuncturists found a successful system to work on this energy body in a regulating and harmonizing way.[158]

The concepts of Western medicine, yoga, and acupuncture represent different aspects of the same subject of investigation—man. The various aspects, however, have given rise to different methods; established medicine and psi healing attack disease on different levels. A fruitful coexistence of both systems is possible. Acupuncture, for example, could be the ideal way to prevent serious illnesses; but it fails in advanced severe organic illnesses, since it attacks the causative energy scheme of the body rather than the advanced degenerative process in the cells and tissues. When something has been destroyed, acupuncture will seldom be effective. At that stage Western established medicine must attempt to compensate for the disorder, repair or replace inoperative tissues or organs, or remove hopelessly diseased tissue.

7/THE REDISCOVERY OF THE ENERGY BODY

Whenever the atmosphere becomes heavily charged electrically between clouds and earth or even other atmospheric layers, very high tensions may develop and electrical discharges take place. One electrical discharge known to everyone is thunder and lightning. But there are also soundless discharges, where the electrical energy is not sufficient for a violent disruption through the air layer. In days gone by, sea travelers observing singular light phenomena on the masts of their ships considered them a bad sign, for violent storms usually set in soon afterward. We know that this St. Elmo's fire—named after a legendary saint and patron of sailors—is the result of electrical discharges primarily emanating from projecting ledges and pinnacles during states of high electrical tension, before approaching storms, and during snow and dust storms.

Laboratory investigations of this natural phenomenon have yielded some interesting results.[6] Artificial St. Elmo's fire was produced on small objects during complete darkness, and these luminous apparitions registered on photographic plates. Erecting a constant electrical field between an object and an electrode with an opposite charge or a condenser plate produced a continuous luminous apparition that could be used in the darkness to light a photographic film. This process yielded a reproduction of the object from which the electrical discharge emanated. Electrophotography was developed in 1889 by the Czech B. Navratil.[208] The reproduction shows a characteristic crown of rays outlining the shape of the object. Elec-

74

trotechnicians speak of a corona. Sharp corners and ledges show the effect especially strongly.

One is immediately reminded of the aura seen by clairvoyants and sensitives. Living organisms cannot readily be exposed to strong electrical fields of this sort, since as little as 10 milliamperes of current can be fatal. The Russian engineer Semyon Kirlian and his wife Valentina, who died in 1972, found a brilliant solution: during the 1950s they developed "electro-photography in the high-frequency field"[6]—that is, they used alternating-current fields of high frequency, which are much more easily tolerated by animal life and thus allow the study of the luminescence of living objects in an electrical field.

We will not go into technical details,[184] but if the reproduced object is a good conductor (metal), the picture shows only its surface, while the picture of a poor conductor shows the inner structure of the object even when it is optically opaque. The high-frequency picture of a dead object remains constant, while with living matter, the picture is subject to changes. The microscope allows observation of gradations of discharge, some stable, some in motion. These discharges seem to reflect the object's life activity in the most various colors.[6]

High-frequency photography has been practiced for more than twenty years in the Soviet Union, but in the West interest has been shown only recently, for example by Professor Douglas Dean in New York and Professor Philips at Washington University in St. Louis. High-frequency photographs have also been made by Brazilian, Austrian, and German investigators.[216,238] At the ESP Congress in Hot Springs, Arkansas, in May 1972, the well-known pararesearcher Dr. Thelma Moss showed a documentary film she had made about pararesearch in the United States in which high-frequency photography was demonstrated.[155] The color film taken in the scientist's laboratory at the Neuropsychiatric Institute at UCLA depicted the auralike emanations of people's fingers. In the normal state colorful blue and white rays emanate from the fingers. But when the subject becomes excited or angry in the course of filming, a red spotty pattern appears. The fingers of one person, who had gotten drunk in the interest of science, showed murky eruptions of hazy colors. The strongest deviation from the normal picture was evinced when the subject was in a trance.

Soviet psi researchers would have found nothing new in this demonstration. Dr. Viktor Inyushin, an exponent of biological force-field research in the Soviet Union, had already published works detailing interpretations of high-frequency photographs of the human body. Other Russian investigators have for years observed this bioluminescence in a more direct manner and continuously through special microscopelike devices.

High-frequency pictures of living objects are strongly reminiscent of the statements by many sensitives, such as Gordon Turner, concerning the aura of living bodies. A firm analogy would nevertheless be too risky, for the aura is considered a kind of emanation of the living being, whereas the luminescence in the highfrequency field is brought about by a process of electrical discharge.

It has been said that acupuncture points are sites of heightened electrical conductivity; the electrical field at these points will look different and be expressed by a different color in the photograph. In any case, highfrequency photos present a very interesting method for analyzing the electrical conditions on the human skin. But whether the photograph depicts an emanation of the human skin will have to remain an open question at present.

In the West high-frequency photography encountered some skepticism, nor could some of the discoveries allegedly made by Soviet researchers be replicated by Western specialists.[157] Some results were interpreted simplistically in the East, and it was therefore argued that the Soviet researchers had not discovered anything new.[238] For example, Eastern psi researchers cited the fact that a fresh plant leaf exhibits a much stronger luminescence than a wilted one as proof for the existence of the aura; they claimed that it grew weaker as the wilted leaf's life-force abated, that the paler luminescence indicated the "draining of the life-force." In the West this phenomenon was interpreted simply as a manifestation of drying up. A reduction in water content altered the electrical state; this had nothing to do with any mysterious life-force. Some specialists even voiced the supposition that the Soviet photographs were examples of trick photography.

But even if some of the results of high-frequency photography can be explained away on the basis of previous knowledge, other phenomena cannot. Soviets report that diseases can be identified by this device before they can be recognized by standard methods. Leaves of the same sort and freshness are said to give off different pictures if one leaf is healthy while an incipient disease is developing in the other even if it cannot yet be detected in any other way, such as moisture content. Similarly, the picture of the human hand is different when the person is ill or is in the process of falling ill. Apparently for many diseases there is a "preclinical stage" during which the disease cannot be identified by present-day methods, although it is latently present and recognizable in a high-frequency photograph—or by way of the aura.

Perhaps a more advanced form of high-frequency photography will allow us to diagnose many dangerous diseases, which develop slowly and in secret, while they are still in a curable stage. At least, however, high-frequency photography offers a new tool for the study of bioelectrical structures. Years ago Adamenko pointed out that an electrical discharge in the high-frequency field of living objects is a complicated and ambiguous procedure, whose origin cannot always be accounted for only by the radiation of electrons and which does not preclude the presence of another, still unknown form of radiation.

Particularly convincing is the fact that researchers' concepts of human force fields are based not only on high-frequency photography but also on work with different detectors and a great many other methods. A unique phantom effect the Soviet researchers allegedly observed aroused a good deal of interest. During high-frequency photography of a leaf from which a part had been snipped off, the result gave a complete picture of the entire leaf, though the removed part showed up more faintly.[184,208] This would seem to represent a discovery of enormous significance, tending to support the repeated statements of psychics that when looking at amputees they are able to see an astral or phantom member not visible to normal people. Photographic emulsion is obviously much more sensitive than is the human eye, and some photographs of arm or leg amputees made in the presence of psychics also depict these phantom members. If the physically removed part of the leaf—or an arm or leg— remains in the high-frequency picture, then the electromagnetic pattern forming the basis of the reproduction cannot represent any secondary phenomenon, for such a field would have to vanish when its basis—the physiological substratum—is removed. The energy grid formerly contained in the leg is therefore of greater original significance than the material form.

Western researchers have not yet been able to reproduce this phantom effect.[157,238] It can hardly be trick photography, however. The Russians have been concentrating intensely on high-frequency photography for twenty years, while we have only recently begun working with it. Possibly we simply still lack the know-how.

In the meantime the Russians are said to have advanced to the point where they can make moving pictures of the fields or emanation surrounding man and then evaluate them for medical diagnosis.[245]

In the late nineteenth century the famous British chemist, physicist, and pararesearcher Sir William Crookes considered the possibility of a fourth state of matter, partly on the basis of his study of psychic phenomena. This fourth state of matter actually exists; it is called plasma. (This physical concept of plasma must not be confused with what biologists and doctors call cell plasma or blood plasma.)

The matter of which our world is composed occurs

in three states: solid, liquid, and gaseous. When heated, solid ice becomes liquid water, which, when evaporated, turns into steam, a gas. The fourth state, physical plasma, resembles the gaseous state; it could not be recognized until the twentieth century, after we became better informed about the structure of the atom. In this state, the atoms—which were long considered the smallest, indivisible building blocks of our world—continue to dissolve by increasingly losing their electrons, leaving behind electrically charged particles.

When the transition from the gaseous to plasma state occurs at high temperatures, one speaks of "hot plasma." The plasma of the lightest chemical element, hydrogen, melts into helium in the hydrogen bomb. If the plasma state is achieved with low temperatures, the phrase used is "cold plasma."

When the fourth state of matter was discovered, no one would have supposed that it might exist in the human body in any form. But in 1944 the Russian biologist Dr. V. S. Grischchenko voiced the hypothesis that the fourth state of matter also existed in biological systems and therefore in the human body. For a number of years various prominent Russian scientists have postulated the concept of a cold plasma in living organisms as the basis of life.[208] The researchers call it biological plasma or bioplasma.

The concept of the fourth state of aggregation in living organisms—possibly along with further free elementary particles—is new and revolutionary. Not a word about it can be found in any Western medical textbook, whose concepts of the human body rest entirely on the formulations of nineteenth-century physics and chemistry.

In the twentieth century physics has entered on fundamentally new paths and unlocked entirely new dimensions for which no analogies exist in our experiential world. The physicist knows that he can depend more heavily on his formulas than on his so-called horse sense, for example when describing processes within the atomic nucleus.[68,94] Medicine and biology have not yet participated in this daring leap;

their mentality is still largely grounded in the classical natural sciences.[189] But the contemporary atomic model of physics no longer bears any resemblance to the model of Rutherford and Bohr. The contemporary physicist restricts himself to describing the atom with formulas. But the concepts of the essence of the human body—which in the last analysis is composed of these abstract atoms—have not undergone any such fundamental change. This is because the biological sciences are much younger than physics and because the human organism is much more complicated than the physicists' object of investigation. For this reason if for no other, the sciences of living matter have not developed at the same speed as the inorganic sciences.[35] If the theories of the Russian bioplasma researchers can be verified, their discoveries will alter our basic image of man composed over the past two hundred years.

The center of Russian bioplasma research is in Alma-Ata, the capital of the Kazakh Republic in the northern foothills of the Himalayas, only thirty miles from the Chinese border. In one of the many technical institutes of the modern university city, Dr. Viktor Inyushin, a biologist, is at work with his research team.

Until the late 1950s few attempts were made to relate physical plasma to living matter. The results of a number of experiments with living matter seemed to inspire several researchers with the idea that elementary particles (those smaller than atoms), which of course occur in living organisms, may form a complicated biologically organized network or system in the living organism. Inyushin and his collaborators believe that a permanent, stable state of bioplasma is possible in the living organism and that the body is constantly radiating bioplasma.[98] The researchers believe they have clear indications that the smallest particles of the bioplasma influence electrical fields and are therefore visible under high-frequency photography. More recently Inyushin has sought to prove bioplasmic radiation without the use of electrical fields. If this research succeeds, we will know once and for all whether Kirlian photography shows an aura or only an electric corona.

Independently of the Alma-Ata group, and by quite other methods, the well-known Leningrad biophysicist, mathematician, and neurophysiologist Dr. Genady Sergeyev has also discovered the principle of bioplasma. He started from entirely different presuppositions, developed a different instrument, and arrived at the view that the phenomena he had observed were best explained by assuming the existence of a form of cold plasma in the brain.[239,242]

Sergeyev also came to believe that the body radiates bioplasma. When the neurons in the brain are simultaneously stimulated according to a specific pattern, what Sergeyev has called the "biolaser effect" appears. That is, bioplasma seems to leave the brain in bundles, like photons in a laser beam. The bioplasmic ray can attain such a degree of fluctuating electrostatic charges that small objects can be moved by it.[240,241]

There have long been reports of objects being inexplicably moved from afar (psychokinesis). These accounts were at first simply rejected as superstition, charlatanism, or the result of stored-up electrostatic charges. But proof of the phenomenon was already provided by Karl von Reichenbach. There were, for example, people who from a distance could spin a lightweight suspended paper cylinder with a very minimal momentum. These people affected the cylinder solely by bringing their hand within about 4 inches of it or staring at it fixedly.[101] Pioneers in this special area of psi research always assumed that the cause of psychokinetic processes must be a form of energy emanating from the human body. The human organism must either produce it or serve as a transformer for an external cosmic energy. (Mesmer's concepts of animal magnetism were on the same level, though he did not investigate effects of physical motion.)

These phenomena are today being scientifically researched in Czechoslovakia. It has been unequivo-

cally determined that they cannot be explained on
the basis of air currents, electrostatic charges, bodily
heat radiation, or other known effects.[211] The Czechs
believe that everyone possesses certain psychokinetic
capabilities which are said to be generally only very
minimal, however, and buried by other, stronger
known effects; this is the reason for their being largely
ignored until now. Some people, for example, are
able to influence a thin needle carefully floated on the
surface of a cup or bowl filled with water. By staring
at it fixedly or bringing their hands to within 5 or 6
inches of it they cause it to drift to the edge of the
container. Very talented people such as the Czech
mathematician and physicist Dr. Julius Krmessky
can also cause the needle to move in a circle by
staring at it.[120,121] Even when Dr. Krmessky stands
as far as 24 feet from the needle the experiment succeeds most of the time. Other objects, such as lightweight coins, respond similarly; but long, thin objects
exhibit the effect most strongly. It can be further increased through blinking or through strong mental
concentration. Krmessky has used many additional
test situations to demonstrate this effect.

Anyone who wishes to duplicate the experiment
with the floating needle must watch against being
deceived by purely electrostatic effects; for if the
needle and the rim of the cup have opposite static
charges, and if the needle immediately comes to rest
relatively near the edge of a small cup, a purely
electrical attraction can follow which has nothing to
do with psychokinesis.

According to Krmessky's experience, experiments
of this sort require a great deal of patience and do
not allow the presence of many spectators. Curious
and searching looks from others can disturb or prevent the effect. On the other hand, there are said to
be people whose mere presence sets quietly floating
needles in motion. (It is well to recall one Filipino
healer who was said to be able to heal with his eyes
by staring fixedly at the diseased part of the body—
only when the disease was external, however.)

Moving a floating needle by a glance may be very

amusing, but it remains an insignificant feat. However, there are people who produce this effect in stronger measure. Russian researchers presently have at their disposal two mediums who can demonstrate psychokinesis of an apparently fundamentally different kind. Both Nina Kulagina, a housewife from Leningrad, and Alla Vinogradova, a young Moscow woman, are able to move small objects placed on a table without touching them; direct air currents or anything of the sort have been ruled out. During the last two years the press has frequently reported on the case of Kulagina.

Benson Herbert, head of the Laboratory of Paraphysics in Downton, England, visited both mediums in the summer of 1972; in the presence of Dr. Adamenko he also saw demonstrations by Alla Vinogradova in Moscow.[96] The psychokinetic experiments were carried out on a table covered by a large box made of an electrically nonconducting material with one open side. Alla first dropped a cigarette on the table with her right hand and moved her left palm toward the cigarette as if to brush it off the table—but without touching it.

This action was repeated several times without results. After this she picked up the cigarette, lit and smoked it, and dropped another cigarette on the table, again to begin a renewed attempt. This second attempt also miscarried, and finally the cigarette was replaced by a small cylinder-shaped aluminum cigarette holder. When she moved her hands downward, the holder began to move slightly. At first it rolled back and forth while her hands slid over it at a distance of ½ inch. Then the movements began to become more rapid, until finally the aluminum cylinder rolled all the way across the table in two seconds.

When it arrived at the edge, Alla kept it from falling off, not by touching it, but by rapidly moving her hand over the object, forcing it to turn back by the repelling power of her hand and then letting it roll to the other side of the table. In this way she drove the object for five minutes without any diminution of energy. Back and forth across the surface of the table it rolled, and she claimed to be able to go on forever. It was clear that the driving force resulted from a constant repulsion between her hand and the cylinder. Her hand never attracted the cylinder, but by cleverly moving her hand, she could make the object rotate like a compass needle.

At times Alla Vinogradova is able to transfer this ability to others. She asked the witnesses to carry out similar motions, and one Englishman was actually able to set the cigarette holder moving slightly. But as soon as Alla also held her hand over the object, he could no longer affect it. The cylinder seemed nailed down—by the superior power of the medium.

Thereupon Dr. Adamenko placed a stool in the isolation box and laid an aluminum cylinder on the stool. Then Alla, outside the box, held her hand over the cylinder—her hand thus being separated from the object by the lid of the box—and was able to move it in any desired direction. She could move it by concentrating, even if she held her hand perfectly still. Benson Herbert therefore concluded that Alla is able to control the strength of the electrical charge in her hand and the distribution of the charge. For proof, two aluminum cylinders were laid end to end. She let her hand glide first over one cylinder, and as usual, set it in motion. She then slid her hand over the other cylinder, and it did not move at all. Afterward she demonstrated the opposite: the second object moved, the first did not. Thus she could arbitrarily decide which cylinder would move.

High-frequency photographs of Alla's hands in the "normal state" show the standard inch-long corona; photos taken when she was concentrating on psychokinesis (before actually doing it) show an entirely different picture. The corona is now severely reduced in length, less than ⅙ inch. The researcher assumed that in the course of this process of concentration, bioenergy is drawn back into the body, to be transformed into psychokinetic energy. In other words, the energy needed for telekinesis must come from somewhere, and it is obviously siphoned off from the hands into the brain. The color of the rays also changed, from bluish green in the normal state to red in the state of concentration.

Alla maintains that many people can learn to do these experiments. The primary requirement is bringing thought and body under control. Most of all, one must believe in the possibility and thus, she thinks, healing powers can also be developed. She claims to feel the total energy of her body concentrating in one point and then guides it by an act of will into the tips of her fingers.

The Russian medium further noted: "My experiments are as influenced by my emotional state as by the presence of spectators. If many people are present, more energy is needed and I tire quickly."[98] This statement, too, is characteristic of several kinds of paranormal healing. Further, Alla finds her work easier if she is familiar with the object she is to move and can bring about a spiritual and emotional rapport with it.

As Viktor Adamenko stated at the International Congress of Psychology in Tokyo (August 1972), Alla can induce an electrical field strength of 10,000 volts per cubic centimeter in the surroundings of objects without the provable existence of an electrical field between her body and the object. A neon lamp without an electrical source lit up when held against the object, but it did not do so when held against Alla's body. Sometimes sparks almost an inch long were observed to shoot out of her fingertips in the direction of the object to be moved. This unique distribution of the electrical field, says Benson Herbert, seems to confront physicists with a confusing task.

Alla has learned to control and master the electrical field surrounding every living being. But the observed phenomena can hardly be accounted for by electrical fields alone, for Professor William A. Tiller reports that Alla is able to do psychokinesis even when she stands barefoot on a metal floor and wears a grounded metal bracelet.[284] Given these conditions, our physical laws cannot explain how an electrical transfer can take place. The events support the hypothesis that a new kind of energy is at work which

can be transformed into electrical energy and back
again.

Investigations were carried out around 1920 by the
German engineer Fritz Grünewald[88,89] on the medium and magnetopath Johannsen, whose hands at
times exhibited singular, strongly magnetic fields. Johannsen could do simple feats of psychokinesis such
as depressing one side of an evenly balanced scale.
Grünewald found that each time, just before the
scale descended, the magnetic field strength in the
medium's hands—which he held out toward the object to be moved—grew markedly weaker, only to
increase after the psychokinetic act. It looked as if
something which had produced the strong magnetism
in Johannsen's body—perhaps the turbulent cold
plasma postulated by Sergeyev—displaced itself outward and released psychokinetic effects.

A few times Grünewald, by means of iron filings
strewn on glass plates, was able to obtain pictures of
the magnetic field within Johannsen's hands. In this
way he found several magnetic centers in the hand's
magnetic field which Grünewald believed were
evoked by electrical eddies in the medium's hands—
another startling similarity to Sergeyev's theories of
turbulent cold plasma. But strangely, the magnetic
centers seemed at times to lie *outside* the medium's
hand. We must recall the hypothesis that the biofield
can move outside the body. Sergeyev believes he has
proven that bioplasma can actually move outward
and that psychokinesis is a causal agent.[241] Therefore
it is no longer surprising that the psychokinetic medium Nina Kulagina is said to have paranormal healing powers as well.

While Alla Vinogradova works in part with electrostatic forces, Nina Kulagina seems to demonstrate
what may be called "pure" psychokinesis. To prove
her effect on the body of another, she grasped Benson
Herbert's arm above the wrist and concentrated. First
he felt only a slight warmth from the grasp itself. But
after two minutes, quite suddenly, a sort of heat set
in, reminiscent of a slight electrical current. The sensation became unpleasant and finally so unbearable

that Herbert forcibly freed himself from Kulagina's grasp.

The striking aspect was the very sudden onset of the feeling, after Kulagina had held Herbert's arm for some time. The subject had expected a pleasant, relaxing sensation, quite different from the feeling he experienced so abruptly. This does away with the objection that suggestion or hypnosis was at work here. Kulagina can obviously control the biological potential in her arms, and this ability seems crucial to her healing powers.

Nina Kulagina says that she can quickly heal infected wounds by laying her hand next to them. In cases of pneumonia she is said to lay her hands on the patient's sides. In the course of a three-month treatment under the supervision of Dr. Sergeyev, she is alleged to have removed a partial paralysis of the legs in a twenty-six-year-old so that the patient could walk completely normally again.

Another experiment by Dr. Sergeyev with Nina Kulagina strikes us as uncanny. The medium was able to control a frog's heart—checked by EKG— through psychic concentration and to bring it to a standstill. Efforts at reviving the frog failed. The frog had been killed by psychokinesis.[96]

Biologists working with Dr. Inyushin in Alma-Ata and Dr. Sergeyev in Leningrad believe that all living beings radiate bioplasma but that some psychically gifted people possess this ability to an especially high degree. In states of spiritual excitement or psychic shock the intensity of bioplasmic radiation is sometimes doubled or tripled even among normal people.

Various parts of the body radiate bioplasma with different intensities. It seems most strongly concentrated in the brain; the Soviet researchers, however, also noted particularly strong radiation from the fingers and solar plexus. (The sages of ancient times attributed a special significance to the solar plexus as an energy center for the generation of magical powers.)

Since all psychic and physical states are reflected

in the plasma, Dr. Inyushin contends that the concept of bioplasma offers the greatest possibilities for the objective investigation of the diverse psychoenergetic phenomena, including telepathy.[105]

In later works Dr. Inyushin and Dr. A. S. Roman have addressed themselves to bioplasmic effects during autosuggestion and autogenic training.[219] Experts in this technique are able to direct their thoughts in order to relax, induce a sensation of heaviness in their arms and legs, produce a feeling of warmth in the hands, and so on. During this aspect of autosuggestion characteristic changes appear in the electrobioluminescence, both in the structure and the intensity of the rays, which cannot be achieved by any other method—not even by dipping the hands in hot water, although in this procedure the skin gets considerably hotter than through autosuggestion.[219]

If someone not properly trained suggests the sensation of warmth to himself, only a few sporadic additional lights are added to the normal background luminescence; the same is true for some forms of emotional tension. When a trained person puts his hand on the arm of an untrained one and suggests a sensation of warmth in his own hand, similar changes occur in the pattern of luminescence of the untrained person, who—and this is the astonishing part—does not know what the trained person is suggesting to himself. When the trained person brings his hand within only an inch or so of the arm of the untrained one, the same effect occurs, though sometimes less strongly.[219]

This would appear to be objective proof that the laying on of hands has an effect not psychogenetically generated by the frequently cited "power of faith," and that positive results are possible even without direct contact.

Inyushin and Roman's findings throw the first light on the workings of various forms of paranormal healing. The investigators began by asking: How does the human organism react to any stimulus, as observed through electrobioluminescence? Various factors can serve as stimuli: emotions, autosuggestion, chemical stimulation, and so forth. They learned that the organism begins by responding with a generalized reaction, regardless of the specific stimulus, as if to lay the groundwork for a further, more specific reaction. First of all the organism marshals its forces. Not until the second phase does a case-specific reaction set in, if the occasion warrants it, pointing in the specific direction.

In healthy human beings the first reaction phase is characterized by a steady pattern of luminescence, now and again reinforced by bright flames, and the organization of the specific reaction runs its course clearly and steadily.

The luminescent background of emotionally disturbed people barely changes when outside influences are at work. Rather, the pattern is marked by a constant readiness for reaction which rapidly leads to exhaustion. During this exhaustion, stimuli can lose their significance and occasionally fail to generate any reaction. Reactions to disease-causing factors may, at least in many cases, be similar.

This explains why many people under strong emotional stress are susceptible to particular diseases such as head colds and hay fever. Their condition robs them of the bioenergetic reserves to erect a healthy barrier against these pernicious influences. In magnetizing or laying on of hands, bioenergetic reserves seem to be transferred, enabling the organism to carry out the specific curative reaction. This is why the Philippine psychic surgeons often apply magnetic healing before they undertake severe operations. The preliminary treatment strengthens the organism's bioenergetic reserves. The healers are apparently able to sense the patient's bioenergetic state and know how much it can be expected to accomplish.

Examples of the transfer of enormously strong bioenergy was furnished by the healer Phil A., to whom the journalist Ruth Montgomery devoted an entire book.[146] His ability to "fuel the patients' magnetic fields with new energy and to revitalize them," as he put it, seems literally wonderful. For four years, until

1930, he "revitalized" the patients of Dr. C. Hill, a physician active in the San Francisco Bay Area, and helped many in convincing ways. Using his hands, Phil sent an energy charge into the patients. What he has to say about controlling and guiding the energy in himself is reminiscent of Alla Vinogradova's statements.

Subsequently Phil collaborated with the surgeon Dr. Dena L. Smith after curing her of a heart ailment of long standing in 1956, when she was a medical student. Through Phil the surgeon constantly witnessed events which her medical studies had taught her were impossible.

For fifteen years Patricia Lucille Golden, born in 1949 in Powell, Wyoming, was a happy and healthy child. Then she began to complain of headaches, and in the course of the next few years her behavior changed remarkably: she became rebellious, antisocial, and unmanageable. Her parents took her to see neurologists and psychiatrists, without success. Finally in 1968, after a long series of negative test results, a hospital in San Jose, California, discovered a tumor at the base of the brain. Meanwhile the nineteen-year-old patient had grown almost blind and paralyzed. She could no longer leave her bed. Medical prognosis held out little chance for the successful removal of the tumor. Even if she survived the approximately seven-hour operation, she would probably have only a few months to live.

The girl's father had read Ruth Montgomery's recently published book, *A Search for Truth,* in which she wrote about the remarkable healer, whom she simply called Mr. A. Golden was able to reach the author by telephone, and she agreed to persuade the healer to treat the suffering girl after the operation. Ruth Montgomery explained that Mr. A. would not come to the hospital, in order not to offend the medical men. The operation was carried out on November 11 in the San Jose hospital by first-rate surgeons, resecting the tumor located in the fourth ventricle. A histological examination of the excised matter revealed that it was a malignant form of ependymoma.

At the beginning of December, Phil A., together with Dr. Smith, visited Ruth Montgomery. The two of them intended to fly on to California and promised to call Patricia's parents during a stopover in Dallas, to find out how the girl was. Before the plane landed in Dallas, the healer suddenly had an intuitive flash that it would be best to get off and continue on at once to Houston, since that was where the girl was. In fact, on the morning of that same day—December 5, 1968—the very sick girl had been flown from San Jose to Houston, where she was to be admitted to the M. D. Anderson Hospital. However, the patient insisted on being taken to her parents' home since—as she later said—she had the feeling that she would die otherwise. Finally her wish was granted, since her condition was considered hopeless. Her parents described her facial color as green, her knees swollen and thicker than her emaciated thighs, her eyes glassy; she could not keep anything on her stomach.

The healer arrived in Houston at two o'clock in the afternoon and treated Patricia for half an hour, "sending . . . the energies through her lower abdominal area—the magnetic field." After this first treatment Patricia was able to get out of bed and move around the room a little. At six o'clock the second treatment took place, after which Patricia was able to eat a full meal. At ten o'clock that night, when her skin had regained its normal color, her eyes had become clear, and the girl could again speak coherently, the third treatment began.

The following morning, after the fourth treatment, the patient was overcome by a ravenous appetite. The fifth and last treatment took place at noon. Afterward the healer said that she would experience no more difficulties so long as she led a sensible life. He refused a fee, accepting only repayment for expenses.

Three weeks later Patricia was already back to driving her car, had regained her normal weight, and was in the best of health, though she continued standard medical treatment for some time longer. In 1972 Patricia was hale, hearty, and happily married. There is no doubt in her mind that Mr. A. saved her life.[146]

Some patients remain in touch with Phil A. after their recovery and have themselves recharged once a week. Ruth Montgomery reported several who lived to be more than ninety years old. The oddest case was that of an old lady who at the age of ninety-eight broke off her treatments because her financial reserves were about to be exhausted and she did not wish to live longer than her money would stretch.

The possibility of transferring bioenergy from one person to another no longer seems the imaginative product of superstitious minds. To be sure, most physicists will argue that physical plasma cannot exist in the human body as either a dynamic or a static system. Physical plasma in the human body should recombine—the negative electrons and positive ions should join into normal atoms—unless a totally different form of energy or physical element which we have not recognized before is at work. Because of the electrical charges, moving plasma currents in the human body would vanish almost immediately in the material aggregate of the human body. But the Hungarian biologist and Nobel prizewinner Albert Szent-Györgyi has said that the biologist must be on his guard when physicists tell him something is not possible.[195]

Further, physicists have examined the plasma state almost exclusively in connection with inorganic matter. Perhaps bioplasma represents an entirely new state of plasma which we do not understand, or a genotype of the material world beyond physical plasma (let us call it a transplasmic state) which can occur in connection with organic matter. Compared to familiar physical plasma, it may be almost nonelectrical and more subtle, but it may transform into a plasmalike state with electric particles (perhaps under the influence of particular high-frequency fields in Kirlian photography?), at which time it will be detected by our instruments.

Our biological and medical concepts do allow for the generation of electromagnetic rays able to extend their energies into the spectrum of visible light, in the magnitude of a few electron volts (units of energy used in nuclear physics). Possibly one can imagine further ultraviolet rays in the body, if only to a minimal degree.[91,195]

X rays, on the other hand, are over a thousand times richer in energy, gamma radiation even a million times or more. But in investigating the psychokinetic phenomena of Nina Kulagina, X-ray films or other photosensitive material were used as the surface to hold small objects. The developed films showed the tracks of the moving objects. It is said that in this process occasional extremely hard but energy-laden rays appear which lie in the range of X rays or with even greater energy charges.[240] If these assertions are correct, it would be understandable that a number of Russian researchers are firmly holding to the concept of bioplasma.

A great many researchers in the West and the East have investigated the effect of emanations from healing hands and have discovered some quite puzzling effects.[299] Unrefrigerated foods radiated by healers' hands have kept much better, without spoilage, than comparative samples which the healer did not hold. If decaying processes are stopped by the bioplasmic radiation, it can be assumed that the radiation affects germs and bacteria, killing the microorganisms. It seems probable, then, that the healing radiation can similarly kill microorganisms causing infections. In fact, quite a few healers investigated by American researchers were able to remove or prevent infection from wounds by a laying on of hands. The same effect has already been reported for Nina Kulagina.

Good healers have often proved the power to promote growth. Sprigs planted by them flourished much better than those planted by others. At Newark College of Engineering, Professor Douglas Dean and his students sowed barley seed under controlled laboratory conditions and attempted to mentally influence the growth of the plants during germination. The results showed that seeds germinated most quickly and seedlings grew most rapidly when "cared for" by persons who had achieved significant scores in

ESP card tests. Curiously, according to Dean, not
only those students who scored higher than normal
with five correct guesses had a positive influence on
plant growth, but those whose results lay distinctly
below average also had a marked effect on growth.
On the other hand, no influence was exerted by students whose number of correct answers exactly corresponded to the average.[299]

The Bulgarian physician and parapsychologist Dr.
Georgi Lozanov has also investigated the influence of
healing on the growth of plants. Some of the radiated
plants grew three times as rapidly as under ordinary
conditions and were considerably more vigorous.[184]

Equally interesting are laboratory experiments with
anesthetized mice. Statistically evaluated experiments
gave unequivocal proof that artificially numbed mice
regained consciousness considerably more quickly if
radiated from a distance by healing hands.[84]

This new energy is probably at least partly identical with Reichenbach's Odic force and with the vital
energy called ch'i in Chinese acupuncture. It is interesting that Reichenbach claimed this new biological energy could be transferred to lifeless objects, for
psi researchers have recently noted that water irra-
diated by magnetopathic healers affects the growth of
plants, although the water cannot be distinguished
chemically from untreated samples. Plant seeds watered from a bottle which a psychic healer has held in
his hands for a long time germinate and grow considerably more rapidly than seeds of the same species
watered normally. Reichenbach's hypothesis, articulated 120 years ago, that water absorbs and stores
biological energy from healers seems confirmed.[206,207]
This energy seems to originate in the bioplasmic body
of the healer or medium. But from where does the
energy body get its energy?

Most paranormal healers speak of a power that
surrounds all of us and with which sensitives charge
themselves. Many call it the divine power, others say
simply that God does the healing and that it is not
they who heal. Filipino healers say that one must
simply open oneself to the flow of this divine power

through concentration, meditation, and prayer. One healer of the Unio Espiritista Cristiana Filipinas also told me, however, "If the healer feels this power waning, he grasps the flag of the Unio Espiritista and charges himself with new power."

The healer Alexei Krivorotov, investigated by Soviet researchers, has the sensation of receiving the power from outside. Ambrose Worral said, "I consider myself merely as a 'channel' or 'conduit' for the healing current, not the generator of the power that heals."

In 1962 the stigmatized Therese Neumann died in Konnersreuth. Besides the stigmata, she maintained her body without material nourishment. From Christmas 1922 until her death she took in almost no solid food and gave up liquids in 1926. In July 1927 she was observed day and night by four nurses under oath. During this time she took 0.014 ounce of host in 3 tablespoons of water. Besides blood and regurgitated bile, she voided 32 cubic inches of urine. She weighed 121 pounds on the first day, 112 pounds on the fourth, 119 pounds on the eighth, 116 pounds on the eleventh, and was back to 121 pounds on the fifteenth day.[226,304]

During the period of National Socialism, Therese was investigated and watched over for a protracted period of time by members of the SS, obviously ordered to detect any fraud. The observers had to abandon their project without having achieved their object.

What source of energy maintained Therese's vital functions? Established medicine holds that life energy must be wrested entirely from the process of metabolism taking place in the body. But there are probably other possibilities which are unfolded in exceptional cases.

Perhaps we are living in a sea of energy which can quite simply flow into us, but we shut ourselves off from this source through our false concepts. The Filipino healer Tony Agpaoa told me why every year he maintains a rigorous fast for at least sixteen days, eating nothing except a little honey and drinking only water: "I need it to provide myself with new power for my work. Afterward I have the feeling of being recharged like a storage battery."

During long fasts (Agpaoa is said to have fasted for as long as 45 days) Philippine healers eat a teaspoon of honey a day, although it is unlikely that they have heard of the significance of the blood-sugar level. In fact, a spoonful of honey is also administered to patients in Western reducing sanatoriums, since a lowered blood-sugar level can cause unpleasant side effects.

Fasting as a healing, regeneration, and rejuvenation cure is also practiced by several doctors in Western sanatoriums. It is by no means primarily a treatment for loss of weight, as most people suppose. The German specialist in fasting Dr. Otto Buchinger labels the fasting cure as "the king" of cures.[32]

When external nourishment is no longer available, the organism begins by demolishing fatty deposits and metabolic remnants stored in the connective and unhealthy bodily tissue. In proper fasts healthy substance is drawn on only as a last resort. This process results in a great "cleansing" of the organism in two to three weeks, during which time the fasting person, curiously enough, experiences hardly any hunger pangs, as he would if he continued to take in at least 500 calories a day. The fasting person continues to take light exercise and goes for walks. If instead he spends his time in bed, the body begins to break down the active muscular tissue, so that after three weeks of fasting the person is really ill.

In the early 1960s curative fasting without these safeguards was "tested" in a German university hospital, with the insane outcome that curative fasting was said to be dangerous and to be avoided. According to an interesting report in the *Medical Tribune*, mice who were not fed every third day lived 50 percent longer than similar mice reared without fast days.

I have undergone two two-week fasting cures and recuperated marvelously during them. One time, also, following the animal experiments reported in the

Medical Tribune, for a period of six months I did not eat on two days of the week—I still do this once in a while when in a stress situation. A proper fast can be enormously relaxing and can restore a disturbed spiritual and bodily balance. In the Gannushkin Institute near Moscow psychotherapeutic and psychiatric treatments are carried out by means of fasting cures—allegedly with a high success rate.[182]

A properly conducted fasting cure does not weaken the patient but strengthens him. Though the ability to think analytically generally diminishes slightly during the cure, intuitive thinking and readiness to meditate —factors related to paranormal talent—can awaken or be increased.

In his book *Das Heilfasten* (Healing Through Fasting) Otto Buchinger touched on the unresolved question of bioenergetic powers:

> I am tempted to make a totally "unbelievable" and heretical assertion. . . . Besides air and water, is solid and liquid digestible matter really the only form of nourishment? After observing many people who have undergone long fasts, one cannot avoid the thought that some additional cosmic power of vibration maintains and "recharges" the fasting organism. It must have something to do with *religio,* with the renewed attachment to a creative original energy. The years-long *inedia* [lack of nourishment] of Therese Neumann refers us to a literal interpretation of Matthew 4:4: "Man shall not live by bread alone, but by every word that proceedeth out of the mouth of God." Is it really possible for man to recharge himself from the universe by finding the Word, the creative logos? I have heard of two cases of *inedia* at the Sorbonne in Paris, but they were never published. I daresay they could not be fitted into the pigeonholes of academic bureaucracy.[32]

8/PSYCHIC SURGEONS

Zé Arigo

A man who was called the "eighth wonder of the world" by journalists and scholars worked for twenty years as a healer and psychic surgeon for the benefit of the very poor people of his homeland. When he died after an automobile accident in January 1971, he was accompanied to his grave by 30,000 people, among them the daughter of a former president of his country. This was the Brazilian healer José Pedro Freitas, known as Zé Arigo. He was active in Congonhas do Campo, a small, quaint city of 17,000 in the state of Minas Gerais. The townspeople—of every color—live in wooden huts, primitive houses, and deteriorated mansions. But in recent years the attraction of Congonhas was not the artful baroque facades of its inner city but Zé Arigo, whose reputation stretched far beyond the South American continent, and whose followers numbered in the millions.

Certified reports from scientists and patients agree that Arigo carried out serious operations of every kind while the patients were fully conscious. Generally he used only a kitchen or pocket knife, a pair of scissors, and a few clothespins. In this incredible way he removed tumors and other organic disorders. Little or no blood was lost during his operations, and the incisions closed as soon as he laid his hands on them, leaving only a thin pink scar. While the well-known American physician and pararesearcher Dr. Andrija K. Puharich, together with Henry Belk, investigated Arigo's work, the healer removed a small tumor on Puharich's arm with a simple knife—without sterilization, and without pain. Afterward a scar could bare-

ly be detected to show where the tumor had
been.[200,248]

Arigo's eye examinations were famous. The patient
was usually asked to stand against the wall of the
examination room. Arigo firmly held the patient's head
against the wall and asked the patient to look upward.
With one finger Arigo held the upper eyelid and
guided a sharp, pointed kitchen knife—which had
been carelessly lying on the table among a jumble of
papers, a jar of honey, and writing materials—between eyeball and eyelid, so far that the knife point
became visible under the skin and could be felt with
the fingers as a prominent swelling over the brow.
With strong circular motions (which he often carried
out without looking at the knife) Arigo sometimes
pulled the eyeball almost completely out of its socket,
examined it, and, if necessary, rapidly removed a gall-
like mass. Then he let the eyeball slide back into its
proper position, pulled the knife back out of the eye,
and pressed the lids firmly together; sometimes a puslike fluid ran out of the eye.

Not until then did the patients move again. They always assured spectators that they felt no pain of any
kind but had observed and clearly perceived the
whole procedure. Arigo's eye treatment has often been
filmed and shown on television.

The knife was never sterilized; at best, Arigo wiped
off the most obvious traces of dirt on a piece of paper
before operating. Nevertheless, the most delicate abdominal, cranial, and optic operations succeeded. Although not a single case of infection and failure could
be proved against the healer, one day one of his
"operating scalpels" was confiscated and he was forbidden to perform any more operations.

Dr. Mauro Godoy, director of the municipal hospital in Congonhas do Campo, spoke to journalists about
Zé Arigo: "From a medical standpoint, I am a great
admirer of his manual and intuitive arts. I am not an
unskilled surgeon, and I can carry out a cataract
operation in eighteen to twenty minutes. But in my
presence Arigo accomplished the same operation,
flawlessly, in two minutes. He used an unsterilized

pocket knife, without any detrimental consequences.
It is a pity that this blessed man is forbidden to operate. He is much too law-abiding to openly act in de-
fiance of a court order. But he could save many lives if
he were allowed to operate."

Arigo was accused of quackery and sentenced to
ten months' imprisonment; but he did not have to
serve his full time, since people with influence, who
owed him a great deal, saw to it that he was released
early. Though he had to stop operating, he continued
to counsel everyone who sought his help.

Arigo worked from Monday to Friday, generally
from early in the morning until late at night. In a
trance state he often diagnosed more than a thousand
patients a day and wrote prescriptions for effective
remedies. Arigo had followers on every level of society, but his most prominent adherent and friend was
Dr. Juscelino Kubitschek, until 1954 governor of Minas
Gerais, and Brazilian president from 1956 to 1961.

Kubitschek, the spiritual father of the modern me-
tropolis of Brasilia, was himself trained as a physician.
His daughter Marscia suffered from advanced leu-
kemia, and her condition grew steadily worse. Renowned specialists from the United States and Europe
appeared powerless against the progress of the disease. When all the possibilities of Western medicine
had been exhausted, Dr. Kubitschek took his daughter
to see Arigo, who cured her.

Scientists—among them Dr. Puharich—examined
over a thousand patients, using the most recent medical methods and tools, before they were seen by Arigo.
Medical and paranormal diagnoses were compared.
Not one erroneous diagnosis could be charged against
the Brazilian.[200]

Antonio Agpaoa

Coincidentally, a few days after the great Brazilian
healer's funeral a small German-speaking group traveled to Asia in pursuit of rumors that there were a

number of psychic surgeons in the Philippines who performed successful operations which seemed to dwarf whatever had been reported of Zé Arigo.

Among the surgeons, Antonio Agpaoa—usually simply called Tony—was said to be the best known and the best. Agpaoa allegedly worked without a knife or other surgical instruments. He was said to open the patient's body by a mysterious power or emanation of his hands, without the patient's experiencing any pain. He then allegedly removed the focus of infection—at times even cancerous tumors—and closed the body again without leaving a scar. In most cases the patient was said to be able to get up right after the operation and to resume work after a day or two.

In the last few years many Americans have traveled to the Philippines to be operated on by Agpaoa or other surgeons of the same school. The well-known pioneer in extrasensory perception Harold Sherman, currently president of the ESP Research Associates Foundation in Little Rock, Arkansas, visited Agpaoa together with Henry Belk and other surgeons in 1966. On his return he wrote *Wonder Healers of the Philippines*.[248]

The group now planning to fly to the Philippines to study the native lay surgeons included three physicians, several patients, and myself, a scientist. One of the physicians was Dr. Hans Naegeli-Osjord from Zurich, president of the Swiss Society for Parapsychology. The trip had been organized by the Freiburg journalist Hans Geisler, who published reports during the 1960s of the singular operations performed by Agpaoa and other psychic surgeons of the Philippines. American reports on psychic surgery in the Philippines were very different and at times contradictory. Many were favorable, others hostile. There were said to be about forty healers, most of whom belonged to the Unio Espiritista Cristiana Filipinas.

American patients told us the most contradictory stories about Agpaoa. Astonishing achievements and unsuccessful operations were reported; one group asserted that an appendix removed by Agpaoa had been identified as chicken intestines. Such accusations naturally disturbed us, but we considered it unlikely that a healer who had been practicing for over twenty years and had attracted patients from all over the world could be nothing more than a clever illusionist.

In Bangkok a number of Filipinos got into our airplane, and I asked several of them in English (the second national language besides the native Tagalog) whether the name of Antonio Agpaoa meant anything to them. They did recognize the name but knew nothing further about him, which astonished and irritated us. Was it a matter of the proverbial prophet being unsung in his own land, or were we pursuing a mirage?

Our first stop was Manila, the seething capital, bordering on the South China Sea, of the republic of seven thousand islands. Our ultimate goal was Baguio, the country's second capital, situated 4500 feet high in the mountains, some five hours by car from Manila. It was the charming summer residence of the upper classes, where Agpaoa lived. We had asked for an appointment, and he let us know he was expecting us.

After our arrival in Manila three members of our group immediately hired a car to Baguio. The rest of us spent the night in a hotel; the following morning at seven Agpaoa's chauffeur came for us. Because of preparations connected with a national holiday, traffic was already extremely heavy; astonishingly, it seemed to regulate itself in a most wonderful way without traffic lights, policemen, or any visible adherence to traffic laws.

We traveled first on a highway, then on a country road through a flat landscape—the so-called lowlands —and passed many tiny settlements with simple wooden houses. The inhabitants were clean and colorfully dressed. Now and again we could see elegant Filipinas, arrayed in latest Western fashions, peeking out of the most wretched huts. The temperature grew increasingly tropical as the hours passed, until we finally came to the highlands, where the straight country road turned into an increasingly curving mountain road and the climate became more bearable. Our ride resembled a summer tour through the foothills of the Swiss Alps, with some magnificent deep chasms and

waterfalls, where pines and other tropical and sub-
tropical plants flourished. We reached Baguio around
two o'clock. Agpaoa's chauffeur let us off at the small
hotel Villa La Maja, on the southern edge of the city
in the midst of pines along a steep mountainside.

Agpaoa was waiting for us. He appeared in the
doorway of the hotel and came toward us up the
steps to the street: a handsome Filipino, thirty-one
years old, fashionably dressed. He was friendly, his
handshake was likable and firm; there was no immediate sparkling radiance, as might have been expected from a "wonder healer." He welcomed us in a
neatly articulated American English; he spoke with a
pleasant slowness, so that we understood him more
easily than we had expected. In the hotel lounge we
were introduced to his wife, Lucy.

After we had been assigned our rooms, we ate dinner with the Agpaoas. The Philippine midday meal
reminded me of French cuisine with its lavishness and
variety. Agpaoa turned out to be an eloquent companion who knew how to keep his guests entertained.
He simply mentioned that he had operated that morning and that he intended to let us take part in the
next day's operations. That evening we again dined
together and talked for some time afterward. Agpaoa expressed a special interest in life in Germany,
since until this time he had met American tourists almost exclusively and had had few dealings with Europeans. He parted from us quite early because, as he
told us, he needed the rest of the evening to meditate
in preparation for the next day's surgery.

After a hearty Philippine breakfast the following
morning, we walked up and down in front of the hotel,
waiting for Agpaoa. Toward ten o'clock a large American Plymouth drove down the street. A rich American
had given Agpaoa this car in 1966 in gratitude for a
successful operation. Agpaoa was accompanied by a
somewhat older, slender gentleman—his father,
Moises, who, as we had already been told, often assisted the son in his operations.

Agpaoa seemed somewhat more reserved and at the

outset more taciturn than the day before. As we went down the stairs from the street, Agpaoa pointed up to the second floor. Apparently that was where he was going to operate.

We had prepared still cameras and movie equipment and went to the second floor. It was chiefly made up of the little hotel's large lounge, with couches, armchairs, and a fireplace. At the left, separated by a glass wall, was a room that contained a sink and could be used as a kitchen. Here Agpaoa washed his hands after operating. At the left of the lounge, in front of the kitchen, stood a long, solid, transparent glass table.

The other members of our group stood around the fireplace with Agpaoa as he told them about the cases he intended to operate on today. I observed the father as he prepared the glass table to be used as the operating table. No matter how you tried, this table offered no hiding place. Moises placed a white sheet over the glass and covered it with a plastic cloth. That was all.

We began to set up our tripods and motion-picture cameras. In the meantime Agpaoa chatted with patients who had arrived for their operations, inquiring about their symptoms and the medical diagnosis. It seemed unlikely to me that a fraudulent operator would wait until just before surgery to worry about details; a fraud must be thoroughly prepared beforehand, at least when doctors are going to be present. Agpaoa, after all, could hardly bring along chicken intestine and pork "props" suitable to every possible disease: he was coatless, dressed only in tight-fitting trousers and a turtleneck sweater. The fact that he performed the operations in a hotel also spoke against any hypothesis of fraud; for he could hardly improvise a deception in a strange building.

During the preparations Agpaoa chain-smoked mentholated cigarettes. Finally he gave a sign that he was ready to begin.

Suspense was now at its height. For the first time in our lives we were going to see a bloody operation without surgical instruments—or a trick as clever as it was vicious.

The first patient was an aging American woman with severe breast cancer. She lay down on the prepared table and took off her clothes. Her genital region remained covered with a towel. Agpaoa and his father, as well as nine spectators, among them three doctors, stood around the table in a circle; the inquisitive hotel staff kept in the background. The American's right breast had already been completely amputated in the United States. The left showed a huge cancerous growth, with several additional nodes the size of corn kernels.

Agpaoa allowed his slightly outstretched hands to pass over the patient's body at a noticeable distance. Apparently he was attempting to feel out the nidus.

Now the healer stopped above the right abdominal section and pointed to this place on the body. Agpaoa said that he would begin today by removing a metastasized section.

Among us we had six movie cameras; some were already in action. One of the spectators held a strong light which Agpaoa had procured for us, since he wanted to be sure we had enough light to get good pictures.

We were asked to stop filming for a moment and to join in a short meditation. Agpaoa held his hands over the patient as if blessing her, closed his eyes, and said a short prayer in English, calling on God for help and success in today's operation.

Agpaoa had pushed the sleeves of his black turtleneck sweater up above the elbow so that his forearms were bare. We observed each of his movements and were later able to use our motion pictures to reconstruct the entire procedure. His hands were empty; nothing was concealed between his fingers, which were spread wide at times. After stretching out his hands as if in blessing, he never again brought them near his own body; he could not, therefore, transfer from a hiding place any material he might have brought along.

Agpaoa dipped a wad of cotton into a plastic bowl full of water and laid it on the body of the patient, who lay on the table with open eyes and seemed fully conscious. Agpaoa's fingertips lightly touched the patient's abdominal wall and began to massage it gently. While the healer continued his massaging and kneading of the abdomen, it suddenly looked as if blood were seeping through the patient's skin. After this had gone on for some time, something like raw flesh glimmered under his steadily moving fingers, which now seemed to push diagonally into the skin. After a few more moments Agpaoa used his right hand to pull out of the body something like tissue, without severing it. Agpaoa kept his left hand steadily inside the wound in order, as he explained, to keep the body "open."

The patient appeared to feel no pain whatever. She addressed some remarks to her husband, standing beside her. Then she briefly raised her head so as to be able to see the operation. She exclaimed in surprise when she saw the bleeding, apparently open wound, and the raw tissue which Agpaoa steadily worked over with his fingertips until he let it slide back into the cavity. Immediately afterward, it seemed he worked his way deeper into the body, his hands heavily smeared with blood.

Next to the site of the operation lay blackish-red clumps of coagulated blood.

Now Agpaoa jerked his right hand inside the body, as if he were applying slight force to tear off something. He threw something bloody into the slop bowl —presumably the wad of cotton which he had placed on the patient's body at the beginning and which he may have used to get an easier grip on the smooth tissue. Immediately thereafter, Agpaoa inserted his right hand back into the wound and slowly pulled out a plum-sized piece of tissue which he laid on a cotton wad and held out for the patient to feel; his left hand remained in the wound. Finally he pulled out his left hand carefully, until only two fingers remained pushed into the abdominal wall. "One, two, three," he said. On the word "three" his left hand became completely separated from the patient's body, and all that remained on the body was a tiny puddle and a few clumps of coagulated blood. When these were wiped away, the abdomen lay undamaged as before. The sheet placed across the patient's loins below the site of the operation had also become heavily smeared with blood.

The spectators, especially the doctors, looked at each other in perplexity. The whole procedure had gone so smoothly and quickly—perhaps two or three minutes in all—that we had not yet taken it all in. The physicians touched and examined the excised tissue. There was no doubt that it consisted of organic fleshy matter.

In the meantime Agpaoa had washed his hands, and we all gathered around the fireplace again. Tony lit a mentholated cigarette, and we questioned him.

The first question, of special interest to the doctors, was whether Tony had had any medical training. "I'm sorry," Agpaoa replied, laughing, "but I've got to tell you that I've had no training—as you understand the term—in the medical field." Surely it was impossible to perform surgery without anatomical knowledge, we countered.

"Is it absolutely necessary for a homing pigeon to be able to read a map?" Agpaoa asked in reply. He said further that in the course of time, through dealing with patients and physicians, he had acquired some knowledge of anatomy, but he did not need it for his operations. While operating, his hands were in a trance and only partly controlled by his conscious mind. In earlier times, especially during serious operations, he had required a complete trance before he could operate; during the surgery he had no conscious control and was not consciously in contact with his environment.

We were curious about his way of diagnosing. "I'm sorry, but I can't say it any other way than to say that I know without knowing how. When I concentrate on the patient, I know what's the matter with him."

He also feels certain emanations from the patient's body, he told us, and palpates these with his hands. In this way he is able to form a picture of the patient's condition. He can also see the patient's aura, which guides him during the operation.

"If a patient comes to you with a confirmed medical

diagnosis," a doctor asked, "do you base your treatment on that?"

"I always diagnose my way. Often I agree with the clinical diagnosis. In the final analysis, I always go by my own diagnosis."

"What kind of power allows your hands to penetrate the patient's body? Is it based on electromagnetism?"

"That's hard to say. Maybe some electromagnetic phenomena are involved. But basically a spiritual power works through me. This power does not come from myself. I have the feeling of being only the 'channel' through which the power flows, or maybe a tool of the power."

While we talked, Agpaoa's father had rubbed an ointment on the patient's stomach. She arose now, put on her wrapper, and left the room, supported by her husband. She asserted again that she had experienced no pain whatever and had been fully conscious throughout. We did not doubt her, since we had spoken with her several times during the operation.

The next patient was a German who had asked to be treated in her hotel room. A degenerated lymph gland was probably removed from the upper right quadrant of the abdomen. Since I worked the patient's movie camera during the operation, I do not have any visual documentation of this case, nor can I recall the details well enough to repeat them here.

In the following cigarette break we questioned Agpaoa further: "Do you operate on everyone who comes to see you?"

"No. Sometimes I am not allowed to. But I always know whether I'm allowed or not and whether the time is right."

"How can you tell?"

"By the color of the patient's aura and the color of my hands. My hands change color when I direct them at the patient. If I see yellow, I'm allowed to operate, but if my hands seem orange-colored, the time isn't right. If my hands turn orange or red during the operation, I have to stop right away, otherwise I endanger the patient. Sometimes, too, there's need for a magnetopathic treatment, for strengthening. In cases like that, I can often operate later on."

"Can normal people like us see your hands change color?"

"No, I'm the only one who can see it."

"Do you operate even if a doctor says the case is inoperable?"

"I always operate unless I see unfavorable colors."

"Can you cure every disease?"

"Of course not. But we Philippine healers can often bring about improvements in apparently hopeless cases or at least alleviate the symptoms, sometimes even remove them completely. It's important not to lose faith! Even if I can't cure everyone, no patient has ever died from my operations, and there has never been a dangerous infection, even though some doctors who have seen my work believed that there *had* to be infection."

We had now twice seen the apparent opening of the body without instruments and its closing without leaving a scar. We could not seriously doubt Agpaoa's ability, unless the entire procedure should turn out to be a form of mass hypnosis, which the films would prove or disprove. Agpaoa could not give us any explanation that satisfied scientific Western thinking. He said that he opened the body by a "spiritual force" that worked through him whenever he was operating.

We further learned that Agpaoa had performed his first "wonder healing" at about the age of eight.* Even before this, he had had strange experiences for several years. Agpaoa told us that when he was a child he had seen "higher beings," invisible to others, who invited him to come with them to the mountains to prepare himself to become a tool of a "divine healing power." He did follow them and often spent days meditating in the mountains. At the age of nine, after more than eight days of meditation and fasting in a narrow cave, it was vouchsafed to him that he was to fulfill a mission in this world.

*See below, p. 111.

His account reminded us of the initiation experiences encountered in shamanism, whose parapsychological aspect has hardly been investigated at all.[65,112] It is a grave mistake, typical of our times, that we consider everything in the area of so-called mysticsm as imagination. However, man consists of the totality of his expressions, whether they are clearly visible or only "latent." Both personal observation and external investigation should be used together; there is no reason to assign a higher value to one than to the other.[36] If the mystic states of consciousness bring about tangible, real effects, some reality must underlie them.

After this conversation with Agpaoa it was the turn of a patient from Hamburg. He suffered from an intestinal disorder whose symptoms were localized in the left side of the abdomen. The operation proceeded like the one I first described, except that Agpaoa's right hand evidently went further into the body. Agpaoa removed a larger piece of tissue, which looked like an adhesion from the intestine. After this he performed a hemorrhoid operation on the same patient, entering the anus with his bare hands. After feeling around for some time, he laid bare the vein to be removed and asked a member of our group to tear it out with a forceps. This operation was relatively unbloody. The patient finally had a slight pain in his gluteus maximus muscle (in the buttocks), and Agpaoa finally removed something bloody which the doctors present regarded as a degenerated lymph gland.

It was now approaching noon, and Agpaoa ended his surgical activity for the day.

During the following days we saw still other operations, most of which we filmed. Surgery of the prostate was performed on an American patient, and a small benign tumor was removed from the testes without the patient's feeling any pain. We saw operations for hemorrhoids and varicose veins, the success of the latter being somewhat in doubt. An alleged cardiac operation on a German patient did not allow the spectators to tell a great deal about what was going on.

In this case he was dealing with a valve defect with cicatrization, the consequence of a rheumatic infection in a twenty-six-year-old patient who also suffered from severe cardiac insufficiency.

Cardiac surgery is among the most serious procedures, as far as Agpaoa is concerned. He began with prolonged stroking of the patient's head and chest, a method familiar from magnetopathic treatments. Then the patient's eyes and ears were covered or stuffed with wet cotton pads. Finally the healer, his eyes occasionally closed as if to enable him to concentrate better, approached the chest obliquely with his hands; the spectators were almost completely kept from observing the procedure by a towel that blocked the view. We got the impression that during very serious surgery Agpaoa is disturbed by onlookers' curious glances.

After a short time his hands were covered with blood, and he brought out what seemed to be small bloody substances. He claimed to be removing calcium deposits and "cleansing" the mitral valves. The success of this operation was doubtful. Later the patient was operated on again without the presence of spectators. His shortness of breath—which admittedly could be largely psychogenic—was not, according to the patient, improved by the surgery. Perhaps Agpaoa did remove sclerotic deposits by paranormal means but was unable to remove the valve cicatrization. The patient had the impression that Agpaoa had not penetrated all the way to the heart. This need not be held against Agpaoa; for in many cases Philippine surgeons seem also to operate psychokinetically.

At the end of a morning of operating, Agpaoa pulled out a roll of sturdy adhesive tape about 3 inches wide and asked one of us to hold the free end. He held the roll in his left hand. Then he concentrated and with the edge of his hand or the edge of his middle finger "cut" through the tape as if with a knife. Next the free section was pasted on the other unrolled tape, and in the same way Agpaoa severed the doubled strip from the rest of the roll.

He repeated this maneuver several times, until finally, instead of using his hand, he cut through the adhesive tape with his stuck-out tongue; he could also do it simply by blowing on the tape. By the end he had created a strip about 8 inches long made up of six thicknesses of tape pasted one atop the other. He asked two members of our group to hold this by both ends, and without visible exertion he "cut" through this layer of six adhesive tapes with the middle finger of his outstretched hand, starting the cut several times.

Adhesive tape of the sort Agpaoa used can sometimes be severed by a short, hard tear. As our developed films later showed, however, on that day Agpaoa carried out the separation without employing any mechanical force worth the name; he rubbed the tape very lightly with his finger. If the tape had been loosened beforehand, it would have torn as soon as it was unrolled, which in itself requires considerable energy. But even a previously loosened piece of tape cannot ordinarily be torn by a tongue or blown apart. Subsequently Agpaoa repeated these experiments, going so far as to paste eight layers together—in all probability, a psychokinetic achievement.

Ever since accounts of Agpaoa's surgery were published after Harold Sherman's trip to the Philippines in 1966, there has been no lack of scientists eager to minimize Agpaoa's operations as pure fraud. The best-known adherent of this theory is the American physician Dr. Seymour Wanderman, whom Sherman asked to come to the Philippines in 1966 as scientific star witness, as it were, to the genuineness of Agpaoa's operations.

But matters turned out quite differently. Anyone who has studied the psi phenomena gets the impression that at times, powers with a downright intelligence of their own seem intent at the last minute on putting a spoke in the wheel of the serious researcher looking for tenable, objective proof. In this case Agpaoa welcomed Sherman's plan to call in a physician from the United States. He even postponed some interesting operations to the following weekend, when Dr. Wanderman was expected. But difficulties in obtaining a visa forced Dr. Wanderman to postpone his trip twice; when he finally arrived after several days' delay, Agpaoa had taken care of some urgent cases; other patients, annoyed at the long waiting period, had left, so no patients were available—though at other times Agpaoa is beleaguered by them.

Dr. Wanderman missed several interesting operations because he had gone to visit friends in Manila. On his return there was a new patient; Agpaoa pulled one of his molars with his bare hands. The American physician assumed that the tooth had already been very loose. When another patient had the same complaint a short time later, Agpaoa offered to let Dr. Wanderman test the tooth's firmness. The physician had to admit that the tooth was steady in its socket. After Agpaoa removed this tooth painlessly with his bare hands, Wanderman said that this was not interesting.

Finally there was a patient with a superficial cyst in the abdominal area. When Agpaoa opened and squeezed out the cyst, the American doctor was outraged at such a primitive method, which he believed must lead to serious infection. Wanderman witnessed another cyst operation and was finally shown one or two abdominal operations.

Besides Harold Sherman, the previously mentioned Dr. Hiroshi Motoyama was also present. Agpaoa requested Dr. Wanderman to reach into the operation site, but he refused; nor did he accept blood and tissue samples. After a short stay he departed and claimed Agpaoa's operations were fraudulent.

Dr. Wanderman suspected that Agpaoa did not penetrate the patients' bodies while operating but cleverly spread some kind of membrane over the patient's body, at the same time squirting a red fluid over it. He would manipulate around this prop, creating the impression in outside observers that he was

actually operating. When Agpaoa actually opened the
patient's body, he was using a razor blade concealed
in his left hand. Wanderman admitted he had not
actually seen such a blade, but he knew it is not possible to make an incision with the bare hand. In an
American television program Dr. Wanderman said
that he did not consider Agpaoa worth further investigation.[248]

Practically all the circumstances under which
Agpaoa worked speak against deception. Most of the
surgery we saw took place in the hotel Villa La Maja
and was observed by our entire group. Agpaoa worked
by ordinary indoor daylight. We stood around the operating table more or less in a circle; the movie
cameras were also working from several angles.

If at times Agpaoa holds his left hand somewhat
cupped, this is not because he keeps a razor blade
concealed in the palm, but because during surgery
the left hand plays a more passive role and is used to
hold open the site of the operation. I made a point of
looking under Agpaoa's left hand from behind while
he held it suspiciously still during operating, but I was
never able to see a razor blade or any similar tool.
The only material I was able to detect in Agpaoa's
operations was a piece of cotton or gauze, which he
quite openly soaked in water and applied to the site
of the operation; at times he seemed to take it into the
wound itself—perhaps to get a better grip on slippery
tissue, or to have a foundation of separation for a
subsequent "materialization process."*

When I was a youngster I was very interested in
magic tricks and illusions; I was myself an amateur
magician. To this day I attend performances by outstanding international acts whenever I can. I know
that a great many illusions are possible, but every
magician needs certain preconditions for performing
his tricks, whether it is a special suit with adequate
opportunities for concealment or a special table with
a false bottom. Most of the time he requires free
space at his back. A magician cannot tolerate camera

*See chap. 10.

people surrounding him on all sides, working movie cameras with time exposures. If Agpaoa were such a unique supermagician, it's a sure bet that he would have become a star in the world's foremost variety theaters.

Our films, developed after our return to Germany, unequivocally contradicted the possibility of mass hypnosis. Rather, they proved that our observations in Baguio had been accurate.

Other American doctors have claimed that on examination, some of Agpaoa's blood and tissue samples turned out to be chicken blood and flesh. Agpaoa is hardly so foolish as to hand American doctors chicken blood, but the rumor continues to circulate and be given wide credence. Agpaoa's reaction to the accusation was to stop giving away samples of blood and tissue.

We too became suspicious because Agpaoa did not leave us any blood or tissue samples. But in these paranormal processes the specific character of blood and tissue might be changed, since in all probability Agpaoa's hands give off a much stronger emanation than that of Western magnetopathic healers. But one of our doctors who was a specialist in pathology recognized the tissue removed in the hemorrhoid operation as veins and in the prostate operation as prostate tissue.

Some tissue seemed to puzzle the physicians, however. From the outset these samples looked different from tissue excised with the knife; but tissue of this form could not have been normally removed from animals either. What is at work here seems to be a severing mechanism of which we know absolutely nothing—which makes sense, for we are dealing with a knifeless operation.

Among the physicians in our group, one, Dr. H., could stay in Baguio only a few days and saw only the operations described above. After his return to Europe he was therefore the most skeptical. A few weeks later, when he had gained sufficient distance from his observations, he summed up the results somewhat as follows:

Standing 3 feet away, I saw the inside of the gaping wound. Quite clearly the body seemed ripped open at this place. Astonishingly, one saw some bloody yellowish-looking body tissue. But I could never orient myself and determine which anatomical parts were lying before us. This is in complete contrast to incisions in our surgical clinics, where the trained eye can usually determine more or less at once which bodily area is involved. It is true that during my short stay I witnessed no intestinal surgery, in which case I might have been better able to determine the anatomical facts.

The physician further stated that without histological examination of the removed tissue he could not be specific:

Some looked like lymph node tissue, some had the external appearance of connective tissue, still others of arterial wall sections. The sections were not handed to us, nor was the blood examined, and therefore I speak of bloodlike, serous-looking liquid.

My findings are limited to the astonishing fact that Agpaoa apparently wields a mysterious power to open the body at any desired spot merely with his bare hands. He then removes something from the body; and after he takes his hands away, the body closes up again completely. After the superficial bloodlike puddle has been wiped away, no visible scars remain.[92]

This is the thoroughly considered, very carefully weighed judgment of a physician. He had no doubts that Agpaoa was able to open the patient's body, but he makes it clear that in Agpaoa's case we are not dealing with "normal" operations like those of the standard Western operating theater, but with "paranormal" ones.

Of course none of us was able to judge the therapeutic value of Agpaoa's performance. The subjective well-being of some of the patients after the operation was considerably improved; others, however, showed no such evident relief.

At the suggestion of Dr. Naegeli-Osjord, members of our group with a scientific bent met in his room every day after the surgery session. At these meetings we wrote down our common observations and discussed attempts at an explanation. We were unanimously of the view that one or another demonstration could be simulated by an artful trick but that this could in no way be true for *all* the operations performed in any one morning.

The question of the absence of pain was, in our view, not explicable through hypnosis or suggestion. Around 1830 the British physician J. Esdaile, practicing in India, was performing the most complicated surgery without the patient's feeling any pain and without the use of an anesthetic, simply by hypnotizing the patients and suggesting painlessness.[46,307] In those days total anesthesia normally had to be used, since local anesthetics were not in use until near the end of the century. Because of insufficient experience and inadequate circulation remedies, death from anesthesia was very frequent. By comparison, Esdaile operated on his hypnotized patients with a sensationally low rate of fatalities, and hypnosis also seemed to lower the incidence of infection. Despite these clearcut results, Esdaile's method was characterized as "unscientific"; he was called a charlatan. Under the pressure of these attacks, he discontinued operating on hypnotized patients.[46]

Over a hundred years later his process was adopted in the United States and practiced with much success. It lost most of its practical value, however, after Carl Ludwig Schleich discovered local anesthesia, which is much more convenient in many cases. Techniques in total anesthesia have also significantly improved in the past 140 years. Prejudice, narrow-mindedness, and perhaps wounded vanity suppressed a discovery until it lost its practical value almost entirely.

Today we know that to eliminate pain we need not employ deep hypnosis; waking suggestion is also used. The patient is aware of everything going on around him and normally conscious of himself; but as a result of the suggestion he feels no pain. The Bulgarian physician and parapsychologist Dr. Georgi Lozanov demonstrated this method on August 24, 1965, in connection with complicated inguinal hernia surgery. His procedure was shown on Bulgarian television.[184] Suggestive language gives the patient the assurance that he will experience no pain whatever, that the site of the operation is completely desensitized, until this concept so completely dominates the patient's thinking that it comes true.

On the basis of extensive observation, however, I must state that in carrying through suggestion as we understand the term, it is ordinarily necessary for the hypnotist to impart verbal suggestions. Before the many operations by Agpaoa and other surgeons which we observed, absence of pain was never suggested. True, before their own surgery most patients watched operations on others and thus gained assurance that pain would not occur. But such knowledge would not suffice to achieve total absence of pain in all sorts of cases and operations. Even a number of patients who were pathologically afraid of pain did not experience it.

We observed surgery on an older man during which a benign tumor was apparently removed from the left testicle. Even if this tumor had consisted of fake tissue, the patient would have had to feel pain during Agpaoa's manual treatment of such a sensitive organ. We further witnessed Agpaoa's giving an injection to an American woman suffering from an advanced form of cancer; the large hypodermic looked more like the instrument of a veterinarian. He injected her directly into the breast, without her experiencing the least pain. A paralyzed Australian was given an injection directly into her back without her feeling anything and without any infection setting in.

Very skeptical patients did not feel any pain. Note too that even after lengthy preparations the ablest hypnotists are unable to hypnotize 100 percent of patients and spectators, let alone when no verbal suggestions are given.

Besides normal hypnosis or suggestion, however,

there is also "mental suggestion," as we called it earlier. Motoyama's experiments, the attempts by Vasiliev, and Durov's demonstration of telepathy with animals show an impressive spectrum of possibilities. But transmitting absence of pain telepathically would probably exhaust the surgeon's total power of concentration, which he surely needs for other paranormal processes in operating. Perhaps "Philippine anesthesia" incorporates normal-suggestive and mental-hypnotic components, but these would not seem to suffice as explanation.

It is much more likely that the primary effect is called forth by a strong bioplasmic emanation from the surgeon's hands, either interrupting nerve transmission or affecting the patient's biofield; perhaps there are certain similarities to the mechanism of acupuncture. In the last analysis, however, the healer's force fields would seem to play a crucial role during paranormal surgery.

At the time we tried to account for the opening and the unscarred closing of the body. To date we know very little about the forces that hold human body cells together in tissue. It is fact that the cells structure the firm form of the body, but there is no clear agreement about the causal powers that effect the bond. The American healer Olga Worral claims that the body's formation and the unity of its cells come into being through the force fields of the astral body, which according to her represents the causal field of the biological structure.

How the infinitely many forms of animate nature come into being has always been a mystery; morphology continues to be a purely descriptive science. Some people believe the solution to the problem is DNA, desoxyribonucleic acid, but these are nothing but information symbols. Though they represent the cellular code, they cannot order the cells into particular forms and patterns. This necessitates a force field—a superordinate, organizing biofield.

When we were in Baguio we believed we might find an explanation for the penetration of the body without a knife and the closure without scarring: perhaps the surgeon partly disturbs or temporarily suspends the energy body's force field (which allegedly holds together the material structure). By this process the material or morphological structure loosens or even dissolves at the site of the operation, so that the surgeon seems to penetrate the body as if it were soft butter or opens it altogether. After the normal structure of the energy body is reestablished, the cellular order returns to its original form, and outwardly everything is as before.

A primitive comparison may clarify this hypothesis. Strew iron filings over a piece of paper and apply a magnetic field to them. The filings will order themselves into specific patterns and figures, held in this position through the magnetic force. They can be moved out of their positions only after a degree of resistance is overcome. But if the magnetic field is suspended, the rigidity of the filings is dissolved, and they can be moved out of their original pattern with a minimum of effort. Then, if the pattern was not too extensively disturbed, when the magnetic field is switched on again the field will reestablish the original structure.

Just as the iron filings are held in their rigid positions by the magnetic force field, so the cellular structure of the body is directed by a superordinate force field. The only difference is that the biological field is structurally more complicated, in connection with physiological and physical forces. Through a partial suspension of the energy body of the patient at the site of the surgery the unity of the tissue structure is loosened, and the surgeon can quite literally "dive into" the body.

I clearly observed this diving into the closed body cover later when I observed the healer Marcelo Jainar. He once inserted his extended middle finger directly into the stretched popliteal space (back of the knee) of an extended leg. There wasn't the slightest possibility of optical illusion, since it is not possible to depress the flesh deeply at this location as Jainar would have had to do to simulate penetration. Since no blood appeared, it was clear that Marcelo had stuck his finger one or two knuckles deep into the tissue.

In the course of our group's discussions, the talk turned to a postwar occurrence in Switzerland, with which Dr. Naegeli-Osjord was familiar. It had an undeniable resemblance to several aspects of the Philippine operations and was unusually well documented by scientists.

The Dutchman Mirin Dajo—his real name was probably Henskers Arnold—was born on August 6, 1912, in Rotterdam. In 1947, in public performances at the Corso Theater in Zurich, he left his audiences breathless. In plain sight a fencing foil was stuck through his body, piercing vital organs, without the European fakir's breaking down and—equally clearly —without his experiencing any pain whatever.

He had turned up with two countrymen—his partner, de Groot, and one Otter who had allegedly discovered Dajo's unique talent. Dajo declared that he had developed it through psychic-spiritual training. It was based on his absolute conviction that the sword could not hurt him. He felt, as he said, not the slightest tinge of fear; no doubt this was an important precondition for his performance. He worked with the suggestion "Wherever the sword touches, there I am not."

All he felt was a slight resistance when the tip of the foil went in (some patients made similar claims after Philippine surgery). When the weapon was pulled out of his body, only a slight scar remained. Many spectators are said to have fainted. When one of them suffered a heart attack, Dajo was legally stopped from performing in public.[186]

Dr. Naegeli-Osjord was personally acquainted with Mirin Dajo and told me further details. Dajo several times presented himself to scientists, once on May 31, 1947, at the Zurich cantonal hospital. Along with professors, students, and journalists, Dr. Werner Brunner, the chief of the surgical division, was also present. Dajo appeared, accompanied by his two Dutch companions; he bared his chest and concentrated. The spectators smiled. Most, presumably, were expecting an impressive magic trick. De Groot took a blade and pierced Dajo through from the back so that the tip of the weapon projected a good two handbreadths out of the upper abdomen.

No blood flowed. The spectators had stopped smiling; they were turned to stone.

Nevertheless, the scientists were not convinced. They wanted to take an X ray. Dajo agreed. For this procedure they had to go to the next floor; he steadily climbed the stairs, sword through his body, and without apparent effort walked down the hall to the X-ray room. The X ray was taken and developed at once. The result was plain: Mirin Dajo was pierced by the sword. Vital organs would by rights be damaged, and the fakir ought to be in a critical state. Twenty minutes later the foil was withdrawn; only an insignificant scar remained.

Dajo was also tested by scientists in Basel, and according to authenticated reports he allowed himself to be run through by the scientists themselves. (As is also true of the Philippine surgeons, his condition was subject to ups and downs; on some days he was not able to give his demonstrations.)

A rich private person made Mirin Dajo an extravagant offer. For a large sum of money he was to swallow a spherical object attached to a spear. This wedge-shaped steel pike was about 4 inches long and ⅛ inch in diameter; the thin side was highly sharpened; the pike was welded to a ball somewhat smaller than a fist.

The "sinister presence" of the two companions of Dajo was Otter, who also controlled the purse strings. He encouraged Dajo to accept the offer, but the fakir was not certain. He hoped that he would be able to rid himself of the spear and ball by the same principle he used when he was pierced with the foil. He seemed to have faith in a temporary dissolution of the structure of his bodily tissues during the blade's intrusion, and he apparently hoped that a similar dematerialization would allow the ball to pass through to the outside.

Of course this project sounds fantastic. Dajo agreed only reluctantly to the experiment—which in itself is a bad start for difficult paranormal experiments.

The fakir swallowed the steel monstrosity, but his hopes were not fulfilled. Finally he had to seek out the surgeons, not for a sensational demonstration this time, but for surgery. They operated—not entirely without some understandable satisfaction. Dajo's body was opened and the ball and spear removed.

After a day and a half Dajo demanded to be released from the hospital on his own authority. His request was granted after he signed a release form. The following day he visited Dr. Naegeli-Osjord to obtain his agreement for medical supervision to his further experiments. Dr. Naegeli-Osjord first examined Dajo, especially the site of the operation. Two and a half days after the surgery, the wound seemed to have undergone three weeks' normal healing.

Nevertheless, the failed experiment seems to have paved the way for Dajo's end. He had planned a fasting cure and intended to go 80 days without food, with only minimal amounts of liquids. With this in mind he went off to visit friends in Winterthur.

Dajo frequently engaged in bilocation experiments. Like Robert Monroe,[152,168] he was convinced that his "spiritual self" (perhaps his bioplasmic body?) could leave his physical body and return to it. Following the example of Indian yogis, by a sort of self-hypnosis he put himself into a state in which his vital functions were sharply reduced, and he often remained so for many hours, while he claimed to go on psychic travels. Such experiments are also carried out in the Philippines during the training of psychic surgeons and mediums.

A few days after Dajo left Zurich, Dr. Naegeli-Osjord received a worried phone call from Dajo's friends in Winterthur. He had said that he intended to "leave his body for a day," as he had often done before. Now, after a day and a half, they'd looked in his room and found him lying there as if dead. As it turned out, during these experiments in extreme consciousness transport, Dajo had encountered death.

Although these medical miracles were precisely and scientifically documented, they have had no influence on scientific thought. As an individual case, it can easily be ignored.

Both Dajo's swordplay and Agpaoa's surgery leave the impression that at the deepest causal level, our material organic structures are held together by spiritual forces, following quite particular models—"ideas" in the Platonic sense. Any influence on this deep causal plane can bring about effects and suspend force fields, practically leading to a loosening or dissolution of the material structure, which immediately rearranges or reforms when the bioplasmic disturbance is removed.

Philippine surgeons penetrate deep into the body at times and afterward the original structure is restored, undamaged. Dajo carried out this loosening of the organic structure and its subsequent restoration on his own body.

The Philippine healers are convinced that a mental-spiritual power works through them and enables them to operate paranormally. It is this power, they believe, that opens and closes the patients' bodies by affecting the astral body.

They believe the ability to practice psychic surgery lies hidden in many people but that to activate the force one must have reached a particular level of spiritual development. This requires constant work on the self. It begins with exercises in concentration and controlling one's emotional life. The Filipinos claim that meditation and prayer are most important. They are by nature a deeply religious people, with a strong need for metaphysics. Spiritualist chapels serve as gathering places for men and women for meetings which combine religious services, exercises to develop psychic powers, and healing treatments—just as in early Christian times religious services and spiritual healing were often joined.

Placido and the Spiritist Church of the Philippines

One Saturday, Agpaoa took me to an assembly of the Spiritist Church of the Philippines on the outskirts of Baguio. From outside, the church looked more like a barn. Inside, too, the large clay-floored room had a certain resemblance to a threshing floor. Most of the audience had a poverty-stricken appearance. Natives —slightly more women than men—sat on primitive backless benches. The women had brought small children who slept, wrapped in blankets. At the front, on an elevated platform, stood a large table and chairs. An oil lamp threw off a meager light.

I sat down on a bench in one of the front rows. After a period of time a youngish, good-looking Filipino with fine, spiritual features stepped on the platform and gave a speech in Tagalog, which seemed to be a sermon. He made an exceptionally likable impression. I assume that it was the healer Gonzales, who was to die suddenly a few weeks later.

This speech was followed by a Bible reading. Speeches by other Filipinos followed, each lasting ten to fifteen minutes; this went on for over an hour and a half. The audience listened reverently. Agpaoa had introduced me to a Filipino named Placido who could speak English and explain the proceedings. He too had made a speech and now told me that automatic writing was about to begin.

Automatic writing occurs without any conscious control by the writer. It is, as it were, writing in a trance, during which the writer is not conscious of what he is writing. The hand is guided by a power or intelligence outside the writer's consciousness. Some people are in the habit of doodling while they think about something; in principle this may be a step toward automatic writing. Western psychologists say that the stimulus—or causa movens—is the subconscious.

In doodling, relatively superficial areas of the subconscious are generally at work; nevertheless, properly trained psychologists can often draw interesting conclusions from these scribbles. On the other hand, during hypnosis or in special trance states extremely deep layers are touched and given a chance to manifest themselves unhampered. Thus advanced forms of automatic writing may produce statements that seem completely alien to a person's conscious self. The psychoanalyst will doubtlessly still be able to attribute some parts of these documents to the person in question. But some automatic writings can in no way be explained psychologically; a number of psychics write down pages and pages in foreign languages which they have never learned and whose content often goes far beyond the writers' intellectual level, and about which they know nothing on awakening from the trance state.[12,17,19] The Brazilian Carlos Mirabelli, who died in the early 1950s, is said by reliable witnesses and experts in depth trance to have produced automatic writing on the most diverse topics in more than twenty languages.

The writings often end with the signatures of historical personalities, though at times the content does not correspond to the educational level or character of the signatories. Nevertheless, expert witnesses agree that under normal conditions the psychic himself could not have written on these topics. Medical monitoring of the medium in the trance state has determined an extremely rapid pulse—120 to 150 beats per minute—as well as a body temperature of 99.5°F and insensitivity to heat, cold, and pinpricks.[82]

Two current theories may account for the phenomenon. The animistic theory seeks to derive all phenomena from hidden powers of a person's soul, powers always present in his psyche but not developed. The spiritist theory, on the other hand, assumes the existence of extracorporeal intelligences which can manifest themselves through the psychically gifted subconscious. Both theories rely on the deeper levels of the subconscious.

In any case, authentic automatic writing is a form of psychism; one speaks of "writing psychics." Persons who in a trance state begin to speak—sometimes in a totally altered voice—about things which they could normally know nothing about, often in languages they have never heard, are called "speech psychics."

On this particular evening in the Spiritist church a few women who were said to be psychics took their places at the table. White sheets of paper lay before them; they picked up pencils and poised them over the paper without leaning their arms on the tabletop. They were waiting for guidance by "other powers."

After a while the hands of some writers seemed to begin to move. Some pencils pushed violently against the paper, others flew across the sheet with uncanny speed.

Tony Agpaoa had told us that automatic writing was one of the preparatory exercises for learning psychic surgery, and the analogy seemed plausible that surgeons' manual movements were also somehow "guided" by some intelligence or spiritual power which seemed to lie outside their conscious self.

On a previous evening our German group had made its own experiments with automatic writing under Agpaoa's direction. While Philippine psychics attempted to put us into some sort of trance state with monotonous chants, we waited for automatic movements of the pencils held ready between our fingers. At moments we felt a twinge in our fingertips and felt that the pencils wanted to move. But our European reason immediately took over, asking expectantly what word would emerge or telling us that this was all nonsense, and any impetus to automatic writing was promptly blocked.

I now understood that the Filipinos presuppose quite other possibilities for activating psychic depth layers than Europeans do. Western reason not only creates new possibilities, it also buries others.

The automatic writings in the Spiritist church were interpreted by a trance medium; I cannot say much about this, since I do not understand Tagalog. Placido told me we were dealing with religious statements, references to biblical quotations which were then found and read out loud. Next, many Filipinos, one at a time, came to the table and tried their hand at automatic writing. For the most part it resulted only in illegible scribbles—they were, after all, only beginners.

"Now we will have magnetic exercises," Placido explained to me. A number of people placed themselves around the large table. The leader of the assembly held out his outspread hand and pressed it against the tabletop while he seemed to be seeking spiritual-mental concentration. The others standing around the table did the same. It was almost reminiscent of a table-moving séance. After a while some women seemed unable to remove their hands from the table. With an apparently strong effort they drew their hands to the edge and then succeeded in letting go. These attempts were repeated with others, some of whom fell into a proper trance. A few men stood ready to catch anyone who might fall.

The leader stood outside the group and sharply observed the participants. Suddenly he stepped up to a woman whose hands seemed glued to the table and gave her a light blow on the forehead with the flat of his palm. The woman's eyes turned up and she fell into a deep trance. Tipping over backward, she was caught by the leader. Immediately several others came to join them. The woman was now stiff as a board, her eyes closed. Helpers carried her into the auditorium and laid her down on a bench. Another woman took over the treatment. She began to talk to the unconscious woman, who began to breathe loudly and utter words in Tagalog between rasping noises. The words turned into sentences, the content of which I unfortunately missed. Perhaps it was a sort of hypnotherapy or psychocatharsis, but Placido mentioned "possession."

Throughout, the psychic woman sitting with her spoke soothingly until the woman in the depth trance gradually grew calmer. The rasping stopped, and finally an uncanny silence prevailed.

"Astral traveling," Placido whispered to me. The

Filipinos believe that in such states of deepest trance or hypnosis the spirit or soul can separate itself from the body and perform absent healing by astral traveling.

The subject or the patient—I do not know which term is more applicable—finally lay lifelessly, her face relaxed and very pale, somewhat tinged with gray. All present remained in absolute silence; no sound of impatience could be heard, as might be expected if Europeans were expected to sit still for a long time without anything happening. I can no longer remember whether it was half an hour, an hour, or even longer. Agpaoa told me that such "soul excursions" at times took all night. It was now approaching midnight, and the psychic leader obviously imparted to the woman in the trance an order to awaken. But she did not seem to react. The psychic began to carry out magnetic passes along the unconscious woman's body, but this and repeated vehement talking to were unsuccessful. She gave the appearance of a dead person, and I realized that a huge difference probably exists between Western hypnosis and some of what is practiced in this area of the Philippines. Killing through the mere use of deep hypnosis may be possible.

Now the Filipinos suddenly showed some restlessness. Several people jumped up and massaged the entranced woman's hands and feet; one person stroked her head, others rubbed her body. This activity came to a sudden stop, and everyone waited. After one or two minutes, which seemed an eternity, the unconscious woman's chest began to move imperceptibly. Everyone waited patiently until her features grew lively again. Finally, in response to the psychic's calm talk, the woman opened her eyes and, somewhat confused at first, looked around.

Next came a new phase of the night's activities: magnetic healing. People who were ill or had some sort of infirmity came to the dais, and several Filipinos acted as magnetists. Some patients were placed on the table, others only sat in a chair.

One healer was massaging the abdominal area of a

Filipino stretched out on the table. This treatment did not impress me very much.

Now Placido called to me. He had with him a little boy, about eight years old, whose tooth he was going to pull. It was the first or second molar on the right in the lower jaw. (Unfortunately I forgot to test how firmly it was still embedded.) Placido began by touching the tooth with his finger and said that he would give a "magnetic injection" to produce insensitivity to pain. Then he placed a little cotton around the tooth, in order to be able to grasp it more firmly.

I stood directly behind the boy and brought my eyes close to his head to be able to see exactly. Placido lifted out the tooth by his thumb and forefinger, apparently without effort. The little patient didn't bat an eyelash. Even if the tooth had already been somewhat loose, a short expression of pain could still have been expected from an eight-year-old.

But what came next perplexed me even more. During the evening Placido had mentioned that he might perform psychic surgery before the night was out—"if God wills it." Now a woman was placed on the table and her abdomen laid bare. Placido passed his outspread hand a couple of inches over the bared area, as if making a radiesthetic diagnosis. Then he bared his arms, spread out his hands, and brought them close to the woman's body from above. What followed looked at first like a sort of massage of the abdominal wall, but after a short time a bloodlike fluid seeped from the patient's skin, and now the course of events resembled one of Agpaoa's operations. Placido's small hands clearly seemed to penetrate the body, and after feeling around at length, his right hand pulled out something long, mucous, and pus-infected. In my view, it would have been impossible to smuggle such loose, cystlike tissue into the area of the operation; it would have fallen apart.

After this followed the usual incantation of "One, two, three," and his left hand was withdrawn. Except for a small puddle of blood, nothing remained that would have attested to an operation. Someone else wiped away the blood, and the patient was washed off with water. The woman arranged her clothing, arose from the table, and sat again on the bench she had occupied earlier.

The Healers of Rosales

Since we were eager to observe as many surgeons as possible, Agpaoa organized a day trip to Rosales, a small town in the lowlands and a center of surgeons of the Unio Espiritista Cristiana Filipinas. The Union is said to have more than four hundred centers, spread over all of the Philippines, where healing treatments are performed in a church on specified days in connection with a religious service. The Union was founded at the beginning of the century; since around 1948 it has been in demand by suffering people from all over the country. Its by-laws are on the highest ethical plane.[44,290] They call for the selfless commitment of the surgeons to their patients and forbid its members to take payment for their performances. At an earlier time healers were forced to refuse even voluntary donations. Many of them live in what by our lights are hopelessly primitive conditions.

Agpaoa was reproached because he accepted voluntary donations for his operations. But as we learned, nowadays the surgeons of the Union also accept all manner of fees. As a rule these are very modest gifts, for most Filipinos treated by psychic surgery are very poor.

The entire town of Rosales seems poor. We stopped before a very simple large building, and Agpaoa told us that it was a church. On entering, we saw primitive benches on which people sat or lay, an overwhelming number of them obviously ill. At the front, in place of an altar, a simple table was placed on a dais, as in the Spiritist church of Baguio. Over it hung a yellow-and-white flag with an emblem and the inscription "Unio Espiritista Cristiana Filipinas." On the table, dimly lit by an unshaded bulb, lay a woman; behind the table stood a surgeon who seemed to be proceeding in the same style as Agpaoa.

On coming closer, we saw that he was just about to perform an operation on the abdominal area. The woman lay still with open eyes, apparently feeling not a trace of pain. Her head rested on a well-worn Bible, which functioned as a pillow in all the operations. The healer removed some bloody tissue and took his left hand away from the body; after the bloodlike substance was wiped away, no scar could be detected. The surgeon washed his hands in a tin bowl. The blood on the site of the operation was wiped away by a girl who then took the washbowl and left the church by a side door, to return with fresh water for the next operation.

Before we knew it, the next patient had got up on the table, and the site of the disorder was bared. The surgeon palpated it clairsentiently, without touching it, and then brought his hands closer to the body. Blood appeared very quickly, and after a short time his hand seemed to have penetrated the body. The wounds or body openings were not as large as in some of Agpaoa's operations, but the healer worked at uncommon speed. The operations and treatments— he did not open the body in every case—were carried out almost on the assembly-line principle; fifteen or twenty an hour. A two-year-old child, screaming with fear, was placed on the table, and coagulated blood was removed from his stomach. A mentally ill woman fought back and had to be calmed down first; then her goiter was operated on. The protuberance seemed to have grown considerably smaller after the operation; further surgery on her was planned for the future. Various patients with "weak lungs," as the healer called it, were operated on their backs. The surgeon went into the body superficially and took out "blood clots." Subsequently the patients were magnetized by hand.

After a further operation the surgeon took a rest, and we were introduced to him. His name was Marcelo Jainar, but everyone called him by his first name.

Marcelo was in his mid-forties and had been performing surgery, as he told us, since 1954. He was an entirely different type from Agpaoa. His English was not as good. Presumably he lived much more modestly; he had a family of six children, and he operated all day long for a few pesos. Next to the operating table stood another table, at which sat a bookkeeper and recorder who accepted the voluntary contributions for the operations. Many patients were unable to give anything at all, others clutched a few centavos. Medicines were also handed out at this table. We went outside the church with Marcelo and talked with him. He told us that he worked here twice a week—on Thursdays and Saturdays. People who sought him out were too poor to afford a medical doctor. For the operations in his church, which he had built himself, he asked nothing.

Marcelo impressed us as thoroughly honest, goodhearted, and modest. To think of this decent man as a cunning magician was impossible. He said that his ability to heal had come upon him suddenly, "like the ray of light of God overcame Saul who became Paul." Like Paul, he said, he had previously cursed the church.

Unfortunately there was not enough light in the church of the Unio Espiritista to take movies, but since Marcelo often came to visit Agpaoa in Baguio and operated there, on several later occasions I was able to watch him operate and to take movies.

We went back into the church with Marcelo and were surprised to see another surgeon at work. It was Carlos, a very young healer who worked in the same style. During several of his operations we could clearly see intestinal tissue and loops, which I had not been able to observe in Marcelo's operations.

One patient, who allegedly had no sight in one eye, lay down on the table, his head on the Bible. A towel was placed under his head to soak up excess bleeding. Then the patient's ears were stuffed with cotton, and Marcelo simply entered the eye cavity next to the eyeball with his index or middle finger. He poked around in such a way that a spectator of any sensitiv-

ity—let alone the patient—would have gone into
shock. Blood flowed freely. A second eye operation
was considerably more savage. The patient's one eye
was covered by a white film, clearly a case of cataracts.
Marcelo's fingers picked around in the eye so vehemently that it began to look like a single bloody hole,
whereupon he repeatedly pressed and pushed at the
eyeball with his thumb. The blood flowed across the
entire face and into the other eye; a helper quickly
rushed over with cotton and towel and dried the
healthy eye. Whether something was removed from
the eye was not clear in view of the amount of
blood and clots. The eye was finally cleaned; the
patient got up and declared that his vision had improved—which has no value as testimony, for the
white spot still remained. What astonished me was
that the healer had not destroyed anything with such
a brutal-seeming method, and the patient had felt
no pain.

Completely incomprehensible, too, was the treatment in which several patients apparently had their
bodies opened, primarily in the abdominal region; it
seemed that a wad of cotton soaked in medication was
placed inside. After this, the wound closed again without a scar, the "inlay" apparently remaining inside.
The patient was asked to come back so that the cotton
could be removed. We saw several patients who, we
were told, had had soaked cotton placed inside a week
earlier; before our eyes these were now taken out as
great bloody lumps.

Half a year later, we heard of an experience by
some Germans in the Rosales chapel. The group
included parapsychology writer Rudolf E. Passian,
who vouches for the authenticiy of the occurrence.
His report confirms our observations made some
months earlier, presenting further arguments that
Philippine surgeons can open and close bodies without leaving a scar.

In May 1971 I went to the Philippines to find out for
myself about what they call knifeless surgery. I have long
been concerned with the study of paranormal phe-

nomena. Together with a German woman, a chemist, and a physician originally from Austria, we hired a Philippine travel guide; she and her husband were to drive us in two hired cars through the lowlands to visit several psychic surgeons. Finally we arrived in Rosales and were taken to the chapel of the Unio Espiritista Cristiana Filipinas. A woman healer was performing.

The chemist in our group had already had astonishing experiences among the Indians of the Americas. He had gotten to know a tribal chief who had met a white man for the first time. This chief, according to the chemist, also operated in an entirely inexplicable manner; he opened the body with a bamboo stick, removed pus deposits and tissue, and finally brushed his hand across the operated place—like the Brazilian Zé Arigo—and the wound closed.

This chemist had an intestinal growth which he had acquired in the army; when he pressed it, it was visible as far as the anus. It bled once a week. He had been operated for it a year and a half earlier, in Germany, but without lasting relief. He hoped to get rid of the growth through Agpaoa's work.

Now that we were in the chapel of Rosales, observing the healer's operations, the very high-spirited and talkative Philippine guide intervened. The chemist was invited to bare his chest and to lie on the table. After hesitating briefly, he agreed. The healer opened the chemist's abdomen in the familiar manner. The German woman took movies, standing on a chair. But because watching this operation made her sick, I took over all further filming, which somewhat distracted my attention from exact observation, and I missed a few details. After the operation the patient was told a cotton wad had been inserted into his body. The spectators stated that, when the operation already seemed over, the healer had taken a cotton wad and, rubbing it back and forth on the patient's body between his hands, looking off into the distance, had made it disappear, apparently into the patient's body. The healer told us the cotton was magnetized now inside the body and that it would have to be removed in a few days.

Sleight of hand or genuine paraphenomenon? From

the older specialized literature—which is, after all, much more informative than today's—I know there is such a thing as materialization and dematerialization. But as I said, my attention was distracted by the filming. I let the matter rest.

After a visit to Urdaneta to see the healer Juanito, we returned to Manila. When he said goodbye to our travel guide, she again told the chemist that he absolutely must go back to Rosales to have the healer remove the cotton. But the chemist was not interested in the supposed cotton ball; he wanted to persuade Agpaoa to help him get rid of his growth, and since his stay in the Philippines was short, he had only a few days left.

The following day we were in Baguio with Agpaoa. He had his hands full with a good-sized group of travelers, foreign patients among them. Nevertheless we succeeded in arousing his concern for the chemist's case.

Two doctors were present at the preliminary examination; the tumor near the anus was obvious. Agpaoa said he would have to perform two operations two or four days apart, since otherwise the bleeding would be excessive.

The first operation was performed the same day, in the hotel room. The patient lay on his back, the upper part of his body exposed. The operation was about to begin when Tony suddenly asked: "When was the last time that something was done to this patient?"

I was afraid Tony might refuse to operate if he learned that we had already visited the "competition" in Rosales. Since the patient had had surgery in Germany some time ago, we answered, "A year and a half ago."

"No, no, no," Tony said very firmly. "It has to have been a short time ago."

We had to confess. Names were named, and Tony, who had already bent over to begin the operation, walked backward to the adjacent bed, where he sat down. He seemed nonplussed and uncertain. We did our utmost to persuade him that the chemist had been taken by surprise in Rosales and had not himself planned to let the woman healer work him over.

Finally Agpaoa decided to operate. He concentrated visibly, and we had the impression he was eager to prove he could do better than his Rosales colleague.

The operation took place on the abdomen. He seemed to be inside the body in a trice, blood flowed under his hands, and we heard the familiar smacking sounds that often occur when he penetrates farther into the body.

Tony made his kneading motions, then somewhat separated his hands, and at once I saw the cotton come into view, coated with red clumps of clotted blood. Frightened, Tony stopped and cried, "What's that?"

We had no choice but to explain what his competition had done. Agpaoa quickly regained his composure and gave orders to his Swiss assistant, who used a long forceps, the only instrument Tony occasionally employs, to pull the cotton out of the wound. She threw it into a bucket and explained that some healers placed magnetized cotton into the body to attract "diseased matter." Then unless it was demolished in the normal course of metabolic change, the cotton was removed.

Tony continued to operate in his usual manner; although we had barely three days left before our departure, he promised to do his utmost. The crucial operation took place on the last day before the chemist's departure from Baguio, between 6:00 and 7:00 a.m. Sunday. We filmed the operation with a 16-millimeter camera as Tony Agpaoa took out the entire growth, the size of a hen's egg.

Since then the chemist has had only one episode of bleeding—soon after his return from the Philippines. He is in good health. A full year has passed, and no further complications have set in.

Tony—Portrait of a Healer

After we had stayed at Villa La Maja for a week and a half, most of our group flew back to Europe. I moved to Agpaoa's home on the outskirts of Baguio. By Philippine standards he lives in a very spacious house with large living rooms, though it is not lavish in Western terms. The lower floor holds several bedrooms for guests, as well as a large room also used as a dining room for patients. The upper floor, arranged in the same way, provides living quarters for the Agpaoa family.

One side, connected with the large room on the lower floor by a glass door, houses a smaller room. An opening in the floor about 6 feet square allows spectators to look down into Agpaoa's treatment room on the ground floor. A position at a balustrade directly over the table and patient makes an ideal vantage point.

The entrance, separated from the treatment room by a door, consists of a large, light meditation room with colorful murals. Paintings on the rear wall depict legendary stations in the life of Agpaoa.

Living in Agpaoa's house, I had an opportunity to observe many operations, including those performed by Marcelo from Rosales, who worked here twice a week.

I also had frequent opportunities to talk with Agpaoa and taped many of our conversations on a cassette recorder. Agpaoa is a man of many faces and moods, an interesting and complicated subject. Since he dwells extensively in states of consciousness not yet studied by psychology and anthropology, it is difficult to attempt a complete and fair picture of him.

Tony Agpaoa was born June 2, 1939, in a bamboo hut in Rosales, of poor parents. His mother died some time ago. Tony's earliest memories—and here the skeptic will smile—were of the rising sun, its glittering rays making his waking eyes blink; seen, not from his bed in the bamboo hut, but from the crown of a high caimito tree. This view is followed by shouts of people who place a ladder against the tree and, amid scoldings and threats of dire punishments, bring him down. It is said that as a child Tony often disappeared from his bed during the night and was found at the top of a tree in the morning. He never knew how he had gotten there. To this day his father is prepared to swear to the truth of this statement. A critical European would hypothesize that the story represents either Philippine imagination or a peculiar case of somnabulism—walking in one's sleep.

During these years there first arose in Tony's mind the idea of a spiritual being who watched over and comforted him. For this reason he first called this being "comforter." Perhaps Tony heard adults saying that he must have an alert guardian angel because he had never yet fallen out of a tree, and his imagination turned this into the protector. Tony searched all over for what he came to call his protector, and finally felt guided by him.

Even as a small boy he sensed there were states of consciousness about which people around him knew nothing; he was aware of many things long before he was able to put them into words. He felt at one with his natural surroundings, and nothing seemed alien to him. He seemed to remember much that should by rights have been new to him. (As Plato said, "All learning is only the soul's remembering.")

Without a doubt Tony Agpaoa has a strong eidetic tendency—to use a term from Western psychology— and is capable of the highest achievements of the imagination. He was able to sit in the woods, meditating to the point of self-forgetfulness and "filling himself with the invisible." (Instruction in magical powers in the West also generally begins by developing the imagination.) Since he could "bring back" voices and sounds, such as the song of a bird heard once before, and hear as clearly as if this bird were actually singing, he assumed that sounds must be stored somewhere, on call.

There are obvious analogies to Agpaoa's childhood in Ruth Montgomery's description of the healer Phil A.[153] As a child, he too is said to have spent days away from home in the woods and on the lake shores of his then sparsely populated hometown. When punishment proved useless, his parents finally became reconciled to such occurrences. Little Phil A. felt happy in the woods, alone with animals and plants. It is reported that both Tony and Phil A. were never afraid of sleeping alone in the woods.

From earliest childhood, Phil A. received a steady stream of instructions and explanations from "higher powers" about life and the production of human energies. He could not describe this more fully to others, but it seemed so natural that he assumed everyone must be receiving similar knowledge. He believed these instructions and information were available to everyone who understood how to "listen." (Tony Agpaoa said more or less the same thing when he explained that all human knowledge is somehow stored up—perhaps in some sort of cosmic memory—and that meditation could impart all kinds of instruction drawn from it.)

The most important event of Tony's childhood occurred when he was eight or nine. His playmate Pedro Gonzales, engaging in some horseplay, fell on a sharp object, and a large, bleeding wound gaped in his thigh. The boy's parents and others came running and did not know what to do. Tony saw his friend's bloodied skin and the pain-distorted face. "You will open and close wounds," he heard a voice saying inside himself and felt a warm pulsing in his hands. Slowly he placed his hands over Pedro's wound, and when he pulled them away a few seconds later, the deep wound had closed. Only a little coagulated blood remained.

The news of this "miracle" spread like wildfire. When Tony returned home, neighbors were already waiting for his touch. He touched them, and all immediately felt cured or at least improved. Tony Agpaoa began to believe in his power to heal.

Little Filipino children always went barefoot. Often they injured their feet. Tony touched the bleeding toes and soles, and the blood stopped. Of course the bleeding and pain might have stopped by itself, but no one could be convinced that the wounds had not closed through Tony's agency.

Other Filipinos could remove splinters and thorns, but the ones Tony pulled out almost jumped into his hand. The wounds did not become infected and seemed to heal more quickly then usual.

Tony soon turned to treating internal diseases. A young girl embarrassed him when she pointed to her abdomen and said that it hurt: "Touch it and take it out." Father, mother, and daughter stared at the blushing Tony. Finally he touched the girl where she felt pain. Under his fingers, something in the patient's body seemed to move.

He heard an inner voice: "Push it up to the navel." Tony moved his index finger directly over the mysterious shape under the girl's skin and pushed. The strange thing—soft and unpleasant to look at—suddenly popped out of the navel. Tony had to turn away. The mother took the initiative and examined the thing. The girl said only, "The pain is gone." But the father maintained that Tony had driven the devil out of the girl.[11]

This was the second phase in the development of Agpaoa's surgical skills. He seemed to take something out of the body without opening it—and what he removed was something no physician could deal with. What really happened, in medical terms? In all probability it was not a tumor or growth or specific human tissue, but consisted of products which often appear in paranormal treatment of beginning degenerative conditions.

Tony believes that in internal illnesses something in the patient's body reacts to his touch. He claims to see dark, eerie clouds or shapes within the patient's body, which he can move around and remove through the natural openings and mucous membranes. A pathologist examining the singular substances that emerge would have to report: "Not human tissue."

Presumably the processes at work here belong in the category of materialization. Such internal diseases are probably on an incipient, perhaps preclinical, level, and have a close connection with the bioplasmic body alleged by the Soviets. Today Agpaoa himself says he works on patients' "astral bodies."

The third and highest stage of Agpaoa's surgery

developed later. In some cases, diseases which Tony could "see" as dark clouds or shapes responded only reluctantly if at all to his efforts. Apparently there were miracles he could not perform. Sometimes he was able to push the formations he saw a little way toward the body openings, but they slipped back to their original positions so he could not get them out.

Tony wanted to send away one patient with this kind of complaint. (He was probably confronting a clinically defined, fully grown tumor.) "Your insides hurt," he told her, "but the pain doesn't hear me, it doesn't react to my hands."

However, the woman refused to leave and followed Agpaoa everywhere. Finally Tony decided to examine her again—and he clearly "saw" the core of the disease through her brown skin. But he could not budge it.

"I can't get it to a body opening. If I were a surgeon, I'd just cut the place open." He gnashed his teeth and, lost in thought, ran his fingertips over the woman's body. Horror seized him as he saw the raw flesh of an open wound, as if he had cut into the body with a knife. Blood streamed out.

He heard the voice of his protector. "Hold the wound open with the left hand and reach into the body with the right. Then take out the dark shapes with everything that clings to them." Tony pulled out the tumor—though at that time he did not know the word. His hands were covered with blood that continued to gush out of the wound.

He heard a voice behind him. "Make the bleeding stop or you'll kill the woman."

Tony was deathly afraid. "How can I stop the bleeding?"

"You opened the body with your fingertips. Try to close it by rubbing your hand across it," said the voice. Of course, this was the same technique used by the Brazilian Zé Arigo.[200]

Tony passed the flat of his hand across the wound without touching it directly. The other spectators' eyes followed him. The wound had closed; only a little puddle of coagulating blood remained. No scar could be seen. Tony wanted to thank the person who had given him the correct instructions, but could not see him. None of those present aside from Tony had heard him.

"Then I'm not the one who did this. You are," he said, meaning his protector.

"Neither of us, Antonio," came the answer, "but the Hand which is in all hands. For God is everywhere."

"But please, let me operate without blood. I can't stand it. The sight and the smell of it make me sick," Tony begged.

"Not only you, Antonio, the others as well. But without blood no one would believe, not even those who have been healed. But all right—perhaps a little less blood." In this way Tony arrived at the final stage of his training. He went from place to place, healing the sick.

A corresponding scale of three stages of healing activity may be seen among most Philippine surgeons.

Stage 1: Magnetic healing, also practiced by Western magnetopaths, works according to the doctrines of established medicine, by such suggestive effects as those achieved by Rasputin, the monk at the court of Czar Nicholas II. Rasputin could halt the bleeding of wounds—for example the life-endangering bleeding of the hemophiliac czarevich Alexei (whose blood lacked the normal ability to coagulate, so that even the smallest wound was potentially fatal).

Stage 2: The healer can see some internal diseases as dark clouds or shapes within the patient's body, and he can use his hands to give substance to these shapes and drive them toward body openings without the body's being opened.

Parallels can be found in biological therapy and natural remedy treatments. Natural healers often say that "something must come out of the body" and draw "the sickness out through the skin." Skin rashes induced by biological cures occasionally represent the turning point in a chronic disease and the onset of a general strengthening of the organism. Whether the concept of a cleansing of the body is correct cannot be further investigated here. But surely the Philippine surgeons are, in opposition not to natural laws, but only to facts as we have come to accept them.

Stage 3: The psychic surgeon opens the body, eliminates clinically perceivable niduses, and closes the body without leaving a scar.

In daily practice all three stages of treatment will appear together; they may even overlap. Presumably an increasing amount of psychic energy is required as treatment moves from the first to the third stage, and today there seems to be frequent combination of the second and third stages: the healer opens the body superficially, so that the second-stage process can run its course more easily and smoothly.

Tony Agpaoa went from place to place, healing the sick of his country, opening bodies and closing them without a scar. Whatever he pulled out of the wounds sometimes brought with it peculiar fleshy strands, sometimes of a structure different from the primary tissue—as if a kind of root were attached to the tissue mass.

These unusual tissue formations, found neither in Western surgical operations nor in a butcher shop, caught our attention during our first days in the Philippines and caused perplexity among our physicians. The roots turn up from time to time in the work of several healers and point to the appearance of materialization.*

Tony soon realized that if he operated on a pregnant woman, he started a miscarriage. This led pregnant unmarried girls to seek him out, causing conflicts of conscience for the Catholic Agpaoa. Meditating, he heard the inner voice of the protector, warning against deliberately causing miscarriages.

Young Tony became a celebrity in his region, but he felt that fame would make it impossible for him to please everyone. Girls whom he had refused an

---

*See chap. 10.

abortion were furious at him and spread all sorts of ugly rumors.

When Tony had spent a day in a village healing, the cured patients brought him presents in gratitude. Some poor people brought him an egg, usually already boiled so that it would not be damaged if dropped; others, a melon. Patients who were better off brought chickens, pigs, and goats.[11]

Agpaoa believes that according to metaphysical laws every gift has a beneficial effect on the giver and will somehow be returned to the giver many times. He felt gifts were like money, which must circulate and work if the economy is to thrive. For the most part he passed what he received on to the needy, since he could take only a few things along and could not eat all the eggs and melons himself.

This turned some people against him too. Many who brought him presents were angry when he passed them on; others said it was not right for him to accept anything. He learned that it was pointless to try to defend himself; therefore, he mostly kept silent when attacked on the counts that have been raised against him for more than 20 years, that he is a conjurer and a fraud. He is patient and has learned to wait, convinced that the truth about paranormal surgery will prevail when its time has come.

He believes these phenomena are rejected out of the worldwide materialism of our day but that this materialistic epoch will be followed by a time of general spiritualization in which Christianity's fundamental verities will be revitalized.[10]

Tony Agpaoa is without a doubt an advanced mystic, equally firmly anchored in Christianity and Indian and Far Eastern teachings, though we do not know where he gained this knowledge. Certainly he has read very little, which seems to confirm his claim that he garnered his knowledge and information from meditation.

Each year Agpaoa undergoes a sixteen-day fast, during which he drinks only water and eats a little honey. During Holy Week he spends long hours in

prayer and mystical exercises in his church or, along
with other healers, in the mountains. But Agpaoa does
not consider himself a holy man. He lives not only in
a higher world but just as much in this one; he lives
life on the whole scale of human possibilities. For this
reason, too, he has human failings as compared to
other healers. He smokes a great deal, probably more
than is good for him. He likes to drink in moderation
and would drink more if it did not adversely influence his paranormal skills. He has enormous vi-
tality—probably a prerequisite for his accomplishments. In sum, he is a true Filipino, with the temperament and blood of the islander; he loves adventure and enjoys playing bingo and other games of
chance. It would be naive and erroneous to judge him
by Western standards—but he has become used to
this.

Agpaoa believes that only he knows the way he
has to go—this is not saying that his way is always
right. He makes mistakes like everyone else, but tries
to learn from them. Besides working as a psychic
surgeon, he considers it his task to contribute to the
greater spiritualization of mankind, reason enough
for many materialistic people to consider him "crazy."
This he accepts as part of the price; for his outstanding
calm, patience, and invulnerability to negative
external influences are incomprehensible to Western
minds. Probably they are the result of years of
meditation and spiritual exercises. Hours of waiting
do not disturb him in the least. In the same way he
may keep others waiting—which is apt to annoy
Europeans.

In 1966 Agpaoa was still living in Quezon City, on
the outskirts of Manila, where Harold Sherman observed him for three weeks and later described the
trying atmosphere in which Agpaoa was forced to
work.[248] Surrounded by indescribable street noise so
that at times one could not hear one's own words,
and by crying children whom the Philippine women
had brought along; besieged day and night by regi-
ments of patients clamoring to be treated—in the
midst of hectic activity, which would have discon-

certed anyone with a normal nervous system, Agpaoa performed his work with unchanging repose and helpfulness.

When he was younger, he was a member of the Unio Espiritista Cristiana Filipinas, but he resigned because many of the association's tenets seemed too narrow. (At that time the healers of the Union worked only after hours of performing specific religious ceremonies. To Agpaoa all this seemed unnecessary: "Why should we have long religious services and let the very sick lie waiting, so that they may even die before we operate? Praying can be done at night, the day should be used for healing.") Nevertheless he valued the members for their uprightness and selflessness and respected their beliefs without sharing them on every point.

Professor Guillermo Tolentino, for many years a supporter of the Union, today claims that Agpaoa was expelled because he commercialized his healing and had come under the influence of "evil powers." In 1966 he predicted that "Tony will come to a bad end." A German magazine, perhaps relying on this source, claimed that Agpaoa had fallen into the clutches of a local mafia.

Still another source claims that Agpaoa practices "black magic," using his powers for evil purposes. Anyone familiar with the lively Far Eastern imagination will not take such speculations too seriously, although Agpaoa has clearly had to surmount crises in his life and probably faces still others. Such a rapid rise from poor boy to healer with an enthusiastic following could go to anyone's head.

What most irritates Tony's opponents is his penchant for publicity, but without it, hardly any outsiders would have heard of Philippine surgery to this day—even though the American Medical Association has officially declared the Philippine operations a fraud.

In October 1967 Harold Sherman went on a second trip to the Philippines. A charter flight had been organized by Joe Plaza, James Osberg, and Joseph

Ruffner, who a year earlier had been cured of a serious back injury by one of Agpaoa's operations. More than a hundred patients categorized as clinically incurable or resistant to treatment were to be operated on by Tony Agpaoa. Practically all had available medical histories, so that the success of Agpaoa's surgery could easily be evaluated. Sherman, accompanied by F. J. Liddon, a prominent American businessman, had flown on ahead and awaited the charter flight's arrival at Manila Airport.

On the afternoon of October 5, 1967, the plane landed. The airport was besieged by an army of reporters and photographers. Official representatives of the Philippine Medical Association had come to extend a welcome, as had Agpaoa himself, having only recently moved from Manila to Baguio. When he discovered that officers of the Philippine secret police had also come—to apprehend him for unlicensed medical practice—he considered it the better part of valor to mingle inconspicuously with the crowd of onlookers.

The secret police had obviously been told to prevent treatment in order to "protect" the Americans—which would have meant the whole long journey had been for nothing. Agpaoa, for his part, had ordered twenty-three hired cars, to which the patients were transferred. According to Sherman's account, the transfer of these patients—many seriously ill and further exhausted by the long flight—in the Philippine heat and extreme tension defies all description. It was assumed that the patients were to be taken to Baguio. The police seemed ready to begin the pursuit, but as if on command, the hired cars scattered in every direction, and the confused pursuers were successfully shaken off. The patients were taken by great detours to a hotel at the seashore about 60 miles from Baguio. The route went over steep, impassable mountain roads, dangerous in the approaching twilight, and Sherman later called it a miracle that all the patients arrived alive. Since the hideout might be discovered at any moment, Agpaoa began to operate at once.

James Osberg, who felt responsible for the junket, meanwhile attempted to effect a "truce," at least for the period required to operate on all the American patients. He was prepared to offer himself as a guinea pig: in the presence of representatives of the Philippine Medical Association, the healer would operate on Osberg, resolving once and for all the question of fraud.

A Philippine physician, Dr. Padua, demanded that test patients be selected by the Philippine medical society. He personally suggested two drastic cases: a patient with a large cystic calculus, and one with a bullet in his head.

There was a great deal of suspense about whether Osberg would find a healer prepared to operate on such critical cases, but to the physicians' great uneasiness, the offer was immediately accepted. Thereupon the medical society's representatives sent word that even if a healer could successfully perform both operations, he would nevertheless be arrested for performing surgery without a license.[250] Harold Sherman called this "the incredible admission that, even when the authenticity of psychic surgery can be proved . . . the medical authorities will do their utmost to prevent its practice."

The surgery was performed under this incredible pressure. When the police finally discovered the hotel, it is said that Agpaoa—disguised as a waiter, serving guests—was not recognized. Most operations were subsequently performed in a remote place in the mountains, where patients were smuggled during the night.

Given such conditions, we need not be astonished that not all the expected results were achieved. After a week's work Agpaoa was totally exhausted. He told Sherman that many of the selected severe cases required additional magnetic healing in a calm and relaxed atmosphere.

In order to forestall further complications, the organizers of the trip kept the patients' names secret even after their return to the United States. Even before the trip, however, Sherman had been in touch with some of the patients. According to him, genuine and lasting cures were effected on some cases.

It is hardly astonishing that these unpleasant experiences have had their effect on Agpaoa. His opponents, however, have interpreted Agpaoa's increasing mistrust as a swindler's deviousness.

Agpaoa's house at the edge of Baguio is situated at the bottom of a valley, surrounded on three sides by mountains. To the south it has an open view. During the day it is very warm, even in winter. Nevertheless, I was unable to shake a stubborn head cold I had acquired at the beginning of my stay at the Villa La Maja; it grew more pronounced.

Ever since my tonsils were removed over twenty years ago, I had suffered a strong disposition to sinus infections—about ten a year of varying intensity and duration—and frequent bad head colds. The sinusitis I developed this time was not the acute kind which quickly leads to a crisis and rapid relief, but a creeping, chronic form. I suffered from a headache and slightly raised temperature, especially in the evening, but even during the day I felt weak and reluctant to make any effort. When I blew my nose I expelled purulent, sometimes bloody mucus. At the hotel, one of the European doctors gave me acupuncture treatments, without the slightest effect. Subsequently, over a period of several days, Agpaoa's father, Moises, inserted little rods with a menthol-smelling salve in my nostrils; this always brought a period of relief but had no effect on the sinusitis. Toward the end of my stay in Baguio I asked Tony if he could relieve my sinusitis surgically. He agreed and also planned to perform a procedure in my abdominal and intestinal region the following day. Thirteen years earlier I probably had had a severe abdominal or duodenal ulcer and suffered frequent symptoms in this area, though not so extreme that I would have agreed to an operation at home.

I believed Agpaoa could improve my sinus condition but did not count on a complete cure. Among the numerous operations I had seen, some did not give the patients significant relief. In fact, before the operation I thought about how I could obtain a cure when I returned to Germany. In short, I was not in a highly emotional state and expecting a miracle, ready for a psychogenic cure. But I was not in the least fearful of the operation, since I had not seen even one operation where the patient felt any pain or where anything else went wrong. Having seen so many paranormal operations, I was curious to experience one myself. I had not yet taken movies of any head operations, and I planned to have a compatriot take one of mine.

When Agpaoa appeared the following morning, ready to operate, I realized the light in the operating room and in my bedroom was insufficient for filming. It occurred to me that it would be ideal if the operation could be performed outdoors, but I did not dare say so. But Agpaoa, noting my disappointment, said, "Let's operate in the yard."

Tripod and movie camera were quickly set up. Herr G. was happy to man the camera. I took my place on a chair in the middle of the little yard, surrounded by a swarm of puppies, chickens, and a turkey. Pigs grunted in the background. Tony waited until his father brought a bowl of water, a towel, and some cotton. But I had already placed my own towel around my neck. Now, to avoid the bright sunlight, I closed my eyes and concentrated completely on my own feelings. The only mental distraction that occasionally intruded was the question whether Herr G. was managing to cope with the film equipment.

First I felt Tony's outspread hands slowly stroking my temples and head. This motion may have gone on for half a minute or more; then I felt two fingertips of one hand press against my nose from below, while the other hand pressed against my forehead and the bridge of my nose. At once my nose began to bleed profusely, and Tony shouted, "Say 'Ha,' say 'Ha.'" I did, and immediately the top of my nose seemed somehow to soften under his touch—I cannot describe the sensation any other way. (Later I tried to imitate the feeling by pressing with my fingers, a wet cloth, or cotton, but it was absolutely impossible.)

Next my whole forehead seemed to grow soft, as if Agpaoa were pressing a squashy, pulpy substance, but I felt no pain or any other discomfort. I did feel blood or a bloodlike liquid at body temperature flowing, at one time, down my throat.

As the film showed, Agpaoa's procedure took place at the upper edge of the bridge of my nose. My feeling that my forehead had softened probably arose because—as Agpaoa later explained—blood and pus were drawn from the frontal into the nasal cavities by means of his magnetic power. From here, however, the infection was not withdrawn through the nostrils or throat; it was probably externalized by paranormal dematerialization around the bridge of my nose.

The actual operation may have taken half a minute or a minute. Then I felt a towel being wiped across my face, and Tony's father again placed the same menthol-smelling rods in my nostrils. Then, as a kind of aftertreatment, Tony magnetically stroked my head, forehead, and temples. And the operation was over.

Father Moises pointed to the washbowl, where a loose, bloody piece of tissue floated. I learned that Tony had removed this too, apparently through the bridge of my nose.

I realized for the first time that I could breathe better than I had for years. In the course of time the nasal passages must have narrowed—a condition to which I had adapted so that I no longer knew what it meant to breathe freely. As the same time I became aware that a steady chill, caused by the constant slight fever, had disappeared. I felt well in every respect. No matter how vehemently I blew my nose, all that came out was some crystal-clear mucus; a few minutes earlier I had produced only suppurative matter.

Two years have passed, and since that day I have never suffered from another cold, much less a sinus infection, although I have often been exposed to climatic conditions which would invariably have led to a head cold earlier.

This quick, elegant, and entirely painless operation was a masterwork without parallel in Western medicine. Depicting Agpaoa's success as psychogenic appears totally absurd to me.

Six months later my film of this operation was shown on German television; I had naively allowed the network to borrow my movies and medical record. The program's commentator summed up more or less as follows: "Agpaoa took some cotton soaked in blood or a red liquid and pressed it against the patient's forehead, producing the illusion of an operation. The relief the patient felt was due to the mentholated rods placed in his nostrils after the so-called operation." This method of reporting speaks for itself.[261]

About ten or fifteen minutes after the frontal operation, surgery on my abdominal-intestinal area was performed. Since I had to lie down for it, the operation took place in my room. There were some half-dozen spectators—Philippine women visiting Lucy Agpaoa, who had already watched through the window during the operation in the yard. Tony began by palpating my abdomen lightly. I found it interesting that he felt the area of my appendix and seemed irresolute, perhaps irritated by some kind of deformity left over from the appendix irritations I used to suffer repeatedly. Finally he moved on and turned his entire attention to the area of the stomach and the duodenum.

I was asked to raise my knees slightly. As I was about to raise my head, he instantly sensed tension in me and said, "Relax." Then I felt his hands moving very softly, near my navel. When I peered around again a few moments later, I saw his right hand already partly inside my body, and to my great surprise I saw a puddle of blood. I would have thought liquid on one's body would be felt. Now I could hear gentle splashing or smacking noises and had the feeling that Agpaoa's kneading fingers were searching around in my body; I could not tell whether this exploration was superficial or went deeper. Then I felt very clearly that he tried to pull something out of the depths of my body that put up a certain resistance—and still I felt no pain. Something seemed to give inside me, and at the same moment Agpaoa pulled out a longish piece of tissue that looked like a section of intestine; it probably came from the jejunum (part of the small intestine) rather than the duodenum.

The familiar incantation "One, two, three" followed, and Agpaoa's hands separated from my body. On my stomach a small puddle held a few clumps of coagulated blood. Moises toweled the area and rubbed an ointment into it. After resting briefly, I got up. I felt no weakness or pain, and I looked forward to dinner.

But I had an unpleasant surprise. I sat down at the table with a hearty appetite, as usual. But after a few spoonfuls of soup I could not go on eating—though I did not feel sick in any way. That evening, too, I ate only a little and with reluctance. My appetite slowly returned the following day. In the afternoon I drank two cups of coffee and ate a piece of cake without any ill effects. In the following weeks I became aware of a distinct change in my eating habits: I ate less than before—which did not disturb me. Immediately after surgery I was also abnormally sensitive to cold—even to cool food and drinks, which gave me sudden, cramping stomach pains.

Now, two years later, my difficulties—which were, at worst, intermittent—have lessened or stopped altogether. Some foods I used to avoid do not bother me any longer, but of course I cannot be sure that this is the result of the operation.

On the last day of my stay in Baguio, a Sunday, I spent the morning at the balustrade in the small room, observing Marcelo at work in Agpaoa's treatment room one floor below. The patients were locals. For skeptics who still believe in a trick, I want to mention that this Sunday morning Marcelo arrived from Rosales on the mail bus. He was wearing no jacket, only a short-sleeved shirt. He had brought nothing but a thin briefcase, which throughout the morning's work stood on the floor against a wall 6–9 feet from the operating table. He never left the table, though the patients changed constantly. He was given only occasional assistance, by two young men in Agpaoa's employ: seventeen-year-old Robert and a nineteen-year-old gardener, neither of them "sorcerer's apprentices." Agpaoa and Marcelo change assistants very often, and it is absurd to assume that all the occasional helpers are trained on the spot as accomplices in an elaborate fraud. From my vantage point above the table I could closely observe the healer's and assistants' every move. Marcelo often produced considerable quantities of tissue, which was thrown in the plastic bucket placed next to the table. After only an hour's work the matter in the bucket had reached an amount that could hardly have been concealed somewhere on Marcelo's body—let alone during hours of riding on a bus in very hot weather.

Two other guests of Agpaoa's were also observing Marcelo's work: Herr G. and Miss Cheryl Baker from Australia. Twenty-three years old, she had become confined to a wheelchair at the age of seven. According to her account, she suffered from paraplegia, the result of a botched lumbar puncture performed in Australia. Cheryl Baker had no family, had sold her few possessions, and had traveled to the Philippines, where she had spent the last six or eight weeks with Agpaoa. At that time Tony's efforts resulted in increased sensitivity in her paralyzed legs. Unfortunately, during her stay the paralysis did not retreat. Later she flew to England by way of Hong Kong, Nepal, Israel, and Germany, working as a stenotypist at all intermediate stops to earn the money to continue her travels. An admirable example of courage which might well be held up to many hypochondriacs, Cheryl Baker intended to write a book, *Around the World by Wheelchair*.

After we had watched Marcelo at work for a while, Tony Agpaoa joined us, and we began to chat about his legendary ability to produce inexplicable results by the power of his gaze. As a child, Agpaoa told us, he could sit fascinated in front of a fire for hours, watching the flickering flames. He believed that he could influence the fire by spiritual-mental concentration.

One day, he told me, his friend Alfredo threw a ball at him across a hut, and the ball fell into a gutter on the straw roof. The boys' efforts to get it down failed. Finally Alfredo challenged his playmate, who even then was credited with wondrous abilities in handling fire, to use his gaze to burn a hole into the straw roof where the ball had come to rest. Goaded by his friend, Tony fixedly concentrated on the straw roof. "Burn it through, burn it through, burn it through," he thought intensely.

After a while Alfredo, speaking in a slightly unsteady voice, said, "Antonio . . . there's smoke coming from the roof."

Tony saw nothing, however, and concentrated even more. Then he too spied a glimmering circle around the ball on the roof. Without burning openly, the hole grew even wider. Finally the ball fell.

Alfredo ran and caught it, but he dropped it again immediately, for it was very hot.

"Put out the fire!" Alfredo called, but Tony had lost control. The roof was already ablaze. Both boys ran into the hut to carry out all the objects. Immediately thereafter the roof fell in.

Later, as a demonstration for Alfredo's father, Tony was asked to set fire to a small heap of straw in the same way. This experiment, he told me, also succeeded. In the same way, he claimed, he had brought about burns on Alfredo's angry father's chest.

Tony is said to have melted blossoms and leaves in their own juice by fixing them with his gaze, so that they were suitable for prescription to his patients. Agpaoa claimed he had healed or removed external disorders such as skin diseases by a concentrated gaze. This ability, he said, had been taken from him again when he was fourteen, because he had not been mature enough for it. Tony expected that someday this power would be restored to him.[248]

Western and Eastern scientists have recently explored the effects of the human eye, a particularly complex organ. Developmentally it is an extension of the brain and remains connected to it. Besides its function as a sensory organ of the visible electromagnetic spectrum, the eye probably commands a number of further skills, latent in most people and still hidden from established science.

Let us remember the significance of the gaze in hypnosis. Gazing plays an important role in the animal kingdom too. The Brazilian giant python stares at rabbits and other prey until they freeze then he devours them.[307] In India I learned about the mongoose, a small catlike carnivore that is one of the best hypnotists in the animal world. It engages in regular duels of mutual staring and fascination with various poisonous snakes. The mongoose usually wins. (Of course the fights staged by Indian street performers represent rather uneven duels, since the snakes' fangs have been drawn.)

These effects have been explained only in psychological terms. But the theory that a mysterious radiation emanates from the eye was proposed as early as the 1920s by the Russian animal trainer Vladimir Durov and the telepath Yuri Kamensky. Years of practical experience had convinced Durov that the human gaze could tame the wildest animal. Durov also investigated the effect of the gaze on the back of the neck by staring at people's necks without their knowledge. They turned around, it is said, 100 percent of the time.

The gaze is also instrumental in some psychokinetic performances. As previously stated, the origin of psychokinesis can probably be found in the bioplasmic body. Old Indian yoga teachings and Asian scientists who have extensively studied progressed yogis affirm that the bioplasmic body possesses a series of energy centers, called chakras, connected with bioplasmic and paranormal processes. There are said to be seven such energy centers or chakras in man.[158] One center in the forehead—the ajna chakra —seems related to the paranormal effects of the gaze in several forms of psychokineses, as in the Israeli Uri Geller, under whose "magic" gaze forks and spoons sometimes bend.[9] Experiments involving Nina Kulagina seemed to make a particular demand on the optical centers in her brain.

Agpaoa's setting straw roofs ablaze with a look may

be nothing more than a very impressive psychokinetic effort, for heating is an increase in molecular kinetic energy. Sufficient increase in molecular movement can bring about a chemical process such as combustion. It is said, incidentally, that Kulagina can cause psychokinetic burns on skin,[98] such as Agpaoa allegedly produced on Alfredo's father.

Toward noon that Sunday morning Tony Agpaoa gave us an involuntary demonstration of his telepathic powers. Herr G. had come to Baguio because, over fifteen years earlier, he had been involved in an automobile accident abroad and had broken his left leg below the knee. The break, treated in a South African hospital, did not heal, and Herr G. had to strap on an awkward brace in order to walk. Because his legs grew to different lengths, his spine became affected, causing severe back pains. Western medicine had not been able to solder together the break after fifteen years or to get it to grow together in some other way.

Agpaoa had already operated on Herr G.'s back; according to the patient, his pains substantially diminished. But Herr G. had been waiting three weeks now for the actual leg operation. Tony had scheduled it for today, but he had not mentioned it.

Tony was sitting on the couch in the large living room and had barricaded himself behind the newspaper. Herr G. began to grow impatient. Probably Tony had come downstairs to operate but seemed undecided. Herr G. asked me to talk to Tony about his operation, but I thought he should ask himself.

While Tony was hidden behind his paper, Herr G. sat on a stool on the opposite side of the room in front of the bar, concentrated on Tony, and mentally kept asking, "Am I going to be operated on today?" After the third mental question, Agpaoa suddenly jumped up, angrily threw the paper aside, said loudly, "No, not today," and left the room.

It became clear that when difficult operations were at stake, Agpaoa could not work whenever he wanted to; rather, he had to reckon with an incalculable, scientifically indeterminate factor—mood, inspiration,

contact with some other dimension, or something else
out of the deepest levels of the psyche, which simply
cannot be controlled by the conscious mind. By contrast, a magician can perform a well-rehearsed trick
at any time; he does not have to postpone it for three
weeks.

That afternoon we were all surprised when Tony
suddenly appeared again and said that he would perform the operation on Herr G. The surgery was carried out in the patient's room. He lay on his back in
his bed. His leg was bared and a large towel was
placed under it. Except for Moises Agpaoa, I was the
only spectator.

Obviously Tony Agpaoa was now "very strong."
He squatted at the patient's bedside, and enormous
concentration showed in his bearing. Almost before
his fingertips touched the leg, blood began to spurt.
In seconds a large wound appeared, and I could see
the open place of the break and the bones. The wound
presented a most unpleasant sight, like a "salad" of
blood and raw flesh.

Agpaoa seemed to think he could join the broken
bones paranormally, with some kind of plastic peg.
I do not know whether he inserted one, for I stood
on the other side of the bed, and now the towel was
pushed upward and hid the operation from me. I assume that at this point in the operation Agpaoa realized that inserting a peg would not work and that he
tried a different course. He seemed to work in the
wound for a while, then applied a large bandage.
The patient was told to stay lying down. I could not
follow the subsequent treatments, since I left Baguio
the same evening.

There is no doubt in my mind that Agpao opened
the leg. I took a photograph of this phase of the operation; though underexposed, it clearly shows the
opened site of the break.

Two or three months later I had an opportunity to
speak with Herr G. again in Germany. Unfortunately,
according to him, his condition was unchanged. The
broken ends of the bone continued to scrape against
each other, and he could not walk without support.

He was not charged for the operation, and although he
spent almost four weeks in Agpaoa's house, he only
paid board for ten days.

In this case, neither Western medicine nor Agpaoa
helped. Agpaoa had not undertaken complicated bone
operations before; he had hoped that a forty-day fast
had intensified his ability in this area. But even today,
such operations confront him with his most serious
problem. Interestingly, Zé Arigo is alleged to have refused categorically to do bone operations. Later, when
Agpaoa visited Germany, he told me that his fingers
were "too soft for bone operations." But it is said that
there are paranormal surgeons among the North
American Indians who successfully perform bone
surgery.

Agpaoa planned to drive to Manila the following
morning, and he was going to take me along. But
typically, he suddenly decided to start out that very
evening. There is nothing Tony dislikes more than a
rigid schedule. Subconscious inspiration cannot be
regulated. He is especially attracted to improvising,
and he loves surprises above all. Probably his paranormal talents would suffer if he were forced to adapt
to a "normal" daily schedule and submit himself to
rules we routinely accept.

Juan Blance

Before leaving the Philippines I wanted to meet the
healer Juan Blance in Manila, whom I had read about
in American parapsychological periodicals. His methods of operating and treatment were said to be entirely different from those of the healers in Baguio
and Rosales. I had heard that Juan Blance could open
the patient's body without instruments, but he could
not close it again: his operations left a wound that had
to heal naturally.

I had been given the address of a taxi driver who
would drive me to Blance's house, but he was ill when
I arrived. I was left to my own devices; all I knew was

that the healer was supposed to live in the suburb of Pasig, but when I got there, not a single passerby, policeman, or taxi driver could tell me the exact address. Of course he had neither a listed telephone nor a sign on the door; that I found him nevertheless is almost a paraphenomenon in itself.

Slowly and at a loss, I asked my taxi to drive back and forth through the streets of Pasig, with its countrified little wooden houses set in handsome gardens. On a narrow path through a row of arbors I saw a number of people sitting and chatting animatedly. As we stopped and I rolled down the car window, the woman who had been dominating the conversation laughed and shouted to the others, "Want to bet he's trying to find Blance?"

A friendly Filipino led me along a narrow path, through gardens, past huts and rabbit hutches, cats and dogs, under drying laundry and across hen yards. Just as I was thinking the road would never end, my guide pointed to the open door of a small wooden house. A staircase led upward, another led down into a cellarlike room in which stood a garden bench— probably some sort of waiting room. A young man sat on a chair—Blance's assistant, as it turned out.

I expressed the desire to be allowed to watch Mr. Blance at his work, and he was sent for immediately. As he came down the stairs, I recognized him at once from the pictures in Harold Sherman's *Wonder Healers of the Philippines*.[248] Blance was forty-three years old, tall and massively built. Though he was quite willing to let me observe his operations and treatments, he regretted that no patients were available at the moment. They tended to come very early, he explained, between three and ten o'clock.

I was about to leave until the following day when another patient came after all—an elderly man. Blance invited me to watch. He pushed aside a curtain and we entered a small, simply furnished room without windows. An oblong table was furnished as an operating table. There were a couple of chairs and a kind of writing desk. A ceiling fixture threw a bright light.

"High blood," Blance said to me in reference to the patient; he obviously meant high blood pressure. The old man lay down on the table on his stomach and bared his neck. Blance reached for my right hand and said he would transfer his power to me. I was told to ball my right hand into a fist and stretch out my index finger. Then, holding my hand about 8 inches above the patient's neck, Blance made a short jerky movement in the air and at the same time pointed to a spot on the patient's neck. I saw a delicate short incision, as if etched by a razor blade.

Now Blance applied a procedure known in Western folk medicine as cupping. The assistant handed Blance an old coin, which he placed on the neck incision, where no bleeding was to be seen. On the coin was placed some cotton soaked in alcohol or coconut oil. This was set alight, and the healer turned a small glass, about two or three times the size of a liqueur glass, upside down over both coin and cotton and pressed it tightly against the skin. The flame under the glass went out quickly, since the oxygen in the air was used up almost at once. The suction thus produced under the glass produced a swelling, growing ever larger, at the incision, and the wound began to bleed.

The blood rose in the glass until it filled about halfway. Then Blance tilted the glass away, some of the blood remaining in it. The rest of the blood, containing coagulated clots, was wiped off the patient's neck. Blance pressed the edges of the cut together and said that it would heal soon.

This patient was followed by another, who seemed to be suffering from a cold or from sinusitis. While he sat on a chair, Blance drove a cotton-covered swab deep into his nose. When he pulled it out, a dark brown clot larger than a pea was attached to it.

A woman was last. She complained of pain on the right side of her abdomen, perhaps an inflamed appendix. In any case, Blance palpated the patient's bare body in the region of the appendix, then kneaded the skin with his fingers, moved his hands aside a little, and stared as if hypnotized at the massaged part of the body. I too stared; not hypnotized, but perplexed—for out of the skin was seeping a yellowish fluid like very thin pus or lymph matter. Blance took a tablespoon and spooned away the liquid. I decided to return to my hotel and return the next morning, well rested and with a clear mind.

I was back in Blance's waiting room at 6:00 a.m. The healer and his assistant were reading newspapers; there were no patients. The assistant told me that they saw an average of seventy patients a day. No one came until 6:30; then a group arrived, obviously a family.

"Ulcers," declared Blance, pointing to the father. The patient lay down on the table, his abdomen was bared, and the procedure was basically the same as I had observed the day before. Blance again used my finger to make a "cut from a distance," this time not in the neck but in the patient's abdomen. I concentrated on looking at the place where the cut would appear, but as if he wished to trick me and to punish me for my curiosity, Blance moved his outspread left hand between me and the patient—definitely without touching the patient—so that I did not see the small, delicate incision until he removed his hand. He repeated the procedure with the coin and the cotton soaked in alcohol, burning the cotton under the glass, collecting the blood in the glass. When the glass was removed Blance used his fingers, still smeared with blood, to press against both sides of the wound. I could not trust my eyes: something came out of the wound which looked almost like a fat caterpillar. It was a bloody but rather firm substance; its basic color was reddish brown, and it seemed to be a couple of inches long. Blance put it in a small bowl filled with water.

"The root," he explained. The small cut, enlarged by the "root"'s passage, remained open. Blance said that it would have to heal by itself.

Immediately thereafter an older woman—obviously the grandmother—sat down on the "operating chair." She pointed to her eyes, where her trouble apparently lay. Blance lightly massaged her closed eyes with both

thumbs, then drew the lids apart slightly and waited.
At the inner corner of the eye a dot appeared; it
grew larger as it made its way outward. Finally a
lentil-sized, elongated light brown mass worked its
way out in slow motion, as it were, and fell directly
into Blance's cupped hand.

There was a steady stream of patients after that.
The treatments always went extraordinarily quickly.
The patients hardly had to wait at all. Usually it
was Blance who waited for patients, reading newspapers or working crossword puzzles. If a break lasted
long enough, he went upstairs to his living quarters.
He always impressed me as totally relaxed and apparently did not need any preliminary period to
think about the case or to concentrate on his powers.
He gave the impression that he was not doing the
work but was guided from outside, like a robot. Sometimes after applying the cupping glass he went into
the waiting room and paced back and forth, only to
return at the exact moment when the blood stopped
rising and the glass had to be taken off. Whenever a
"root" seemed to crawl out of the incision after the
glass was removed, he seemed in a sort of trance but
intensely concentrated.

As his assistant told me, Blance has been healing
since 1958. He must have treated a sizable number of
American patients after he became famous in the
1960s for curing an American boy. Danny Guin of Sun
Valley, California, the son of Mrs. Donna Morel from
her first marriage, suffered from a nonosteogenic fibro-
ma on his left femur—a benign tumor of the connective tissue in the hip area, diagnosed in May 1962,
when the child was five years old. The cause was unknown. His symptoms were inflammation, loss of
weight, exhaustion, and locomotor disorders. After
extensive treatment, surgery was performed on December 29, 1964, and March 18, 1968. The tumor re-
curred, however. Danny was fitted for crutches.

After years of unsuccessful medical treatment in the
United States, Mrs. Morel heard about Philippine
surgery. During the Second World War her husband
had been stationed in Germany and had had occasion

to observe the stigmatized Therese Neumann of Konnersreuth on Good Friday, when the wounds of Christ appeared on her body. He therefore believed that there are things we cannot explain and raised no objections when his wife drew on all their financial resources to fly to the Philippines with her son. Donna Morel was also ready to assume the risk of appearing ridiculous in the eyes of people who knew her.

On April 13, 1966, they arrived at the home of Professor Tolentino, whose downstairs living room was fitted out for psychic treatment. In humidity we would consider unbearable, about twenty patients were waiting when the brown-skinned Eleuterio Terte —a veteran Philippine healer sometimes called the teacher of Agpaoa—came down the stairs from the next floor. When Terte immediately looked at her son and beckoned to him, terror seized Mrs. Morel. The mother vehemently shook her head, wanting to see for herself before entrusting her son to this dusky man. She watched a number of operations before she encouraged Danny to hobble toward the healer on his crutches.

The boy was placed on the table, and Terte touched the site of the illness before there was time to explain the disease to him. He said the case was too serious for immediate surgery; the patient required strengthening magnetic treatment first.

Terte reached into an open Bible lying nearby and gestured as if he were holding a hypodermic, which he appeared to direct at Danny's left thigh. Although nothing could be seen, the little patient felt the sting.

The operation was scheduled for a later time in Baguio, where Terte was going the following day. But then it was learned that Juan Blance was going to work in the Tolentino house that very evening and would be able to operate on Danny.

Blance performed the operation at 6:00 p.m. Accompanied by two assistants, the healer immediately inspired trust in the Americans by his calm, assured, and friendly manner. He laid his heavy hand on Danny's head and said after a while that Danny was now strong enough; the operation could take place.

The usual procedures followed: the opening of the body with a psychokinetic incision, the coin, the alcohol-soaked cotton, and the cupping glass. Blance reached into the wound, pulled out three-quarters of the mass to be removed, and stopped to let Mrs. Morel take a snapshot. Then he pulled out the entire matter and pressed the skin together—again, without closing the wound paranormally.

Two further operations by Blance followed on subsequent days. The last treatment was performed on April 17, 1966, by the healer Ading, who applied massage and carried out magnetic and chiropractic treatments.

On his return to the United States, Danny Guin was soon walking without crutches and felt pain only when he overexerted. His limp is gradually retreating. On April 26, 1966, an X ray was taken, but because it was lit badly, it furnishes no clear conclusions. Another X ray taken June 24, 1966, revealed there was no longer any tumor or the preconditions for a new one to form. The atrophied (underdeveloped) muscles in the left leg have almost completely normalized and adapted to the healthy leg. There remains a slight anomaly of the position of the femur in the hip socket, but the American physicians believe that this will straighten out as the boy grows.

While I was visiting Blance, a man accompanied by wife and child came to see him. He walked with great difficulty and complained of severe pains in his hip. Blance told me this case was very similar to the little American boy's; they were not very frequent.

The patient crawled onto the table with much effort, lay on his well side, and bared the diseased hip. A considerable swelling bulged at the site, indicating a large growth. Blance seemed to concentrate with particular intensity and used the wife's index finger to "open." Then the usual procedure followed. When the glass was removed, with a great deal of blood, the crucial phase of the operation began. Blance, his glittering eyes fixed on the site of the operation, his body enormously tense, stood before the patient. With a quite unexpected agility, the otherwise rather phlegmatic-seeming healer put his fingers at specific places next to the wound. A light red mass of tissue pushed its way through the small opening, and a roundish tumor, larger than a plum, emerged.

Before the operation the skin had been closed but swollen from the tumor. Now, after removal of the growth, there gaped a large, unpleasant-looking wound, which was washed with water and cleansed with cotton. Blance seemed no more afraid of infection than Tony Agpaoa. Finally a piece of adhesive tape was strapped across it, and the patient got off the table. During the whole treatment he had not given any indication of pain.

I saw that two or three pesos were pushed into Blance's hand—less than a dollar for this extraordinary performance. The patient, in turn, was handed his tumor and a piece of paper to wrap it in. Limping only slightly, he and his wife and child walked out of the healer's little house.

Of course I can say nothing about this treatment's final outcome, but possibly it was the same as for Danny Guin. In this operation, clearly, the body was opened and the tumor removed psychokinetically. It is probable that in the performances I witnessed, Blance's ajna chakra was very active; for sometimes the healer stared with the utmost concentration at the diseased part of the body without seeming to do much with his hands.*

Sometimes Blance massaged the abdomen lightly with his fingers without opening the body. Under his hands doughy substances, predominantly gray or brown, seemed to form or come out of the body. Sometimes they had very special shapes; what I saw would ordinarily be considered sleight of hand, but is described in exactly the same way in Harold Sherman's book.

Sherman described a case of a woman suffering from the extreme itching of herpes. I saw one patient who had obviously had leg ulcers, now closed, which

---

*See pp. 81–83.

still caused severe itching or pain. Blance's fingers touched the affected skin. Each time he removed his hands, small fusiform seedlike substances clung to his fingertips—particles exactly like those described by Sherman.[248] Blance threw them into the washbowl with a little jerky motion each time, as if they tended to stick to his fingers.

This process seemed absolutely inexplicable, and I stared attentively at the healer's fingers. Blance's nails were cut very short. The rim normally present on the nails was almost completely cut off—as I noticed among most Philippine healers, probably to prevent scratching. Thus Blance could not have concealed the "seeds" under his fingernails. Again, these strange substances sometimes seemed to emerge from the skin as if in slow motion. Blance moved calmly and deliberately, wearing a short-sleeved shirt. Such processes can probably only be explained on the basis of materialization. The process is somewhat similar to the third stage of Agpaoa's surgery. The difference lies in the techniques for opening the body and in the fact that Blance is apparently unable to close the wound. Nevertheless, his operations are completely painless.

In other cases—perhaps with less advanced diseases or ones not so sharply localized—Blance brings peculiar doughy or liquid substances out of the body without opening it. This looks like a process of diffusion, as if the body were exuding something naturally, as during sweating or skin rashes; but such natural procedures take much longer and are usually not so localized. Perhaps there is an analogy between this form of treatment and the second stage of Agpaoa's surgery.

I spent several days with Blance and observed a great variety of operations and treatments on almost all parts of the body. Given Blance's working conditions, deception was impossible in most instances. He appears uncomplicated and calm and very good-natured. Since he gives the impression of indolence, it is all the more surprising to see him working briskly without pausing to reflect. It is likely that he is in an anomalous psychic state during his operations.

I tried to find out more but could get nothing out of him beyond the claim that while he operates he is "guided by God." He spoke with such conviction and matter-of-factness that I had to be content with his answer. He added that he was not allowed to ask for fees and would accept only voluntary donations; otherwise he would lose his healing powers.

I asked whether he could also heal himself if he should ever fall ill. He smiled like a wise man at a very naive question and said that he could not possibly get sick, for God was keeping him healthy. He had never been ill a day in his life.

I asked how he knew which organ was diseased in patients. When he makes passes over the patient's body with his hands, he told me, he can "see" the diseased organ or the disease itself. He feels something like an electric current flowing through his arms and hands, and thereupon he is guided in his treatment.

At the beginning of my visit I tested his diagnostic skills by asking him to examine me. He passed his hand over my body at a distance of 4–8 inches; like Agpaoa, he paused over the area of my appendix and seemed undecided. I asked whether my appendix was all right. After some hesitation he said, "It is OK now." His hand also hovered over my forehead until I told him that this was the place where Agpaoa had operated on me.

I allowed Blance to give me a chiropractic treatment, which was completely different from Western chiropractic and probably represented a mixture of normal and paranormal usage. The year before, I had sought out a chiropractor perhaps ten times, but I never needed to consult one thereafter—not that I can state unequivocally that this is due to Blance's efforts.

This reservation may seem ungrateful to some readers, but necessary caution has always caused me to minimize phenomena I observed in the Philippines. For after our return a violent difference of opinion was to develop which rose to passionate heights and continues to this day.

9/THE CONTROVERSY
ABOUT PSYCHIC SURGERY

In mid-May 1971 a group of about twenty patients flew to Baguio to consult Agpaoa. Reporters from two German picture magazines, *Der Stern* and *Neue Revue*, accompanied them or followed about a week later, as did Dr. Peter Wartenberg, an internist from Hamburg, and Professor Hans Bender, director of the Institute for Marginal Areas of Psychology (Institut für Grenzgebiete der Psychologie) at the University of Freiburg. *Der Stern* financed Wartenberg's and Bender's trips.

It can be questioned whether the two scientists were unbiased, since even before Bender's departure for the Philippines one of his coworkers had produced a film which "unmasked" the "bloody opening" of a body as a trick.

The group spent about two weeks in the Philippines. Immediately upon its return the *Neue Revue* published a laudatory piece on Agpaoa. The surprise of most of the patients was all the greater when, five weeks later, *Der Stern* came out with a long picture report representing Agpaoa's operations as a swindle.

"The Savior with the Nimble Fingers," read the headline. The text accompanying the pictures was larded with irony:

> The Savior does not ask for money—he takes what he can get. . . . What Tony says—"I am the tool of a divine power"—sounds like the reported miracle cures of Jesus Christ—with only one difference: Jesus did not accept money of any kind. . . . Tony has raised himself to a state of affluence; he owns a travel agency, a beauty parlor, and a tailoring establishment.

In the West we do not begrudge prosperity to any hard-working person. If Agpaoa has managed to achieve a decent life for his family, now numbering six, he should hardly be reproached for it, especially since his long-range plans cannot be realized without funds. After working as a healer for twenty years, Agpaoa owns his own home, which is comfortable by Philippine standards but hardly up to exacting European expectations. Not one room is allotted to Tony personally; half of it is assigned to patients' board and treatment.[243] If he lived and operated in a miserable hut under primitive conditions, would be have found favor in the eyes of the Hamburg team?

Der Stern displayed a full-page photograph intended to expose Agpaoa. The text accompanying the picture stated that Agpaoa spread a thin transparent sheet over the abdomen, clearly visible, the text goes on to say, distinct from the depressed abdomen.

This filmy layer is also the source of the removed organs. Tony manufactures them in the hollow of the abdomen, with the help of cotton, and even shows them to the patient before his assistant makes the "organ" disappear in the wastebasket. Kneading around in the cavity produces a puddle of simulated blood. The explanation: Tony presses a special dye out of the cotton; at first it looks like water, but it reacts with another dye, previously rubbed into the patient, and turns red.

During our stay in Baguio in January three doctors were present at the operations, one with a specialty in pathology. We handled and examined the tissue Agpaoa removed. Surely three doctors and a chemist are able to tell plastic sheets, cotton, and dyestuff from animal or human tissue.

The "plastic sheet" continued to float through the land for a long time. More than six months later Dr. Naegeli-Osjord and his coworkers in parapsychology requested the magazine's editors to lend them the film containing the picture in question. They were told that there was only a slide. Dr. Naegeli-Osjord asked to borrow it. After a renewed request, he was

finally sent twenty slides, all of them completely irrelevant, the crucial slide not among them. Further
requests were never acknowledged.

Many articles derived from *Der Stern*'s report presented the plastic sheet as undisputed fact. But although in the meantime hundreds of Europeans and
Americans have been to Baguio and observed Agpaoa,
to this day no one has brought back one of these
sheets.

Concerning the assertion that the ointment or liquid
rubbed into the patients contains dyestuffs that produce a red dye simulating blood, I brought back several boxes of it, which I found in Agpaoa's treatment
room; I also own several bottles of the liquid that is
occasionally rubbed into the patients. The ointment is
made from Asian curative herbs. I am still waiting
for someone to show me how either can be turned
into a bloodlike liquid that coagulates.

As for "prepared cotton" said to contain a dyestuff
that can turn red, on several occasions Sigrun Seutemann took some cotton out of a sealed package she
had brought along and handed it directly to Agpaoa
during an operation. Agpaoa used it, quite guilelessly.
The operation and the blood produced were the
same as usual.[248]

Further, anyone with the patience and interest to
observe enough operations will see some during which
Agpaoa and other healers produce an enormous
amount of blood—more than could be produced from
the little bit of water absorbed by a wad of cotton.
And some operations require no cotton at all.

When a scientist makes a claim rather than a
hypothesis, he should make sure he can prove it. Laboratory tests should have been made before the sentence was so lightly pronounced. How far-reaching
such manipulation can be is shown by a report in a
scientific publication, the *Schweizerisches Bulletin für
Parapsychologie*. Its November 1971 issue published
an article entitled "Mental Operations—Genuine or
Trickery?" The piece stated, "What has been written
above as well as the clarification supplied by Professor Bender and the internist Dr. Wartenberg (see *Der*

Stern, July 1971) lead to the conclusion that Agpaoa practiced deceit at least in a number of cases." The evidence is dubious, however, when scientific journals base themselves on popular illustrated magazines. And the parapsychologist with *Der Stern*'s team stayed in Baguio only a few days, saw no operations except Agpaoa's, and met no other psychic surgeons.

According to the magazine, analysis of a spot of blood showed that it was not blood. The obvious question—if not blood, what was it?[76]—has not been answered to this day. The article's remark that "potassium rhodamine" mixed with ferric chloride produces a blood-red dye is pseudoinformation that only misleads the reader. In January our group had already suspected that blood produced by paranormal processes might well lose its original specific properties. We can say that ferric chloride and rhodamine were certainly not involved, for they would have been found immediately by easy chemical analysis.

Ted Serios can produce a picture on an unexposed plate through purely psychic power, which he originates in his imagination. That is, purely mental powers can effect a chemical process in the emulsion of a photographic plate protected against light. When there is no doubt that healers and psychics can bring about chemical changes using only mental concentration, it should not seem improbable that chemical changes take place in the blood spilled during Philippine surgery.

The presentation of Agpaoa's therapeutic successes in *Der Stern*'s article differs in at least a number of cases quite markedly from the testimony of the patients involved. The end of the report cites the case of Arnold Koops, a chemist:

Koops suffered from a growth on the anus. He had no objection to the presence of the professor, the physician, and us two journalists while Tony operated on him. We stood right next to the cot. Tony had not counted on this, but he was reluctant to send us away. At first he attempted to press the chestnut-sized growth back into the intestine. Then he covered it with a great deal of

cotton. Mr. Koops turned his head and encouraged
Tony: "Go ahead, I want to go home tomorrow." Tony
looked angrily at Dr. Wartenberg and said he would
have to postpone the actual operation to the next morning. At 6:00 a.m. he appeared in Mr. Koops's hotel room
and worked without witnesses. The patient, reached by
telephone after his return, told us, "The growth remains
in the same position." On July 10 at 6:30 p.m., an airplane filled with believers left the Frankfurt airport,
headed for Manila. These travelers were unshaken in
their belief that Tony would cure them. Hail Tony! To
preserve the patients' privacy we have changed their
real names, known to our editors.[131]

The chemist, Rudolf E. Passian, referred to on page
175 is the Koops discussed in *Der Stern*'s article. Passian's report read:

Two doctors were present at the preliminary examination; the tumor near the anus was obvious. Agpaoa
said he would have to perform two operations, two to
four days apart, since otherwise the bleeding would be
excessive.
      Both doctors interpreted this as an alibi on Agpaoa's
part so as not to have to operate on this clearcut case
in their presence. We were angry at this prejudice and
therefore did not notify the doctors of the time for the
crucial operations.

The first operation, performed that day, removed
the cotton inserted by the healer in Rosales. Passian
continued by saying that in the final operation

Tony took out the entire growth, the size of a hen's egg.
      Since then the chemist has had only one episode of
bleeding—soon after his return from the Philippines.
He is in good health. A full year has passed, and no
further complications have set in.

Der Stern calls another patient "Frau John from
Bochum." When she came to Baguio her general
condition was very poor. She had large gallstones. Her

blood count and spectrogram, evaluated by computer, as well as tissue tests, were unfavorable and indicated an advanced precancerous condition emanating from the lower abdomen. The findings had persuaded her to travel to the Philippines, especially since she had been told that she was unable to tolerate anesthesia because of previous liver damage. In addition, she had to wear thick glasses as the result of retinal damage in her youth.

Frau John returned from the exertions of the Philippines in a state of considerable weakness. Agpaoa had performed seven operations on her. She was completely depressed when she learned that according to X-ray findings, Agpaoa had *not* removed her gallstones. But in the case of her abdominal operation, blood and tissue samples and computer-evaluated spectrographic blood analysis showed that a definite turn for the better had set in. Even if cancer tests are not invariably accurate, a decidedly positive change cannot be dismissed lightly. The psychogenetic theory seems questionable, as the patient, disappointed by the findings concerning her gallstones, no longer had blind faith in Tony. Monitored by spectrographic blood tests, her condition continued to improve; she gained weight and became much more energetic. The eye operation was also a success. Immediately after surgery the patient realized that she needed different, weaker glasses. Later examination showed a distinct improvement in her sight.

Der Stern's article mentioned only the gallstones result. Both results that spoke in Agpaoa's favor were passed over in silence.

The patients who took part in *Der Stern's* trip unanimously reported that a very tense mood prevailed in the group during their stay. No doubt this ambience strongly interfered with Agpaoa's work. *Der Stern's* article states—ironically, of course—"Tony maintains that Dr. Wartenberg was sending out 'baleful vibrations' that disturbed him."

Edward Naumov, a Russian scientist who worked for many years with Nina Kulagina, has stated:

It is difficult to explain to some scientists that emotions have a profound influence on the medium's achievements. These scientists believe people can be turned on and off like machines. They do not seem to understand that their own force fields can also affect the medium. Some of them, who have no understanding of psychology and bioinformation, radiate hostility and mistrust, emanations caught by the medium. Generally we can give demonstrations of psychokinesis at any time, but if the observers include people with a negative attitude, the medium often requires up to four, even seven hours before phenomena take place. On the other hand, if the medium is surrounded by people with a friendly attitude, it only takes five minutes.

That first evening after the arrival of the German group, Agpaoa appeared at the hotel, ready to perform a middle-ear operation on one patient. Two years earlier Frau L.H. had suffered a punctured eardrum after a botched treatment of a middle-ear infection; the puncture did not heal. A year later, in a German university hospital, a 2½-hour operation with local anesthesia inserted an artificial tympanic membrane. It did not fit tightly, however, and caused a constant tendency to inflammation and infection, headaches, and vertigo. After an examination in the same hospital in January or February 1971 another operation was considered necessary. A doctor friend told Frau L.H. about Agpaoa's operations. Although warned that the outcome would be doubtful, she went to Baguio.

Agpaoa asked the patient to sit in a chair. When he began his preliminary treatment, observers rushed to surround him. Photographers' flashbulbs popped, reporters' movie cameras whirred, and Agpaoa grew so nervous that he interrupted magnetic treatment and postponed the operation to the following day.

The next morning Agpaoa came to the hotel very early and performed the operation in the patient's room. Only Agpaoa's assistant was present. Tony placed Frau L.H. in a chair in front of the mirror so that she could observe the operation. After he had concentrated, he made magnetic passes along her head and then pressed his fingers lightly on a space behind her left ear. The patient suddenly saw blood flowing from her head and neck. A short time later Agpaoa allegedly laid her blood-smeared plastic membrane on the table, saying, "Give it back to your medical doctors."

It looked as if Agpaoa had removed the membrane not by way of the external auditory canal but through a space behind the ear. (In my sinus operation, too, the infection and probably an additional polyplike formation were removed not through the natural nasal openings but directly at the bridge of the nose.)

The patient, who was quite skeptical, was not altogether convinced of Agpaoa's accomplishment. Two days later, during a swimming trip to the South China Sea, a particularly high wave dislodged her life belt. Her bathing cap was pulled off and water rushed into her ears. She grew extremely frightened, for normally she would faint after such an experience. But to her great astonishment, nothing happened. Then she realized that Tony had apparently closed the hole in her eardrum. This supposition was later confirmed by her doctor in Germany. Although the healed eardrum was extremely thin, two years after Agpaoa's operation, the patient told me on the telephone that her ear was still functioning well.

Agpaoa took two minutes to close a hopelessly punctured eardrum after an operating team at a university hospital had worked for over two hours with inadequate results. Der Stern's report made no mention of this achievement.

Der Stern gave its readers a picture distorted by one-sided stress on certain points and omission of others; moreover, the reader was not informed that there are many other healers in the Philippines besides Agpaoa.

The article's publication unleashed a regular posse on Agpaoa's trail. On July 10, 1971, shortly after Der Stern hit the stands, a new group of twenty-five Ger-

man patients set out for Baguio, accompanied by a
German television team which clearly intended to
continue exposing Agpaoa.

On August 2, 1971, the television program "Report"
showed films taken during the trip. Here, too, statements differed markedly from the testimony of other
witnesses. First the text of the television report, Immo
Vogel acting as commentator:

> A tourist enterprise in Freiburg arranged the trip, includ-
> ing the flight, accommodations, and the expectation of
> a cure for chronic disorders.
>
> In mid-July another group of ailing German tourists,
> filled with hope, flew to Manila. Before their departure
> we had some of them examined once more by a reputa-
> ble physician; we obtained medical histories on others.
>
> The right kidney of Frau W. had been removed in
> earlier operations. The left contains a relatively large
> stone.
>
> Herr A. from Basel suffers from considerable dimming
> in the lens of his right eye and would like severe
> varicose veins removed from his left leg.
>
> The practical healer Jürgen S. suffers from an old
> head injury. One symptom is deformation of the pupil
> in his right eye.
>
> These three, along with twelve other patients, under-
> took the eighteen-hour flight from Frankfurt. It takes
> another seven hours by car to reach the domicile of
> the wonder healer Tony Agpaoa.
>
> Tony Agpaoa is said to have turned his back on the
> Catholic Church when he was only two years old° and
> to have gathered like-minded companions around him-
> self. Since then he feels he is the tool of a divine power.
> He does not avoid comparisons with Jesus Christ. He
> prepares his new patients for their cure with a kind of
> religious service. He practices a mixture of religion,
> mystic superstition, and his own therapeutic doctrine.
>
> Anyone unwilling to restructure his interior life, to
> purge his soul, runs the danger of not being cured. Each

---

*An error in the script.

healing begins with a so-called operation; after a few minutes something always seems to be removed from the body. Tony does not waste a lot of time on diagnosis. He is said to produce yellow vibrations during an operation—allegedly visible to any spiritualist in good standing—to build up a force field around the patient, all this with a supernatural power which he collects in his head. With his bare hands, so it is said, he can destroy millions of bacteria. Therefore, in spite of the unhygienic conditions, infection is impossible. After the treatments the patient is entirely free to enjoy his stay.

We asked Tony where he got his power and if he was able to heal everyone who came to him.

"I pray, I meditate, I concentrate. Before I heal, I pray and meditate a lot. It is my custom before operating to focus on celestial events. I think that we can heal all those who believe!"

. . . Our attempts to reach into a supposedly open abdomen were blocked at the surface by a smooth, filmy material. So the body was not, after all, open. We built a bridge for the wonder healer by asking, "Do you simulate the operation for the sole purpose of promoting a psychogenic cure through suggestion?"

"No, there are cases where we have to operate. Others we cure by autosuggestion. Still others through absent healing—as we call it. So we have many methods. We do not change anybody, we only try to influence him, and we can cure him as long as he trusts us."

After repeated requests we were given a sample of the squirted red fluid. . . . When, where, and from whom the sample was taken was determined by Tony himself. However, we gained possession of five further samples, all of which we had analyzed. He protested vehemently. . . . Tony knows why he does not allow anyone to analyze this material. The following pictures show that the abdominal openings are simulated. Admittedly, the simulations are clever. Tony spreads a kind of diaphanous sheet over the abdomen. Careful observation makes it clear how the plastic material intended to represent the abdominal cavity slides from between his fingers. . . . Other operations also showed the plastic cleverly slipping between his index fingers.

Tony Agpaoa's subsequent explanation of the sheet over the abdomen—whose existence he had denied earlier—was that it was actually a protective covering made of ectoplasm, a materialized supernatural force which—visible to only a few of the chosen—he pulled out of his head. In some cases, such as an operation for varicose veins, where he could demonstrate immediate, tangible results, his power seems to fail, or he finds arguments to prove that the cure will not become evident for several weeks. After he had operated on Herr A., the patient's varicose veins remained as visible as before.

The tumor on a thigh, seen here, could have been used to convince even the most skeptical. No one could doubt Tony's power if, after the operation, the leg became normal again. But Tony promises the cure for weeks later, when the German tourists are back home, at a safe distance.

And this wart, a trivial thing, Tony considered himself unable to remove. His assistant explained that Tony had forgotten to bring the necessary medication.

Some people cannot be healed because they do not believe until they have seen signs and miracles—so goes one of Agpaoa's twenty-five theses of why he is unable to cure some. How can we believe a man who boycotts our work whenever he can, who will not give us tissue samples, and who has not operated on us?

"How do you feel about people who do not believe you?"

"Oh well, enlightenment will come to them! Sooner or later they will find the truth!"

We found the truth sooner than expected. The Institute of Forensic Medicine in Heidelberg determined that the samples of blood which Tony knew about were human blood. True, at least one of these samples was not of the same blood type as the patient's. Analysis of the samples we had secretly taken gave uniformly negative results: not human blood!

In spite of the out-and-out fraud, many patients feel better after the simulated operations.

Interviews with patients were taped during the flight home. With one exception, all those interviewed said they felt in considerably better health.

Obviously worse than before the departure were two seriously ill men. They, who most needed his help, could not be helped by the wonder healer. . . . Some, it is true, felt better. Even the parapsychology professor, Bender, of the Institute for Marginal Areas of Psychology in Freiburg, called Agpaoa's operations trickery. But how does he explain the sense of well-being experienced by most patients?

Hans Bender accounts for the patients' improvement by psychogenesis, the faith of the patients—which . . . accounts for the prestige accorded the healer. . . . Bender expressed great concern that such patients, returning with a feeling of improvement and new strength, will not consult a physician so that their disorders can be controlled—perhaps out of an obscure fear that nothing has happened after all.

The television commentator ended the program by saying: "In fact, all patients we had examined before the trip refused another examination after our return, although they had earlier given permission. Beginning today, another group of Germans is visiting Agpaoa. Once again, seriously ill patients postpone essential operations in favor of hope in a wonder healer."

In contrast, here are the words of the German healer Sigrun Seutemann, who with her husband was a member of the group. Her report concerning the same trip to Agpaoa was confirmed to me by other group members.

The day after the arrival of the group—which included reporters from German television, headed by Immo Vogel—Agpaoa began treating patients. At first the television reporters were also present at the operations.

The patients had arrived in Baguio clutching the most recent issue of *Der Stern.* Its article presenting

Agpaoa as a mountebank who simulates the opening of the body with a plastic sheet was, of course, immediately handed to Tony. Nevertheless, he allowed the reporters to set up cameras in his immediate vicinity and turn their lenses in every possible direction. I was present at all the surgery. Every operation filmed by the television crew was also recorded on 16-millimeter cameras by other members of the charter flight. No film shows a plastic sheet. Moreover, during Agpaoa's operations none of the eagerly watching spectators could discover a plastic sheet, not even the reporters, although they were asked more than once to point it out.

Agpaoa forbade the surreptitious taking of blood and tissue samples. When he noticed that the TV people nevertheless tried to take samples secretly, he excluded them from the operations for several days. Agpaoa performed many operations, some extremely demanding, including a cardiac operation on me. A disorder of a vessel, evident on an arteriograph, had existed since I was six years old and had grown successively larger, recently causing me severe attacks similar to angina pectoris. The operation was a total success, removing all cardiac deficiency.

The television team did not like to sit around idle and therefore sought out the German ambassador in Manila, hoping for support in exposing Agpaoa. The embassy referred them to Dr. Lothar Lissner, a Filipino of German descent who practiced in Manila and whose publications had earned him a wide scientific reputation.

Dr. Lissner had never heard of Agpaoa, but he was immediately willing to help expose a fraud. He refused the high fee he was offered, since—as he put it—he wanted to render a completely unbiased judgment. He accepted only payment of his expenses for one night in a Baguio hotel.

Since Agpaoa had earlier contracted with the television team that no Philippine physician would be brought in as a consultant, the reporters announced Lissner's arrival the following day by referring to him as a doctor from Hong Kong who happened to be spending some time in the Philippines. Agpaoa had engaged two Philippine nurses to care for the most critically ill patients. As luck would have it, both had trained under Dr. Lissner and greeted him with shouts of joyful recognition. Dr. Lissner's cover was blown.

When Agpaoa arrived the following morning ready to operate, he acknowledged the Manila physician's presence without objecting to his attending surgery.

The first operation was performed on a victim of incurable cancer. Agpaoa gave him only four weeks but hoped to be able to alleviate his situation.

Before the operation Agpaoa stepped up to Dr. Lissner, rolled up his sleeves, and requested the physician to search him for any hidden material. Lissner found nothing. When Agpaoa began operating, he asked the doctor to look closely at the surgery and to describe exactly what he saw. The doctor said that he could see the wound, the opening of the body, a piece of the exposed ureter, and over it a tumor the size of a goose egg. Agpaoa exposed the tumor, loosened it, finally removed it, and placed it in Lissner's hand. The tumor was at body temperature. It smelled accordingly. The wound was closed again in Agpaoa's usual manner.

Dr. Lissner was extremely perplexed for the moment. Later they jointly monitored the patient's urination, which had been blocked by the tumor. It worked properly, although the kidney was incurably damaged.

Thereupon Dr. Lissner dared to ask Agpaoa for help for himself. He had been suffering for a long time from nasal polyps. Agpaoa agreed.

I assisted, and Dr. Lissner's wife was present. A large towel was placed around the patient's neck. Agpaoa opened the nose at the bridge and encouraged the somewhat stunned wife to look at the inside of her husband's nose. Then Agpaoa exposed the polyps and asked me to pinch them off with a small pair of pliers. I did so. Then Agpaoa removed his hands, and the nose closed again. The whole procedure may have taken two minutes.

Dr. Lissner was extremely blood-smeared. After his face was washed, he remained quietly in his seat, somewhat surprised and pale, though he had felt no pain whatever. Next he tried breathing through his nose and reported enthusiastically that for the first time in twenty years he was really taking in air.

At the end of the operation Agpaoa reached for a wad of cotton and dipped it in the bleeding wound. Then he pressed it into Dr. Lissner's hand. "Have it examined," he said. The physician, however, handed the cotton to the television reporter, asking him to obtain and pass on the laboratory findings. Dr. Lissner never received a report.

After this the physician went to his room to rest for a while. There he talked at length to the television reporter and to an American. When he came back downstairs, he said something was the matter with his eyes— it seemed that now, after the operation, his sight was worse with his glasses on than without them. Four weeks later Dr. Lissner wrote me that a Manila eye specialist had prescribed new, weaker glasses for him, and to his great surprise, his eyes were as strong as they had been fifteen years earlier. Dr. Lissner had obtained written confirmation of this fact from his ophthalmologist, who was unable to account for the change.

The Manila physician observed a number of Agpaoa's other operations during the next few days. We traveled together into the lowlands, too, and observed Marcelo and Carlos, two Rosales surgeons. But the one lowlands operation he found the most convincing was performed by Mercado, considered a star surgeon of the Unio Espiritista Cristiana Filipinas. He used to work together with Agpaoa and Eleuterio Terte. Today he works in Agpaoa's style.

Together with a few others, we looked up Mercado without a previous appointment. He was operating in his chapel, with about thirty patients waiting. After we had observed for some time, a young woman was carried in. Dr. Lissner immediately recognized her disease as a uterine abscess formerly called Douglas's abscess, a common and dreaded occurrence in the Philippines. He told me that in his opinion the patient was lost.

Mercado immediately postponed all other surgery and had the woman placed on the operating table. She was very weak and could no longer stretch out her

legs; her abdomen was hard as a board. Our eyes were
hardly more than a foot away from the site of the operation, and we could observe minutely. Before Dr.
Lissner's astonished eyes, Mercado pushed his hands
into the patient's body, and after a little while pulled
out a handful of poison-green pus. "Only one kind of
pus smells like that," exclaimed the physician, "the
kind found with a Douglas's abscess." A little while
later Mercado closed the opening and the patient, who
seemed utterly exhausted of course, was put on another
cot. Mercado ordered an hour's rest for her. After that
she would be able to go home.

Dr. Lissner almost lost his composure during this
event, since he was particularly experienced in treating
this kind of abscess. "I don't want to see any more," he
said. "I've seen enough. I have no more doubts."

When we returned to Baguio that Saturday, Dr. Lissner invited the television team to his room. A few others
were also present while Dr. Lissner gave his final interview for German television. In this interview he
summarized the experiences and events of the past few
days. He pointed out that these operations involved
phenomena which he could not explain. He could say
with certainty, however, that there was no deception.

Not only was this interview with the physician miss-
ing from the broadcast; not even his name was mentioned. Of the three patients mentioned at the
beginning of the program, two were successfully operated on by Agpaoa. The strong dimming of the lens
in the right eye of Herr A. from Basel is gone. He
can now see better with his right eye than with his
generally healthy left eye. Photographs taken before
and after Agpaoa's operation are available. Though
Tony was unable to remove the strong varicose vein
on the left leg, he could improve the condition considerably, so that the patient now experiences very
little difficulty.

As for Jürgen S., suffering from an old head injury,
Agpaoa took his right eye out of the socket and removed from it a remnant of blood that had not re-
sorbed after the accident—a so-called hematoma—

which had caused the patient great difficulties. Since then, Jürgen S. has been able to move his eye without difficulty. The deformation of the pupil, present before the operation, has disappeared.

On August 9, 1971, a week after the first program, another television series broadcast a long piece of misinformation on Tony Agpaoa's surgery. It included excerpts from films which I had put at the network's disposal in the firm faith that they would be neither tampered with nor erroneously commented on.

The second of Agpaoa's operations discussed in this television program was the surgery, mentioned later, on Herr W.'s prostate. The program showed the beginning of the film but omitted the part that would have impressed the viewers most. Then the program showed a scene in which, it was stated, one could see the plastic sheet—although I have not yet found anyone who could—and after this, the phase in which Agpaoa, using a forceps, pulled a piece of tissue out of the site of the operation. The commentator remarked, "And now the healer pulls out the crumpled plastic sheet." The commentator did not tell the viewers that when Agpaoa performed this operation on January 28, 1971, three physicians were present, one with special expertise in the identification of tissue. Every piece of tissue, including the "crumpled plastic sheet," was examined, but the television viewer learned none of this.

The program closed: "And thus the talk of operations without a knife must come to an end once and for all."

"Reporters" of every kind now began to "inform" their readers about Agpaoa. The tabloid press embellished the Agpaoa story with the most bloodcurdling and naive details—all of which the editors invented or at least distorted. Such a respected specialized journal as *Ärztliche Praxis*, in its issue of November 2, 1971, wrote: "Antonio Agpaoa became renowned for his extrasensory talents when only sixteen; thereafter, however, he fell into the clutches of a kind of mafia, which commercialized him."

In the second half of 1971 certain authorities actually considered forbidding group flights from Germany to Agpaoa. It is said that solely due to Dr. Lissner's intercession at the German embassy in Manila, such legislation was abandoned at the last minute.

It is not worthwhile to discuss additional defamations of Agpaoa in the German press. Almost without exception reporters had not been to the Philippines, had no understanding of paraphysical processes, and based their statements entirely on *Der Stern*'s report.

A television discussion between the adherents of the psi thesis and defenders of the fraud hypothesis would surely have better clarified the true situation. Indeed, after the first anti-Agpaoa campaign, an enlightening discussion between Professor Bender and Dr. Naegeli-Osjord took place in September 1971. Each parapsychologist stated his case, and both explanations were reprinted in *Metapsichica*, the Italian journal for parapsychology. First, Professor Bender's:

> My impression of tricky simulation of "operations," gained after repeated observation, refers exclusively to Tony Agpaoa. I have never excluded the possibility that other healers' operations cannot be explained by current medical experience. Thorough investigation should definitely be undertaken, especially since the phenomenon is not limited to the Philippines but is also reported in other countries such as Brazil.
>
> . . . Positive accounts of patients who have been treated by Tony Agpaoa seem to me to refer to improvements—some considerable—which could have been brought about by psychogenic means. Certainly Agpaoa radiates a strong power of persuasion which naturally lends him an extraordinary authority with suggestible patients. . . . I am eager to have a subsequent examination of as many as possible of the patients treated by Agpaoa, especially those who believe their bodies have been successfully opened and whose cure seems permanent.
>
> My observation of Tony Agpaoa could not convince me that he actually opens bodies. But I continue to keep an open mind on the problem and will seize the first

opportunity to examine other wonder healers on the same point.

Dr. Naegeli-Osjord wrote:

On the occasion of my research trip to the Philippines, I had the opportunity of observing a considerably greater number of incursions into the body with bare hands and without anesthesia than was granted Professor Bender—operations not only by Agpaoa but also by a large number of other "spiritual surgeons" who—it seems important to stress—are time and again able to penetrate the body in different ways and heal it.

In my opinion Tony Agpaoa and his colleagues command powers only partly understood by conventional scientific methods. For this reason the empirical experiences I share with many observers and patients must be significant. Professor Bender stressed that neither his proofs nor mine are completely objectified scientifically; further investigation and clarification are necessary.

Like Professor Bender, I would like to point out that the phenomenon of "psychic surgery" is not limited to the Philippines but is part of the esoteric tradition of many peoples and ages. I further refer to the investigations made by the Tokyo scholar Dr. Motoyama and the American researcher Dr. Puharich, both of whom, after very thorough scientific study, have declared the phenomenon genuine.

A year after his first trip Dr. Naegeli-Osjord flew to the Philippines a second time and stayed for four weeks; in early 1973 he studied the phenomena on location for a third time. But so far Professor Bender has refused to travel to the Philippines again.

In May 1972 Dr. Naegeli-Osjord and I attended the Parapsychological Congress annually convened by Harold Sherman in Hot Springs, Arkansas. One day of the congress was devoted to the topic of psychic surgery. We met with Harold Sherman, Dr. Motoyama, and physicians from the United States; saw movies Sherman and Motoyama had made in the

Philippines of operations by Agpaoa and Blance; and came away with confirmation of our previous views. In July the movies were shown at the Second Parapsychological Congress in Moscow and met with a lively response—especially among the bioplasma researchers.[130]

During all this time the fight against the supporters of the Philippine operations continued unabated. One Swiss newspaper (*Schweizerischer Beobachter,* Vol. 47, Nos. 4–9, 1973) savagely attacked Dr. Naegeli-Osjord and Sigrun Seutemann to the point of abuse. Defenders of new ideas which offend established scientific dogma are no longer burned at the stake; instead, attempts are made to "burn" their scientific reputations in order to remove them all the more effectively.

Are we to believe that researchers who have meticulously studied the Philippine phenomena in the field did not long ago work through the often simplistic objections of their opponents? Dr. Naegeli-Osjord has been to the Philippines three times. Sigrun Seutemann has accompanied groups of patients about ten times, observed several thousand Philippine operations, and possesses a mass of case histories. Together with her husband she has taken about a thousand photographs, a great number of which would have to cause extreme astonishment in any honest, open-minded physician.

On February 11, 1973, another German television program offered its viewers a report on the topic. Entitled "Victims of the Wonder Healer" and edited by Immo Vogel, the program dealt with a particular selection of the hopeless cases of patients who shared Vogel's trip to the Philippines in the summer of 1971. Following these, professional magicians imitated one of Agpaoa's operations.

In this case it is important that the program was not transmitted live but had been previously taped in the studio, with all the opportunity for retakes that this implies. Nina Kulagina's psychokinesis can also be imitated by a magician on film or in public performance, but that changes nothing about the authenticity of Kulagina's powers. The same applies to Agpaoa's surgery.

The program featured the case of a patient referred to as Alfred K., who died of intestinal cancer at the end of January 1972. The program took up his story in the summer of 1971. Since K. had been to the Philippines earlier, however, the following is a complete account of events.

K. first went to the Philippines in January 1971, remaining only a few days. He intended to stay two weeks but flew home suddenly to save a week's time, since he believed that after Agpaoa had performed two or three operations on him (hemorrhoids, prostate), he was in good health. On his return to Germany, however, his symptoms reappeared. K. consulted me and asked me to say something in English into a cassette tape recorder for Agpaoa's benefit. He told me that his specialist had recommended an immediate operation to deal with a malignant tumor of the colon. Because there was danger of blockage of the bowel, a total operation creating an artificial canal was unavoidable. K. brought me his X rays and said he did not wish to live with an artificial outlet. Therefore he wanted to engage Agpaoa once more —before Easter 1971.

K. submitted himself to a whole series of paranormal operations and returned in a very weakened state. But back in Germany again, he recovered with amazing speed; there was an almost unbelievable improvement in his condition. He gained weight rapidly, although earlier he had been catastrophically emaciated. His intestinal bleeding ceased, and he required very little colonic irrigation. Very soon he seemed ten years younger. If this change was the effect of suggestion, such an effect could have set in after the first trip also.

The patient's original symptoms suddenly returned during the summer, and the medical specialist's examination again recommended immediate total resection. K. went to the Philippines for a third time, this time with the television team. After Agpaoa operated on him, sudden improvement again appeared, and K.

lived for several months reasonably free of complaints. I telephoned him in late October or early November and learned that he was "not entirely satisfied" yet and was planning still another Philippine trip. I did not hear from him again in person, but I learned through others that his condition had improved again. But at the end of January the symptoms reappeared and Alfred K. died within a few days of being admitted to the hospital.

The physician consulted by the television network admitted he could not find any scars on K. that would have indicated surgery. (Philippine paranormal operations generally do not leave scars.) He claimed that the patient might well be alive today had he agreed in time to have the operation in Germany. No one can speak with certainty on that point, but in the spring of 1971 K. would have had only a very few weeks to live if, rejecting resection surgery, he had not been operated on by Agpaoa. It is likely that K. suffered from a critical cancer of the bowel, but Agpaoa maintained him for almost a year with relatively few complaints. Whether Western surgery would have been better is moot. The patient refused such an operation, which was his personal decision. Shortly before his death, I am told, he advised other patients to go to the Philippines. To speak of "A.K.'s martyrdom," as the television program did, hardly corresponded to fact; considering the severity of his disease, the patient lived astonishingly free of symptoms. He worked a full day in his garage, and death came to him with unusual swiftness.

Patients die in Western hospitals as well. Nevertheless, I wish to emphasize that in case of cancer no one can be advised to reject a Western-type operation and to go to the Philippines. If a patient does so nevertheless, he does it on his own responsibility and at his own risk. And with cancer, the risk is very great. I do know of one case of advanced lung cancer which Western surgeons judged inoperable. The patient suffered from debilitating symptoms, but in spite of his weakened physical condition, he traveled to the Philippines. Agpaoa operated on him, after which

the patient lived quite comfortably. But he died at
the end of the period which Western surgeons had
predicted as his maximum survival time.

The television program mentioned three more cases
in which Agpaoa's surgery had allegedly failed. However, these patients were still alive. Then the reporter
mentioned that, inexplicably, Agpaoa had refused so
harmless an operation as the removal of a wart.

Agpaoa considers it risky to remove warts when
they are situated on acupuncture points. Some Western physicians also take the view that some very
large or long-lasting warts represent necessary safety
valves for the organism. Removing them may have
aggravating consequences. Again, some warts are absolutely harmless; they do not indicate any kind
of disease are therefore not removed by spiritual
healers.

The good intentions of this program's producers
are not in question, but they lack all knowledge of
paraphysical phenomena. They revived the old claim
that the blood was not the patients' and once again
brought out the plastic sheet story.

To understand Agpaoa's surgery, we must free ourselves of the limiting thought pattern that tells us:
Either it is an operation—with a clearly visible incision, blood of the same type, specific tissue removed
in the normal way—or it is trickery.

Dr. Lissner was first to suggest that an experienced
magician be asked to give his opinion on Agpaoa. Six
months later Dr. Naegeli-Osjord acted on this suggestion. While he was visiting the International Metaphysical Institute in Paris, invitations were extended to Dr.
Tocquet, president of the Paris Magicians' Guild, as
well as to a specialist from the Solon Cinema Society.
They were shown the movies made in January and
February 1971 during our visit in Baguio. The experts
concluded that what they saw could not be a trick.

In Harold Sherman's *Wonder Healers of the Philippines*, he tells of an American magician who heard
about Tony Agpaoa while staying in the Philippines
in 1966. He went to see Agpaoa in order to learn his
"tricks." To his astonishment he could not detect any,

and when he left he was convinced that these things had nothing to do with deception.[248]

In his statement in *Metapsichica*, Dr. Naegeli-Osjord pointed out that various healers employ different operating techniques. Even the same skilled healer never limits himself to one method. Agpaoa seems able to perform the same operation in different ways. At times he visbly opens the body and inserts his hand deeply; at other times, in an apparently quite similar operation, he sticks to the surface so that his hands seem to be working psychokinetically—from a distance. "Le vrai n'est pas toujours vraisemblable" —what is real is not always realistic.

Surrounded by observers who also possess a certain amount of psychic talent and a positive attitude toward the surgeon, he finds his psychic power strengthened. We still do not understand the mechanism of psychic strengthening, but if the surgeon is surrounded by skeptics his power is eroded, and he can expend himself to the point of exhaustion.

I observed Agpaoa in two situations when he performed in two totally different ways. In both operations a tumorlike formation was removed from the body.

The first took place in his house, in the presence of critical Europeans. I made a motion picture of the operation. Agpaoa worked in a short-sleeved shirt and seemed to open the body superficially without penetrating further. The tumor suddenly came to light under his hands. Two doctors were present during the operation.

I saw the second operation on a trip to the lowlands with Tony to observe other healers at work. After a visit in Rosales we came to the well-known surgeon José Mercado, who had finished operating for the day. We immediately moved on to Urdaneta, where the healer Juanito was working in a chapel. We did not see much, since Juanito seemed exhausted by demanding operations—perhaps he was also annoyed by our sudden visit. In any case, he took a long rest almost as soon as we arrived.

Agpaoa was clearly not prepared for surgical activity that day, but he saw our disappointment and seemed to get "in the mood" all at once in the chapel, in the presence of believers. A high percentage of Filipinos have psychic talent, and thus a mass of people in the Unio Espiritista Cristiana chapel represent a "power-furnishing milieu."

Without any preparation Agpaoa asked for the next patient. A Filipina came forward and was placed on the table. Agpaoa immediately penetrated deep into the body. The blood flowed as I never saw it before or since. Agpaoa almost seemed to fall into a state of ecstasy and splashed around in the bloody wound as if it were a washbowl; spectators had to jump aside to avoid being splattered.

Agpaoa pulled out a tumorlike growth. Trickery in this improvised operation was absolutely impossible. We had been traveling for hours in extremely hot weather; Tony was dressed very lightly, in a short-sleeved shirt.

The different course of the two operations shows that skeptics create a strongly "power-eroding atmosphere," so that they do not get to see the type of operation they want to see. (In assigning blame, no skeptic has ever thought of looking to himself.) Imagine the exertion involved for Agpaoa when he is surrounded by a large group of foreign patients always including a number intent on "putting him to the test," or even "exposing" him. In one medical journal Agpaoa was called a "deceiver" because an appendix he allegedly removed was found still in place during a subsequent operation in Rome. The psychic surgeon does not take his bearings from anatomical facts, as does the traditional physician, but from entirely different factors. Perhaps he attacks the seat of the disorder in the sense of dematerializing diseased cells. The healer's hands at least are in a trance. Healers themselves are often not clear about the exact process—that is why they are called *psychic* surgeons. Some, such as the late Gonzales, work in deep trance during the operation and have no idea what they are doing. Tony Agpaoa is said to have worked in deep trance during his early years. Today he does not require it any longer; nor do Juan Blance and others. Control of the psychic process takes place in the depth layers of the psyche, so when the healer attempts to interpret the psychic process consciously, his statements are subject to a degree of vagueness. He can believe that the appendix has been removed although he has only destroyed pathological cell tissue or treated it without removing it. The healer may believe he has operated on a particular organ while in reality his activity focused only on the general area. After my abdominal-intestinal operation, Agpaoa told me he had removed my duodenum, which of course was not the case.

The paranormal surgeon knows neither exact structure nor Western nomenclature; but he generally knows exactly what is sick and where to focus his treatment. The actual goal of any treatment, after all, is the removal of disease.

10 / MATERIALIZATION—
SOLUTION TO THE RIDDLE?

As mentioned earlier, such phenomena as psycho-kinesis have gained scientific acceptance only since 1968, thanks to outstanding work with Nina Kulagina, discovered by Professor Leonid Vasiliev.[184,212]

Psychokinesis is also involved when Juan Blance makes an "incision" in the body without touching it and when Agpaoa "blows through" a piece of adhesive tape or "raises" a focus of infection from deep in the body without inserting his fingers. No sooner has Blance completed the "incision" than tumors, metastases, and the like rise to the body's surface, having been separated from their original location in the body by psychokinesis.

It is presumably also by psychokinesis that Philippine surgeons pull solidly anchored molars. Such extraction cannot be managed merely with a strong thumb and mechanical skill; for often the surgeon is easily able to pull even awkwardly situated teeth. In 1965 Tony Agpaoa "transferred" this ability to the American chiropractor Nelson Decker,* who was then able to pull molars with equal ease with his bare fingers, without having undergone any thumb-strengthening exercises.

By using psychokinesis Nina Kulagina separated the yolk from the white of a carefully broken egg and then joined them again without injuring the shape of the yolk.[184] Assuming its official confirmation, is this procedure so fundamentally different from the one that separates tissues inside the body in Philippine operations?

---

*See p. 227 ff.

But psychokinesis by itself can no more explain psychic surgery than any other partial aspect of psi research. We must concern ourselves with a phenomenon still as much disputed by science as it was at the beginning of the century: mediumistic materialization.[12,87,88,89,100]

Dematerialization means a dissolution of organic matter, which probably turns into a fundamentally new state or energy beyond the four states of the material world—solid, liquid, gas, and plasma. This form must be much more subtle than atoms—perhaps similar to elementary particles—and quasi-nonelectrical, so that it can easily penetrate solid material structures. Assuming that bioplasma is involved, as postulated by the Russian researchers Inyushin and Sergeyev,* dematerialization would be the transition of normal organic substance into bioplasma. "Rematerialization" or simply "materialization" is used to designate the return or transfer of bioplasma to normal material condition.

Many cultures have reported appearances of inexplicable materialization,[29,44] though European accounts have grown extremely rare in the last few decades. But the onset of materializations is probably also the basis for strong psychokinetic events.

In some mediums psychokinesis seems to come about by the radiation of bioplasma. In special cases it looks as if bioplasma is manifesting an entirely new capability to materialize outside the body, thickening and structuring itself in such a way that new organic matter seems to form.

Nina Kulagina psychokinetically moves aluminum cylinders weighing up to 2 pounds. During these exercises no visible materializations seemed to appear, even though several signs suggest that physical plasma sometimes appears, at least in an intermediate state.[241] Other mediums have moved much heavier objects by psychokinesis, such as solid tables and wardrobes.[100,233,281] Reliable investigators report not only the appearance of an invisible, intangible force field,

---

*See p. 80.

obviously emanating from the medium's body and extending to the object to be moved, but also an obvious thickening and structuring of bioplasma, to the extent that a material form emerges which may be palpable and responsible for the movement of heavy objects. The entire process may happen in a very short time.

This contradicts all experiences of physics, but then psychokinesis also seems to contradict all experiences of physics, as does telepathy. Pascual Jordan has stated that parapsychology must learn to do without the support of physics to explain telepathy; something similar may hold for paraphysical materialization. We cannot restrict potential mediumistic achievements to what is considered possible by previous theories.

Of the primary manifestations of paraphenomena, all of which were originally denied by the official sciences, materialization is the only one not yet considered rigorously proven. It would seem, however, merely a question of time. Such outstanding mediums as exist in Russia could well be brought to carry out materializations—although, under laboratory conditions, these may remain minimal. Although such conditions bring with them a diminution of exertion, the Soviets are known to have trained their mediums to work under strictly scientific conditions.

We know of no materialization mediums in Western Europe at present. The general defamatory campaigns to which persons with such extraordinary capabilitities are exposed may cause their talents to wither in the bud.[90,180,196] In the United States and Brazil there are genuine as well as fraudulent materialization mediums, and it takes a great deal of experience to separate wheat from chaff. This has contributed to most scientists' refusing to consider any appearances of this sort. A great handicap for the appearance of materialization manifestations is their sensitivity to light, most particularly to the energy-laden rays of the visible electromagnetic spectrum. Only very strong and skilled materialization mediums can produce materialization effects by daylight.

Such a medium was the Brazilian Carlos Mirabelli, whose demonstrations were conducted in broad daylight, in the presence of large groups of physicians and researchers. In order to eliminate any possibility of deception, the medium had himself roped to his chair.[82] Such accomplishments are the exception, however. In general, materialization mediums work with red light or in complete darkness—which facilitates deception, of course. However, all sectors of science contain processes which can be researched only under arduous conditions. The phenomena of nature do not adapt to whatever methods scientists find convenient; rather, *we* must adapt our methods.

It is no longer a problem to allow a medium to work in red light or complete darkness and still exclude all chances for fraud. Even in the early decades of this century a number of investigators researched materialization phenomena under rigidly scientific conditions. Professor Julius Ochorovicz, considered Poland's outstanding psychologist, experimented with a young woman, Stanislava Tomczyk, and with other good mediums. Before the First World War the German physician Albert von Schrenck-Notzing held séances with the French Eva Carrière. She was sewn into a gauze leotard from head to foot; before strictly scientifically controlled sessions, she disrobed totally and was forced to submit to every conceivable examination, including gynecological and rectal tests to assure that she could not smuggle in any kind of material (such as veils) for "trick" materializations.[234] Schrenck-Notzing invited prominent guests to the sessions who attested to the authenticity of the phenomena; among them was Thomas Mann.[144] Nevertheless, people attacked the experimenter most unfairly, apparently for nothing more than having any truck with such things in the first place. I cannot stress strongly enough that the scientific method does not depend on the object of the investigation but only on the technique. Any thorough study of Schrenck-Notzing's works will prove that they represent an accomplishment of the highest scientific order.

Some famous Italian scientists, including Cesare Lombroso, Ernesto Bozzano, and Professor Enrico Morselli, also investigated materializations. A skeptic,

Morselli began by rejecting the phenomena but became convinced of their authenticity.[154] Experiments of singular value were carried out in the early 1920s by two Frenchmen. Charles Richet was a physician at the Sorbonne who received the Nobel prize for his work in physiology, especially for the description of anaphylaxis. Dr. Gustave Geley was the director of the International Metaphysical Institute in Paris, an institution founded in 1919 with government support. Eliminating every conceivable chance for deception and successfully employing complex tests, they experimented with the Polish medium M. Franek-Kluski. Richet recorded the results in his lifework, *Traité métapsychique*, where he examined the phenomena of materialization as scientifically proved.[215] During the 1950s Dr. Hans Gerloff experimented with the Danish Einer Neilsen, Europe's last great materialization medium.[83]

Since the concept of bioplasma was still unknown, researchers had no concrete theories about the emergence of materializations. But all these researchers agree that in trance states certain mediums sometimes exude a basic biological substance apparently produced from their own body cells. This is so-called ectoplasm which, once outside the medium, seems to take on the most various shapes before finally returning into the medium's body.

This process bears a formal similarity with what occurs in some single-celled creatures such as amoebas, which consist of a cell nucleus embedded in a mucous mass of protoplasm. Within the protoplasm can be seen dimmer inner layers, filled with little seeds and droplets, the so-called entoplasm. The glassy, seedfree exterior layer is called ectoplasm.

Amoebas are able to change their form. The plasma in the inside is put into flowing motion, so that flaplike protrusions and singular rootlike extensions come into being, somewhat like a primitive form of limbs, though unstable and shapeless. These plasma extensions, also called pseudopods (false feet), can form at any point on the amoeba's edge, reacting to resistance as they do to light. Perhaps the substance emanating from mediums was called ectoplasm because of this apparent analogy, or perhaps it was really thought to be ectoplasm from the mediums' body cells.

In 1915–16 the English physicist W. J. Crawford noted that an extension about 3 feet long extruded from the torso of his medium, Miss Goligher. Comparable to an elephant's trunk, it was able to "suck fast" to objects, exert an attracting and repelling force, and—given the necessary hardening and firming—to function as a carrier for raising heavy objects.[234]

Without the medium's knowledge, Crawford marked the objects to be moved with a dye. After the experiments were done, stains could be found *under* the medium's clothing, on the skin of her abdomen, as if the materialization had returned into the medium's body at these sites. Crawford, as well as other researchers, placed their mediums on scales during séances and checked their weight during the process. At times they noted a considerable loss of weight for the duration of the ectoplasmic exteriorization, amounting to a few pounds, sometimes more than a few. This suggests that substances are actually exteriorized from the mediums' bodies. Today we can assume that the extrusion occurs over the intermediate state of bioplasma, with consequent materialization into ectoplasm at the body surface. But the designation "ectoplasm" is not apt, since nothing has shown that mediumistic ectoplasm derives from the cells' nuclei rather than from entirely different bodily substances. The names "teleplasm"[234] and "medioplasm"[83] are therefore also used. Since "ectoplasm" has become firmly established in French- and English-language literature, the name will be used here.

During the formation of ectoplasm the medium most often sits in a collapsed position. When the phenomenon is very pronouced, the medium is in deep trance, while bodily functions are in a condition of extreme anomaly. Carlos Mirabelli's heart used to race at frightening speed, his face was white as chalk, and physicians present feared for his life at times.[82]

But when ectoplasm formation is slight, the medium can be fully conscious.

Pioneers in ectoplasm research have often tried to photograph the phenomenon, almost exclusively in black and white, since color photography had not been developed at the time of the early materialization séances. A very few infrared films capture the whole process in motion. The Soviets may well be the first to produce scientifically acceptable film about the formation of ectoplasm from a medium. But anyone who has closely scrutinized existing photos, especially those taken by Schrenck-Notzing and Gustave Geley, and who has seen enough of Agpaoa's operations, both in person and on color and black-and-white film, gains the impression that the substances Agpaoa extracts from patients' bodies and Dr. Geley's ectoplasm are one and the same.

The ectoplasm Agpaoa produces probably has its origin in the patient, while during materialization séances it is chiefly furnished by the medium. In the Philippine operations the ectoplasm achieves a stable end form which lasts for a considerable time, so it might be well to speak of it as "stabilized ectoplasm." It feels like human or animal tissue, though no physician can state unequivocally what is really involved. Some of the almost structureless substances which Blance removes from patients' eyes or brings through the closed skin are probably also a form of the ectoplasm described by Geley and Richet.

It is instructive to compare a composite of materialization manifestations published by Geley in 1918 and the phenomena seen in some of Agpaoa's operations. Geley wrote:

> A substance extrudes from the medium's body. . . . At first amorphous or polymorphous, it comes out of the whole body, out of the natural openings, the extremities, the part in the scalp, the nipples, and the fingertips of the medium. The most frequent and easily observed exit is the mouth; one can see the substance becoming exteriorized from inside the cheeks, the soft palate, and the gums.[80]

The substance takes various forms, "now as an elastic dough [as, at times, it is for Blance], again as thin threads, then again as ropes of varying strength, as narrow, rigid rods, sometimes as a broad ribbon, then as a membrane, now as matter and as thin tissue with indefinite and irregular outlines. The strangest appearance is that of a widespread membrane fringed and covered with bulges, looking much like a net." Almost all these forms appear in Agpaoa's operations and have been captured on film more than once. But Geley's membranous form of ectoplasm was found in examined mediums at a time when plastic sheets had not yet been invented. Probably in some of Agpaoa's operations, intermediary membranelike ectoplasmic forms appear, even if they immediately undergo a structural change.

Geley goes on to say: "When it is touched, the substance feels different. Sometimes it is damp and cold, sometimes sticky and tough, less frequently it is dry and hard. The sensation depends on the form." Compare this with the statement of the physician who, according to the report in *Der Stern*, reached into the operation site during one of Agpaoa's operations: "It feels like a lifeless, tight layer of artificial matter. It was not at body temperature."[131] Might it not be that the hypothesizer of fraud has felt an ectoplasmic formation?

In early 1970 Dr. Hans Naegeli-Osjord published a report on the phenomenon of immunity to fire.[173] He cited a number of incontestable cases of primitive cultures, still almost untouched by civilization—among natives of Ceylon, at shaman inaugurations in Malaya, and with the kahunas of Hawaii—where fire walking or fire dancing is a common cultural event. As early as the late nineteenth century Sir William Crookes reported on medium D. D. Home's immunity to fire; this claim caused many to doubt Crookes's credibility.[288]

In 1935, in the presence of twenty physicians and scientists, the Indian Kuda Bux is said to have put himself into a condition of absorption and concentration and walked barefoot across a surface heated to

806° F. It is claimed that he did not even scorch the soles of his feet.

A great number of similar cases are known. Scientists of earlier decades simply rejected all such reports as frauds. But at the International Parapsychological Congress in Moscow in 1972, a film showed a Romanian dancer walking barefoot across glowing coals without burning his feet.[130] It used to be said of Tony Agpaoa that he could immunize himself against fire.[11]

These incredible accomplishments make more sense if we presume that during certain spiritual states the bioplasmic body of the fire walkers can materialize an ectoplasm able to withstand high temperatures.

Perhaps ectoplasm also accounts for the fact, long disputed by scientists, that some Indian yogis are able to ingest poisonous substances and broken glass without damage. The Soviets demonstrated these feats on film. One yogi drank hydrochloric acid, swallowed glass splinters, and lay down on pointed bits of glass and allowed men to trample him. His back showed only slight indentations, but no kind of injury. Can a yogi prevent the intestinal membranes from resorbing the poison by forming an internal protective ectoplasmic layer? Perhaps the yogi whose body temperature did not drop though he was buried in ice was able to surround himself with an insulating ectoplasmic layer. Of course these are unproved suppositions, but according to Dr. Geley's findings, "the substance appears and disappears at times like lightning and is unusually sensitive, especially to rays of light." Perhaps this is why, when the light is strong (or when camerapeople bring additional lamps), Agpaoa instinctively shields the site of the operation with his hands. Without further reflection, this behavior is immediately taken as fraudulent manipulation.

Geley continues:

Nevertheless, nothing is more changeable than the effect of light. In some cases the substance can tolerate even full daylight. [In some phases of his operations Agpaoa shows the open wound.] The substance has an immediate, irresistible tendency to organization, not remaining long in its original state. Often the organization proceeds so rapidly that the primordial substance is not seen. . . . Another time one may simultaneously see the amorphous substance and more or less complete forms or shapes—such as limbs, even heads, faces—incorporated in the mass.

There are parallels for this, too, in Agpaoa's work when tumorlike formations are embedded in tissue of an entirely different nature. As he described his early activities, the tissues Agpaoa brought to light sometimes were attached to strange, long rootlike strands of an entirely different tissue structure. I saw such structures a few times; they are totally different from anything found in Western medicine.

Geley often observed the complete forming of an organ: "Often these formations grew and developed before my eyes, from the beginning to the end of the phenomenon." Geley saw the substance forming between the medium's fingers and hands. When the medium pulled his hands apart, the substance lengthened, and finally changed into various shapes.[175]

During operations by Agpaoa and other psychic surgeons, such manifestations were also observed by Dr. Naegeli-Osjord, Sigrun Seutemann, myself, and others. Under their hands' force field morphogenetic processes probably take place, using the patients' ectoplasm.

After the statement in *Der Stern* that Tony stretches a visibly separate thin sheet over the depressed abdomen, the article claimed that "this filmy layer is also the source of the removed organs. Tony manufactures them in the hollow on the abdomen, with the help of cotton." The above discussion makes *Der Stern*'s error more understandable.

Back to Geley: "Often the formations exhibit errors, omissions in their newly formed organs. All are possible transitions between the complete and incomplete organic structures, and often the change occurs under the observer's eyes."

Sometimes such paltry forms and pseudoformations occur that Geley states, "They are the product of a force whose metapsychic subtlety is minimal and which disposes over still smaller means of execution but does the best it can."

We must visualize Philippine operations as a process by which internal tissues are dematerialized—that is, turned into bioplasma—and externalized, probably through a chakra of the bioplasmic body. Under the force fields of the psychic surgeon's hands the formation of ectoplasm follows as the first step in rematerialization. The primordial tissue continues to structure itself to an extent depending on the quality of the rematerialization. In the ideal case it turns into tissue of the patient in question. This ideal end product is not usually reached, however. In Geley's words, the formation exhibits "errors, omissions." Often, even most of the time, the process remains on a primordial, poorly structured level.

Visiting Juan Blance, I was able to observe materializations with singular clarity when a mass of puslike yellow liquid seemed to extrude through the skin on the abdominal surface of one patient. At first I believed in a singular process of diffusion. Today I believe I witnessed materialization: ectoplasmic phenomena in a liquid end state. At the time I asked myself whether the bleeding during Agpaoa's operations meant he actually opened the patient's body. Might the blood extrude on the surface of the patient's closed body just like Blance's puslike liquid? Sigrun Seutemann's observations indicate this is so, at least sometimes. This explanation also applies to the incredibly large amounts of blood that sometimes appear, as in Marcelo's eye operations, which are in complete contrast to the Western medical experience. Clearly, whether we are witnessing genuine paranormal occurrences cannot be decided by whether the body is "opened" or not.

If the blood appears as the result of materialization, it may not be fully materialized. Tony Agpaoa may concentrate to bring the materialization to the final point of specific blood, but this places a great burden on his psychic power. This may be why he does not want people to take blood surreptitiously, since the routinely performed laboratory analysis will of course read: "Not human blood," leading to the conclusion of out-and-out fraud.

Geley: "Morphogenesis from the exteriorized ectoplasm of the medium is controlled by the medium's subconscious. Mental images . . . can take shape through ectoplasm. The concept or idea materializes directly, which is why this process has been designated by the term 'ideoplasm,' a term intended to refer to molding through the idea of living matter." During Philippine operations, rematerialization is probably influenced by both patient and surgeon—or by an intelligence working through the surgeon's subconscious. This conjunction may give rise to unique formations which at times lose all similarity to human tissue forms.

Rematerialization observed in Blance's work includes the substances he removes from patients' eyes without touching them directly and the structures he pulls out of the nose, having inserted a little piece of wood as a precipitating agent. In cases of skin disorders, seedlike elongated particles certainly do not exist within the body in this form. Sometimes Blance removes as many as a hundred of these substances from the skin—at times in slow motion and therefore clearly visible—allegedly leading to complete cures of tenacious skin diseases.

Some healers have given physicians removed "tumors" which histological analysis subsequently identified as cotton. In such cases the transformation of bioplasma to ectoplasm took place on the cotton wad used during the operation, now covered with stabilized ectoplasm. Materializations often appear to need a backing to "grow" on, much as the condensation of water vapor is facilitated by heavily textured solid forms. (The little rods which Juan Blance places in the noses of sinusitis patients are probably backing for the transition from bioplasma to ectoplasm.) The dissolved interior tissue is rematerialized on the wad of cotton, which is then completely wrapped in and

permeated with the rematerialization product. The
healer thinks it a tumor. Besides cotton, however, this
false tumor actually contains some substance originat-
ing in the patient's body, but because of inadequate
rematerialization, it is unstructured and therefore
overlooked by physicians, who consider histological
examination complete when the cotton is identified.

I continue quoting Geley: "The primordial substance that forms the basis of the ectoplasmic structures returns into the medium, since . . . ectoplasm is
the partly exteriorized medium himself. A close rapport exists between the medium and the ectoplasm."
In physical mediums the exteriorized ectoplasm is
reabsorbed into the body because otherwise the organism would be deprived of healthy cells, often great
quantities of them. On the other hand, ectoplasm materialized on the patient is severed if it is not already
isolated on the skin as it forms. The severing does
not endanger the patient, for only insignificant
amounts are involved. The ultimate aim of the operation must be to remove something from the body.

If Agpaoa's operations involve rematerialization,
what is the source of the bioplasma from which the
ectoplasm arises? It would be easiest to assume it is
generated by the at least partial dematerialization of
the diseased area in the body.

If it were always true that the healer dematerializes
the diseased area and rematerializes it on the body
surface, the actuality of psychic surgery would no
longer be in doubt. In fact, there are cases where the
diseased areas have disappeared by the end of the
operation. I had this experience myself with my sinus
infection, but such spontaneous cures are by no means
the rule. After the healer appears to have removed an
extensive mass of tissue, the patient's X-ray picture
often seems barely changed, but the symptoms have
disappeared; after some time the clinical findings begin to correspond and the patient has actually become
healthy.

This process occurs only if the patient does not
negate it by suggestion—for example, if he is influenced by the X-ray technician's statement that

nothing has changed and that therefore the so-called operation must have been a fraud.

Opponents of psychic surgery argue that such patients have been cured psychogenically at best. The patient's firm conviction that he has been cured keeps him from experiencing the subjective symptoms; for it is said that faith can move mountains. But this hypothesis fails to account for the paradoxical effects that appear again and again. Sigrun Seutemann cites the case of a twelve-year-old boy, the son of a lawyer. Because of an anomaly of the cornea and retina, the boy was blind in his left eye from birth. He flew to the Philippines with Seutemann, and after an operation by Agpaoa, the boy indicated that he could see through the left eye. The boy was tested to the extent possible in the Philippines, and he was able to read fluently with his left eye. After his return to Europe, he was checked by an eye specialist in Basel who could not find any changes in the eye's organic state and could not explain how the child could see with his left eye.

Similar cures are reported from Lourdes. One patient, Mrs. Bire, is said to have regained her sight though no immediate change could be detected in the eye's clinical state. Only after she had been able to see for weeks did the cure become clinically ascertainable.[170,171]

As is proved by psychokinesis, bioplasma may become transformed and grow active at a certain distance from the medium's body. In the same way, the materialization of bioplasma into ectoplasm may appear at a certain distance from the source of the bioplasma, as has been observed time and again during genuine materialization séances by American mediums.

In some unusual cases materialization processes take place in the Philippine healers' hands before they have touched the patients' bodies—and the skeptic is certain he has proof of a swindle. It is not for nothing that people who wish thoroughly to investigate these phenomena fly to the Philippines.

Many aspects of Philippine operations cannot be more closely examined in this book, for reasons of space and because such a discussion would become overly technical. For example, physicists expect that materialization and dematerialization would release enormous amounts of energy, perhaps in the form of very strong electromagnetic rays. But in mediumistic materializations this is clearly not the case. It is not that fundamental laws of physics like relativity do not apply, but that we simply have no knowledge about bioplasma's interaction with other forms of energy yet to be discovered. And if connected cells and tissues actually do dematerialize, so would the nerve structure in the area, so there would no longer be any way to feel pain. The absence of pain during Philippine operations would become more logical on this basis.

In another operation the phenomenon of ectoplasm became especially clear. In February 1973, two years after my first trip to the Philippines, I saw Tony Agpaoa perform the operation in a Manila hotel room. The patient, a young woman, suffered from a brain tumor; various surgeons had been only partly successful in removing it.

Tony had already performed a number of operations that morning and seemed to require a short period of rest and recreation. To the general amusement of the spectators he put on the patient's wig and danced uninhibitedly through the room, only to kneel down at the head of the patient's bed and get back to work with the utmost concentration and seriousness. After an assistant put some wet cotton on the patient's head, Tony began lightly massaging the shaved scalp with his fingers spread wide, so that there was no way to conceal anything. As he worked, a little bloodlike fluid quickly appeared, and under his fingers some tissue became visible. It looked like raw flesh, seemed to restructure itself into a skinlike substance, and after a short while covered most of the scalp.

A layman might easily have spoken of a plastic

sheet. It did look as if the skull were wrapped in the hard layer of a substance like a bat's wing. (The expression "like a bat's wing" for such ectoplasmic formations has been used by Richet and other researchers.)

The ectoplasmic skin now seemed grown to the skull; Agpaoa pressed lightly against the edge of the skin, revealing the skin surface; at times, with his eyes closed, he concentrated heavily. Now, under this skin, processes seemed to unroll that made me understand why Richet, Crawford, Ochorovicz, Schrenck-Notzing, and others often spoke of an "embryogenesis of materializations." Just as fetal tissue develops in the amniotic sac, so here, under the protective cover of an ectoplasmic skin, a paranormal growth process seemed to run its course. The protective skin became more taut, seeming to grow harder and more stretched. After a short while a colored dark mass glowed through it.

Agpaoa signaled his assistant, who cut through the surface of the thick, hard membrane with great care, extending the cut to half an inch or more. A small amount of bloodlike liquid and a large amount of coagulated and clotted blood gushed out, and finally a little piece of flesh came to the surface. At Agpaoa's instruction, the assistant grasped it with a forceps and —with some difficulty—pulled it out. It had to be severed with scissors. The soft, blood-smeared tissue was about the length of a little finger and somewhat thicker. Agpaoa treated the site with his fingers, getting slightly in the way of my observation; finally he threw a membranelike piece of tissue, mixed with many blood clots, into the garbage can. I can guarantee it was not plastic.

This was a type of operation I had not seen before on any of my trips. Again it became clear that Philippine healers can induce human cells and tissues to fulfill their functions much more swiftly than in normal biological processes, as in the astonishingly rapid coagulation of blood during paranormal operations, and the claim that Philippine operations involve "old" blood and "old" tissue.

Materialization processes also occur during some paranormal Western cures—for example, at Lourdes. During World War I, John Traynor, an Englishman, was hit by machine-gun bullets, one of which went through his upper right arm. The motor nerves were severed, so that he no longer had movement in the arm and the muscles atrophied. His right hand was twisted into a claw, and his entire right side emaciated down to the skeleton. He also suffered a hole in his skull with a diameter of almost 1 inch, severe epileptic attacks, and paralysis of the legs, followed by paralysis of the intestine and the bladder.

Traynor endured in this condition for eight years. A complete invalid, he was scheduled to be placed in a nursing home. On July 22, 1923, as a member of a transport of invalids, he arrived, a human wreck, at Lourdes from Liverpool. On July 25, during a sacramental procession, he suddenly felt a strange feeling of well-being streaming through his body. Traynor experienced an immediate cure. He could move his arm, the hole in his head disappeared, he could stand and walk. Within a short time he was strong and muscular. He settled in Liverpool, worked as a coal dealer, drove his own truck, and performed heavy manual labor. He returned to Lourdes often to give free nursing service in gratitude for his cure. He died in his native city in 1943.[81,224]

This case obviously involves materializations of large areas of tissue. The hole in the skull disappears—that is, is replaced by material not previously present. The destroyed nerves and atrophied muscles are regenerated within seconds, probably by way of a dematerialization of diseased tissue and materialization of healthy structures. But does the materialization result from the patient's own store of cells, or does the necessary bioplasma originate with other people present? Or does the substratum for materialization have its source still elsewhere, in a cosmic energy on the order of the Indian concept of prana?

Decades ago the French physician and parapsychologist Dr. E. Osty reported a well-to-do lady of his acquaintance who spent much time in Lourdes as a voluntary helper at the spring in the grotto of Massabielle. Her chief activity consisted in helping the patients into the pool and immersing them briefly. In the course of her long activity, more than once she witnessed extraordinary spontaneous cures of severely disabled persons bathing in the spring. During the patients' submersion in the cold spring water, at the moment in which the cures presumably set in, she always felt as if all her strength were withdrawn from her. She required several days to recuperate from these attacks of weakness.[29]

During Philippine operations, does the healer contribute something of his substance? We cannot give a final answer, but in view of the numerous operations he is apt to perform one after the other without noticeable loss of power, this seems unlikely. Probably most of the substratum for the materializations comes from the patient, but presumably the healer contributes his own substance or power, especially since he feels that again and again he replenishes himself with "divine power."

11 / THE SOURCE
OF PSYCHIC INTELLIGENCE

The human body seems to be influenced or guided by the energy fields of the bioplasmic body. The bioplasmic body, in turn, seems closely dependent on human thought, on thinking and feeling—in short, it seems influenced by the spirit.

Apparently by its nature the coarser system is always guided and influenced by a subtler system. Around the turn of the century the theosophists C. W. Leadbetter and Annie Besant stated: "Each higher world supplies the power scheme for the next lower, less subtle world."[126,127]

Soviet pararesearchers believe that, using high-frequency photography, they have proved that thoughts, ideas, and feelings can influence and structure the bioplasmic field and shape its structures. Accordingly, the bioplasmic or energy body seems to be the link between spirit and physical body.

While we may be on the verge of scientifically grasping the bioplasmic field of living matter and making it visible with appropriate detectors, we still have not the slightest idea of the basic nature of thought. It is an astonishing and generally overlooked fact that human thinking, which has created our civilization and changed the whole world, proceeds without the expenditure of large measurable amounts of the energies known to science. The most intense mental exertion uses up less chemical-physical energy than does an insignificant muscle contraction.[35] Most scientists nevertheless take it as a given that psychic and mental or so-called spiritual energies are closely related to the body and its chemical-physical reactions and cannot appear independently of the body.

This was the view of the sciences a hundred years ago, and nothing has changed to this day.

But there is not the slightest evidence to support this belief. We must remind ourselves that to this day we do not possess any scientific tool—any detector—that can furnish us with direct proof of psychic energies or thought. The measurement of electrical brain waves (EEG) in no way directly establishes thoughts and feelings, as laymen believe; it may indicate nothing more than their secondary action.

Perhaps in the not too distant future scientists will succeed in making thought visible through special new detectors—perhaps with the aid of advanced Kirlian photography. Perhaps then, too, the clairvoyants' tenacious claim that they perceive thought shapes will be verified. For even the concept, the thought, is founded on an objective reality.

In this context it is interesting to note the fact, precisely documented by the American psychoanalyst Dr. Jule Eisenbud, that Ted Serios was able to imprint a photographic plate completely protected against light with an image born of his imagination. [62,64] It seems certain, then, that a concentrated thought, a concept sharpened by close attention, represents an extremely subtle but highly effective force field which appears to work on and "form" the bioplasmic body. The effect seems to pass on to the physical body.

This puts many empirical findings of Western psychology and psychosomatics in a new and clearer light. Now one can see or at least suspect the method underlying occurrences that up to now have seemed mysterious. We can detect how mental images lead to material form. If I may so put it, we know the broad outlines of the way to materialization or realization of an idea. The understanding that ideas, thoughts, or thinking in general influence the bioplasmic body confirms the proverbial "power of positive thinking" of which philosophers of all ages—even thousands of years ago—were aware. Thus Buddha is alleged to have said, "Power over thoughts is power over body, life, and destiny."[223]

The power of thought can heal diseases by influencing the bioplasmic field. Placebo experiments,
described earlier, prove this unequivocally. In the
same way, a hypochondriac can make himself organi-
cally ill. Without analyzing this connection more
closely or knowing the exact method of realization,
many great men have intuitively made proper use of
the fact by practicing and calling for a so-called
positive mental attitude to life.

The German philosopher and psychologist Oscar
Schellbach founded his school of mental positivism in
the 1920s. It called for a radical-positive—that is,
affirmatively oriented—mode of thought as the best
and shortest way to achieve goals. Long before the
concept of cybernetics was established, his laws of
thought showed a way to the proper or optimal programming of the psychic causative level in man.
Schellbach postulated "conviction," which is ultimately
generated by thought, as the "unmoved mover" in the
psychic sphere.[223] Not every concept has a directing
and controlling influence on the body's force fields,
the bioplasmic body, and thus on the nervous system.
Rather, this function is best performed by emotionally charged concepts and convictions. Conviction
probably guides a person's behavior in the highest
realm of the spirit. The so-called power of faith is,
after all, the same thing, except that Schellbach dif-
ferentiates between conviction and faith in that conviction is generated by perceptual processes—that is,
by the manner and method of our thinking, taking
into account all previous experience and amassed
knowledge—while faith is in a way a received attitude,
an absolute belief in the truth without critical process-
ing, resulting in the tension of expectation. In fact, it
can be said that man is the sum of the convictions he
has formed throughout his lifetime. Positive convictions advance him, negative ones can ruin him. Little
is harder to uproot than deeply entrenched convictions,
grown automatic through years of mental habit. They
control a person's judgment and behavior with an
inevitability of which one is barely conscious. Their
persistence also accounts for resistance to the emer-

gence of new realizations. A physician who through years of study and perhaps decades of practice has observed the normal course of disease and surgery, grounding his observations in theory, must be convinced that psychic surgery is a crazy notion—unless he has already encountered apparent exceptions to natural laws which have shaken his fundamental conviction that everything occurs according to the laws of academic science. It is on this basis, too, that Max Planck is said to have noted resignedly that new views cannot be made acceptable by convincing their opponents but only by their opponents' dying out.

But conviction and faith not only control our behavior and our judgment; they also deeply affect the functions of the nerves and organs of the physical body. The power of thought and faith or conviction is no longer in question today, Western psychologists and physicians have long recognized that it can produce extraordinary results. Nevertheless, they do not draw the relevant conclusions. On the contrary, often their basic attitude is one of out-and-out rejection in all areas of life. The impression is inevitable that scientific knowledge and practical evaluation—even in daily life—are only minimally correlated. Soviet scientists, it seems, think more pragmatically. Eastern and Far Eastern psi researchers do not stop at observing and describing paraphenomena from the lofty academic dais; they are also eager to experience the new mental territory for themselves. For example, Dr. Motoyama has been active as an acupuncturist for twenty years and at the same time is a highly developed yogi; several Soviet scientists are themselves extremely talented telepathic mediums and radiesthesists (water diviners).

To return to the power of thought and ideas: ideas influence every effort and all capacities, both physical and mental. The American surgeon and psychologist Maxwell Maltz reports the following interesting experiment: three groups of students were tested on their ability to hit a target with a bow and arrow.

For three weeks after the test one group practiced daily, the second group did not practice at all, and the third group practiced only in imagination—that is, its members fantasized. They spent some time each day visualizing aiming the arrow with great skill at the bull's-eye. Analogous group tests were made with basketballs that had to go through the hoop. After three weeks new tests revealed that, according to a point system used in evaluation, the first group—which had practiced daily—improved by twenty-four points. The second group showed no improvement. The third group, with mental training, improved by an average of twenty-three points.[141] This appears to prove that the cause for such achievements lies in a superordinate level, in the level of ideas and thoughts—in the mental realm.

Mental patterns generated by fantasy and the imaginative faculty may obviously be imposed on the "subtle" causal field in the same way as skills gained in practice and striving for realization—even in the physical realm. Oscar Schellbach put it concisely: "The beginning and cause of every occurrence and effect is the idea as ideal and soul of the occurrences and effects." The statement expresses the significance of ideas and the importance of correct programming of the spiritual causal fields in man, to borrow an expression from computer language.

Dr. Maxwell Maltz claims that the limits of human performance as well as man's total behavior are largely determined by his self-image, which is the picture that a person holds of himself, his capacities, his potential, his limits, his value. According to Schellbach, the self-image largely corresponds to the sum of a person's convictions. For the cybernetician, the programming data shape the self-image.[260] In principle all three definitions have more or less the same meaning. If someone is convinced of his incapability in one area, his self-image is programmed to failure in this area. He must, as it were, jump over his own shadow to achieve something positive. He will only be able to do so when he changes his negative conviction, his negative self-evaluation and self-image. A negative self-image, a negative conviction, block, as it were, the expenditure of energy from the mental causal field. His inner powers—in the language of Western psychology, the power of his subconscious—will not come into play if he is inwardly convinced of the uselessness of trying. Conversely, a person will leave no stone unturned, his internal computer will work at top efficiency, when he has an exciting goal and is convinced of his ability to achieve it.

Maltz reports cases of students achieving top results in an unusually short time in a field for which they first thought they had no talent. It was possible to awaken in them the conviction that they were talented. Their self-image was changed in a positive direction.[141]

Up to a point this also applies to paranormal talents. The Nestor of Czechoslovakian psi research, Dr. Zdenek Rejdak—and he is not the only one—believes that every normal person possesses dormant paranormal talents which have not been allowed to unfold. Nina Kulagina sometimes needs as long as two hours of extreme concentration before the expected psychokinetic effect sets in. What normal person would make a similar attempt, spending two hours in extreme concentration? Nor would Nina Kulagina be able to summon up the necessary endurance and concentration if she were not inwardly convinced of success.

Tony Agpaoa, who has trained other Filipinos in paranormal healing, says that the prerequisite in teaching a student the ability to perform psychic surgery is to impart to him the faith that he does in fact possess the skill. This shows the deep significance of positive belief in the possibility of success and in one's own power. It lets us recognize the crucial nature of a positive self-image. Today many aspects of our world contribute to people's negative view of themselves, producing a negative self-image in the individual, with all its negative consequences. There are,

of course, a number of causes for this effect. Many
blame concepts and values stemming from Freudian
psychoanalysis;[285] they feel that these ideas, derived
from observation of neurotics, are taken out of their
original context and assigned to another realm where
different conditions prevail. This mental set frequently gives rise to the belief that man is a monster composed largely of aggression, sexuality, egotism, and
destructiveness; that he is something of a miserable
creature, controlled by animal instincts from a sinister
unconscious and helplessly at the mercy of internal
drives.[141] This is not meant to be held against psychoanalysis, but only against its misuses—generally by
people who have only a very superficial or no understanding of it but who nevertheless derive from it
confirmation of their own views. They rashly juggle
misunderstood psychoanalytic terminology, only because nowadays psychoanalysis is "in," while only a
few decades ago it was still ostracized.

It is not only our actions that are shaped by mental
images and the convictions thus created; our bodily
functions are also dependent on our thinking and the
power of ideas and convictions. Even the organic
structure of the physical body may be influenced by
mental powers by way of the bioplasmic field. Besides
the common realizations or materializations by way
of the normal physiological functions of the body—
Dr. Hans Gerloff calls them detour realizations or
detour materializations—there are paranormal direct
realizations and direct materializations in which ideas
and concepts apparently are not actualized by way of
the normal physiological functions of the body but become realized directly from the bioplasmic field, as
in telepathy, psychokinesis, and most impressively in
the materialization phenomena described in chapter
10.

A few examples will demonstrate the influence of
ideas on the bodily functions. A hypnotist presses a
cold spoon handle against the back of a subject's
hand, suggesting, "I am touching you with a red-hot
poker. You feel it distinctly." The subject's face con-

torts in pain, and after the spoon has been removed the skin shows an intense reddening, sometimes even a blister. The idea, induced in the subject—or rather, in his psyche—by the hypnotist affects the bioplasmic energy field, the causal field of the physical body, which for its part releases the reaction in the brain and the nervous system.

One day the well-known physician and discoverer of local anesthesia Carl Ludwig Schleich was consulted by a well-to-do businessman; the patient was in a state of total confusion and asked the doctor to amputate his arm. He had stuck himself with a penpoint and believed that he would inevitably die of blood poisoning. Only an amputation, he insisted, could save him now. Several surgeons had already refused, and Schleich, of course, also rejected the request. Though the wound had been cleaned, cauterized, and disinfected and was not dangerous in any way, the patient could not be dissuaded from his fixed idea, which he held without any factual basis. On the following morning the man was dead. The autopsy revealed no recognizable cause of death. Schleich's diagnosis was death from hysteria.[225,230]

Many analogous examples for the great influence of mental and emotional forces on the functions of the body could be cited. By the same means, however, that ideas based on faith and firm expectation can have negative results, healing—often of the most serious diseases—can be achieved.

Schellbach reported in the 1950s the case of an acquaintance, a Swede, who suffered from extensive paralysis and was confined to a wheelchair as the result of spinal meningitis suffered in childhood. The patient's unshakable faith in the dominance of the spirit over matter and very lively power of imagination gave him the strength to spend weeks working himself up to the idea that he could walk again. In fact, after several weeks his motility seemed to increase, giving him renewed courage to continue in his autosuggestive work. After six months he had reached the point of walking with crutches. His ability to walk is said eventually to have returned almost to normal.

A physician must believe that once a nerve is destroyed there is no possibility of regeneration and no chance of a cure. This holds true, of course, under ordinary conditions and circumstances. But given totally new assumptions, totally new phenomena may manifest themselves. In the reported case the constant influencing of the energy fields of the bioplasmic body by a different mode of thought so altered the energy fields that in the course of time it appears that a reorganization and probably even a regeneration of the damaged nerves and muscles took place; finally even a cure, considered impossible, occurred.

Such possibilities seem so incredible to the Western mind that for the most part we do not consider them. No sensible person thinks of such a thing, no one has the idea of even trying anything of the kind, much less assuming for its sake a difficult six-month psychic-spiritual or physical training.

Of course such cases are exceptions, but they are exceptions precisely because such attempts are carried out only by exceptional persons. It is unfortunate that in the Western scientific world exceptions are given very little or no attention. The Russian scientists, on the contrary, throw themselves on every exception, for it may point the way to new scientific territory. Exceptions have causes. A thorough study of altered causal conditions can often indicate how the exception can be made into an ordinary, reproducible phenomenon.

Every modern Western physician knows about psychosomatic connections, although a few decades ago it would have seemed absurd to most doctors to attribute ulcers—an organic disease—to mental causes. Although the Philippine surgeons have not studied the psychological and psychosomatic literature, they instinctively recognize the influence of mental powers on the body, perhaps to a much greater degree than do the Western sciences. Agpaoa speaks of the power of faith and of the necessity for a positive mental attitude and way of life as preconditions for lasting physical health. He knows that negative thoughts and feelings can affect the energy body and thus cause alterations in the physical body. For him, the appearance of disease in the body is only the symptom of a wrong orientation or attitude in the "astral body" and ultimately in the spiritual realm. Therefore, if a permanent cure is to be achieved, the patient must change his thinking. Agpaoa says that a disease will probably recur if after the operation the patient does not correct his false attitudes and switch over to positive thinking. But nothing seems more difficult to most people than changing old, ingrown mental habits. Agpaoa has therefore devised a technical aid for his patients in the form of a record which the patient can use to program his thinking in the direction of physical health and psychic-spiritual harmony. The record is called "Healer's Meditation." It is spoken in English, in a very clear, distinct, suggestive voice, with effective background music. Regular, concentrated listening undoubtedly produces positive effects by correctly programming the psychic causal plane. The whole person profits to the extent that he opens himself to this influence.

This principle—to influence the subconscious through a record instead of a hypnotist—was first tried in 1930 and later elaborated by Schellbach. He called it psychophony. The subject relaxes on a couch or in an armchair, closes his eyes without going to sleep, switches off all distracting thoughts, and lets the record play, aware and inwardly convinced that the words coming from the record will penetrate his subconscious and sink in like the suggestions of a hypnotist. The patient's inner attitude is crucial. By means of suggestion records he can choose specific behaviors to be incorporated in the subconscious, just as data is fed into a computer. There are sleep records which can quickly bring about drowsiness, sometimes after only a few uses, and can considerably deepen and lengthen a sleep period. Others program nervous patients into calm and relaxation as the best preventive of ulcers and cardiac infarction. The possibilities of positively programming the human subconscious are recognized by few people in the West and hardly utilized at all. Instead, the mass media

feed negative or at least worthless, trivial concepts
and motives into the subconscious; these tend to block
rather than promote any creative positive development, preventing the unfolding of the larger potential
dormant in everyone. Decades ago Schellbach maintained that man utilizes at the most 10 percent of his
potential.[223] Some researchers cite even lower figures.
In his method of suggestology the Bulgarian parapsychologist Georgi Lozanov believes he has discovered
a principle that far outperforms the usual teaching
and learning methods.[184]

Several Western researchers have visited Lozanov's
institute in Sofia and reported on it, among them Dr.
Thelma Moss of the United States[156] and Dr. Hans
Naegeli-Osjord of Switzerland. Within a month, it is
said, skill in a new language is fed directly into the
subconscious of students in every walk of life by by-
passing conscious mental work. This claim sounds so
fantastic that, without checking further, we tend to
dismiss it as frivolous. We are predisposed that such
a report is nonsense, and the belief controls our further
reaction. False convictions of the inadequate abilities
of man block potential abilities. We must free ourselves of them. In the Lozanov method the student is
placed in a totally relaxed situation and listens to the
sounds of pleasant music while the teacher feeds him
the new language.

I have tried to imitate this way of feeding in a new
language during a fourteen-day experiment, insofar
as this is possible with tapes and records. I came to
believe that the net efficiency of the traditional school
methods of teaching a language can be enhanced to
a considerable degree by applying the Lozanov method, provided that the student has some ability to relax. It is important not to try to deal rationally with
the material to be learned and not to force oneself to
master a specific amount. One must also discard the
preconceived notion that the capacity of memory is
limited, that the "attic is full," and the like. One must
constantly suggest to oneself that there is no way to
overload the memory.

Learning during a trance state probably also offers

still unsuspected possibilities which our educators have not considered. During the trance state the human mind seems to open up to new dimensions. Western man, squeezed into the straitjacket of rational thinking, usually finds it very difficult to put himself in a trance; many cannot even relax properly.

Western researchers have paid relatively little attention to trance states—perhaps because the influence of Freud and his psychoanalytic school has recently become dominant. Freud became an outspoken opponent of hypnosis, and hypnosis and trance states are related phenomena. It is true that psychoanalysis has discovered many new aspects in man and brought to light new facts; but the orthodox representatives of this school have also created new prejudices and dogmas that bar the way to many of the possibilities latent in man, since they put limits on people which other psychological techniques can easily overcome. It is too bad that Freud did not turn to parapsychology until near the end of his life and that only very little of this work has been made public.[57] The fact that more and more psychoanalysts are becoming interested in pararesearch does, however, justify our hopes.

In the Soviet sphere of influence scientists have paid little or no attention to Freudian analysis. Their theories, based on the works of Pavlov, of necessity led to intensive investigation of hypnosis and all the phenomena connected with it.[307] There is some evidence that the Eastern thrust of research will turn out to be more fruitful for unlocking man's unused potential. Nevertheless, there is no yes or no answer to the question whether Soviet or Western Freud-oriented psychology and psychotherapy is correct. Probably the psychic structures of Western man necessitated the development of Freudian psychoanalysis, just as Soviet methods are better suited to Russians.

This point of view must also be applied to much work by Russian researchers which is judged skeptically by Western psychologists. An example is so-called artificial reincarnation, experimental work which the Leningrad physician and expert in hypnosis Dr.

Vladimir Raikov has been performing for years.[301]
In principle it is nothing more than a special but
highly effective method for changing the self-image
and thus rapidly releasing hidden talents.

Raikov places his subjects in a deep trance and
suggests that they are famous masters in one or another field, depending on the talent the experiment is
intended to unlock. Thus an aerospace engineer was
translated into the role of a great airplane designer.
He immediately began designing a photon rocket
for space travel. When he was put in the role of the
painter Ilya Repin, he began to paint pictures; after
being awakened, he was so impressed by the results
that he could not believe the canvases were his. In
general these experiments are said to bring out extraordinary talent. In any case, it takes only a few
weeks for the subjects to exhibit artistic accomplishments that would have taken them much longer to
achieve by normal means.[202]

During these experiments the hypnotist does not
impart any abilities to the subjects; he only releases
dormant possibilities which the subject may not have
believed himself capable of. Our convictions, shaped
by rational thinking and everyday experience, block
these talents. Raikov's hypnosis eliminates the criti-
cism inhibiting the person's powers, reaching down
into the deepest realms of the personality, freeing
unsuspected possibilities and talents.

Perhaps this method can also be used to develop
the skill for psychic surgery. Though Filipinos seem
particularly adept at this, it should not be assumed
that Westerners cannot also accomplish this paranormal phenomenon.

In 1965 the American chiropractor Nelson Decker
spent some months in the Philippines. After a lengthy
stay with Eleuterio Terte, at that time the best-known
healer of the Unio Espiritista Cristiana Filipinas, he
joined Tony Agpaoa, with whom he spent several
weeks moving from place to place. He assisted in the operations in the hope one day of operating by this method. Agpaoa, as noted, claims that the prerequisite for

psychic surgery is a particular spiritual attitude, which will put one in a position to absorb and pass on to the patient a divine power (prana? mana? bioplasma? or psychotronic energy?) originiting outside the self.

Decker was made to undergo spiritual exercises and to learn to meditate and master the technique of concentration. After several weeks Agpaoa said that he could now transfer the power to Decker—at first in the simplest operation, the painless extraction of teeth without anesthetic, with bare fingers. Decker only needed to place two matches between his fingers and the tooth, so as to get a better grip. After certain preparations, Agpaoa transferred the alleged power to Decker.

The first attempt to extract a tooth failed, since Decker's hand shook with excitement, and Agpaoa had to take over. With another patient a second attempt under Agpaoa's supervision was successful, and thereafter Decker never had any difficulty with the procedure. After a while he is said to have performed more complicated operations.[248] When I spoke with him, Tony Agpaoa confirmed Decker's reports, describing Decker's condition during the operations he performed under Agpaoa's supervision as a kind of trance, though he was fully aware of his surroundings. His hands, however, were completely outside his control. He felt as if an electric current were flowing through him, and the first time he almost lost control when he became aware of the patient's blood under his hands.

Decker could perform surgery only when Tony Agpaoa was nearby. It was enough for him to be in the next room. But Decker was never able to operate independently. On returning to the United States, therefore, Decker was not in a position to perform psychic surgery. Agpaoa told me that Decker was not sufficiently developed spiritually to be able to operate on his own.

The phenomena by which paranormal skills may be briefly transferred to others by strong mediums are also reported in connection with other paraphenomena,

for example fire walking. The Hawaiian kahunas ran
over glowing lava without burning their feet. Supervised by them, Dr. Brigham, curator of the Honolulu
Museum, is said several decades ago to have done the
same.[71] The previously mentioned Indian Kuda Bux is
said to have transferred the same ability to spectators. His presence, however, was always a requirement for others' fire walking.[186] The procedure, which
he demonstrated in London during the 1930s, was
filmed.

These facts seem to indicate that paranormal feats
involve abilities which are to a greater or lesser degree dormant in everyone, the prerequisites for their
manifestation, however, being granted to only a few.
Perhaps the temporary transfer of the skills of a few
is less a matter of direct transfer of energies than of
the master's inducing in the person in question the
mental conditions prerequisite to the manifestation of
the paraphenomena. If this is so, the actual cause for
the ability to perform psychic surgery may ultimately
lie in the mental attitude, in a special condition of
the conscious and the subconscious.

Modern man is strongly influenced by rational
thought—we are in the rational developmental stage.
But according to Jung's depth psychology, everyone's
unconscious depth realm contains sediments of each
previous developmental state of human evolution.
According to most depth psychologies, in childhood
each person repeats in condensed form the developmental stages of mankind—the consecutive phases of
the archaic, the magical, and the mythic.[323] If children enjoy fairy tales, it is because they speak to the
magical facet of their spirit. The interest in legends
and myths from the ancient world of gods is characteristic of the mythic phase. But even after intel-
lectualization, after the development of rational
thinking, the magical elements continue to play a part
in the life of the individual to an extent probably still
widely underestimated today. Freud revealed several such connections and showed how magical elements often exert pressure coming from the

subconscious on the adult; they lead to seeming nonsense behavior alongside clear, rational thinking and may cause absurd forms of superstition.[30,308,323]

Care must be taken in using the term "superstition." Many expressions of superstition are originally based on genuine understanding of magical laws—an understanding that, applied by chosen persons, was by no means nonsensical. It is a sign of presumption to present these things simply as "primitive" or "pathological," since all of us harbor and are influenced by remnants of the magical epoch in ourselves. There is nothing devaluing in this—rather, something positive. It is probable that our fundamental ability to feel and to sense, to be happy or unhappy, goes back to the magical element in our psyche.

Much has been written about the magical side of the psyche. These matters are discussed in weighty tomes, for example in connection with shamanism,[65] but the crucial point, which should electrify every true scientist, is avoided by most authors, who do not dare to mention it. That is the fact that occasionally accomplishments are possible on the magical level which cannot be understood by rational thought and cannot be produced by rational man.[112] We smile at magical acts because they do not correspond to our experiences and understanding of causal connections; but we overlook the fact that on the magical level concrete effects can occur that at times are completely inexplicable and contradict all rational arguments and which a person not functioning on this level cannot produce. Thus the accomplishments of the Philippine surgeons are probably to a large extent accomplishments on the magical psychic level.

Apparently the person who lives on the magical level is, like the animals, linked to sources of information and energy not open to the normal civilized European and North American, who seems to have reconciled himself to the fact that it is so—provided he has noticed it at all. Daily we perceive mysterious manifestations without seeking an explanation, such as the phenomenon of instinct, the sixth sense of animals, which we generally accept without astonish-

ment as a natural given. How, for example, do birds
of passage know that they must keep to specific flight
routes so that their strength lasts all the way to their
winter home and does not give out along the way?
How do salmon and eels find their way to spawning
grounds over long distances and through heavy obstacles? A fox terrier was flown in a box from Frankfurt to Brussels, where he was given to a new master.
After a short time he ran away, and a week later,
ragged and half starved, he arrived at the home of his
former master in Frankfurt. How did he know the
way?

Such cases are not rare. Though they perplex us
for a moment, we accept them without long reflection. No skeptic doubts them or suspects fraud. But
they involve phenomena which are as basically inexplicable as the feats of telepaths, clairvoyants, or the
psychic surgeons of the Philippines.

We should also remember Cleve Backster's experiments, the mysterious communication between plants
and other forms of life.* An exciting concept, certainly; but not an incredible one.

Suspicion arises only when someone dares to claim
that the person living on the magical level also un-
derstands and can utilize such mysterious and exciting communications. Is it possible that the suspicion
expresses envy, the belief that we must defend our
position which we suddenly—"instinctively"?—recognize as the weaker one: without, of course, being willing to admit it.

To the extent that we avoid discussion of the questions that arise in this context we increase the discrepancy between the magical knowledge of others
and our rational thinking. The assumption that emanations come from all living nature and that a communication system exists among all cells would seem
to advance Western science far more than the assumption that such things are impossible.

At the Second International Parapsychology Congress in Moscow in July 1972 the following experi-

*See p. 35.

ment with the "primitive consciousness of cells" was reported. Two meat samples were stored in hermetically sealed glass containers; one sample was contaminated with viruses which destroyed the meat, while the other sample was kept germ-free. When both containers were placed side by side, the same processes could be observed in both; but when they were kept separate, the decomposition process did not take place in the germ-free container.[130]

Perhaps mobilizing energies unknown to us, the Philippine healers affect the primitive consciousness of cells and tissue and "order" them to loosen or open. The magically sensitive person "speaks" with animals, with plants, with nature. The magical-psychic surgeon "speaks" with cells and tissues of the human body, and the body opens during psychic surgery.[200]

As early as the 1930s Alexis Carrel suspected that the cells of the human body possess capacities that are completely novel, still unknown, and never yet observed, which the body has not yet shown to us because the prerequisites have never yet been present.[35] They seem to react to the radiation of specific psychic conditions and fields in man.

Attempts by depth psychology to explain psychic surgery will not satisfy the scientist, but in evaluating these complex phenomena, we must apply all possible methods to circumscribe, describe, and comprehend them. No one method can explain the complex results; we must apply both analytic and synthetic methods.

Specific spiritual states of consciousness, it seems, can also put man in touch with new sources of information and energy.[273] The religious mystic—I mean the genuine religious mystic, not the enthusiast and still less the sectarian fanatic—feels safe in the lap of God and is thus connected with new sources of energy which seem mysterious to the modern rational person.[280] In this context it is well to recall the Capuchin monk Father Pio and the stigmatized Therese Neumann of Konnersreuth. The history of the saints of the Middle Ages provides us with further examples.

The feats of the Philippine surgeons probably result from the unique combination of magical psychic elements and a mystic-spiritual attitude.

From time to time the Philippine healers withdraw from their everyday environment and go into the mountains in order to restore their spiritual-mental condition to the shape necessary for paranormal operations. The influence of their daily surroundings works in time to bring them out of their exceptional psychic state—in the same way that all of us are influenced, as if by resonance, by the thought rhythms of our environment. This is why the Philippine surgeons' capacities are not constant but seem to diminish when the healers deal too much with worldly matters, as they put it—that is, when they allow the comforts of our civilization to overly affect them. It is also said that the healers lose their skills if they take money. Surely the loss is not directly related to the acceptance of money but ensues because they lead a different kind of life and thus their thinking drifts increasingly from the spiritual to the material plane.

Perhaps an advanced form of high-frequency photography or other newly developed detectors will someday enable us to make objective pictures to show how strongly the emotional world of a Filipino differs from that of a Western person. We will then have objective proof that emotions are not unreal fantasies but represent concrete, objectifiable force factors—realities with which science will have to deal.

Entirely new possibilities may result at some time in the future by a combination of Soviet high-frequency photography with the American process of biofeedback—the name given to the recording of particular physiological functions, for example during psycho-spiritual exercises, and their immediate communication to the subject.

In practicing self-hypnosis or during autogenic training, particular physiological functions connected with the psychological processes, such as galvanic skin and brain currents, can be registered and immediately communicated to the student during the exercise. This procedure is derived from the most recent findings of American learning theory[41,42,43] and allows the student to observe the learning process on a special screen. By this means he can learn to consciously control, correct, and even produce certain particular brain rhythms which have previously been random.

In the laboratory of Dr. Elmer Green, a member of the staff of the Menninger Foundation in Topeka, such a process teaches patients to balance their body temperature, thus eliminating headaches. Some persons are said to have learned to produce at will certain brain waves and the states of consciousness connected with them; for example, theta waves can produce a feeling of great happiness and a closeness to God such as the medieval mystics may have experienced.

If after biofeedback training a practitioner were continously shown the condition of his bioplasmic field, perhaps as a colored Kirlian photograph on a screen, it might become possible to unlock psychic and paranormal faculties which today no one can assess. For Kirlian photography most probably allows identification of states of consciousness in a more differentiated and immediate form than can be done by measurements of physiological quantities.

We have noted that paranormal capabilities may lie dormant in all of us. Any effort to awaken them will generally be fruitless so long as clear directions for the effort are lacking, leading as it were to blind groping. Even if at times the effort may come close to its goal, the subject will not be aware of it and will inadvertently drift away from the goal. During the common learning process we profit from our errors, of which we must be made aware. Our subsequent behavior is then influenced by these experiences. If we are confronted with a strange piece of electrical apparatus and on touching it suffer an electric shock, we learn that we should not touch it again. When someone learns to type he immediately sees his errors and knows that he must change this or that. Such experiences and this kind of learning are conscious. Paranormal endeavors, proceeding altogether in the subconscious, do not furnish the student with an immediate answer and do not tell him clearly and distinctly whether he is moving in the right direction.[163] The statistical chances of developing paranormal skills by the usual learning methods are very slight. Some paraphenomena have a long initial period. In the nineteenth century Reichenbach at times had to have some of his sensitives wait in the dark for up to four hours before they became clairvoyant. Who would ever think of staring into the dark for four hours to try to find out whether he is able to see an aura?

By means of an advanced procedure combining Kirlian with feedback techniques, surely many factors connected with paranormal achievements could be made conscious; next we could learn to influence them; and finally, we could learn to practice the optimal state of consciousness for each type of accomplishment. The special states of consciousness necessary for psychic healing might be maintained with relative ease over a longer period of time. Such a procedure would be like a mirror, as it were, for large areas of subconscious processes and functions. Just as the mirror serves to show us our external appearance, and we can use this picture to undertake numerous corrections—in our bearing, clothing, and the like—a Kirlian-plus-feedback procedure could represent a mirror for the invisible aspects of a person's being. A combination of such a procedure with psychoanalysis might produce an ideal means for man's true development.

One day there may be courses of study in which the student, by means of Kirlian-plus-feedback under the guidance of experienced teachers, will accomplish the same feats in a few weeks or months that some yogis can do only after years of complicated training. Perhaps then, too, we can learn to produce the spiritual states that supply the basis for carrying out the Philippine operations. . . . But let us not reach too far into the twenty-first century. Today we do not have an unequivocal answer to the question about the origin of the knowledge and power needed to perform psychic surgery.

To end this chapter, we cite two further theories which attempt to account for the creation of mysterious knowledge in some human beings.

The adherents of reincarnation believe in man's previous existence, from which he has brought knowledge into his present life. The American physician Professor Ian Stevenson has concerned himself with the reincarnation problem for many years; he has studied many cases of alleged rebirth in India, Ceylon, Lebanon, Brazil, and Alaska and has collected extensive material.[265,266] There are various ways of explaining reincarnation, though this is not the place to go into detail.*[169]

The spiritualists attempt to explicate the complex factors. The word "spiritualism" is despised in the West, partly from prejudice and partly on justified grounds, for this area has attracted many charlatans, and there has been and continues to be much fraud. This does not, however, alter the fact that various genuine paraphenomena often take place at spiritualist sessions. The citadel of spiritualism is in Brazil, where genuine phenomena and fraud are inseparably interwoven, though fraud is said to predominate.

The most pronounced and most honest spiritualist among the psychic healers was Zé Arigo, whose surgical and therapeutic feats have already been described. Each working day—at seven o'clock in the morning—Arigo prayed in his workroom and adapted himself spiritually to his "guide from the beyond," the spirit of a German physician, Dr. Fritz, who allegedly practiced in Munich and Vienna and who died in a concentration camp toward the end of the Second World War.[40] Arigo claimed to be Dr. Fritz's medium. When he was in touch with the spirit, his facial expression and personality changed. This change in his expression is said to be clearly noticeable even on photographs.

When he completed his work Arigo would lock himself in his workroom for several minutes and take

---

*For details see Morey Bernstein, *The Search for Bridey Murphy,* Garden City, N.Y., 1965.

leave of Dr. Fritz. But Arigo's wife claimed that sometimes her husband came home inhabited by the spirit of the German doctor, as she could tell immediately from his behavior and expression. The response of Arigo's dogs was notable: ordinarily they greeted him with joyful barking, but when he came home with his "spirit guide," they were disturbed and occasionally hid. Other sensitives are said to have seen a phantom of Dr. Fritz—blond, with thinning hair and a bloody wound across his jaw, the result of a blow before his death in the camp. During the early years of his "collaboration" with Dr. Fritz, Arigo, it is claimed, often spoke German, though he had never learned the language.

The phenomenon of Zé Arigo/Dr. Fritz confronts any thinking person with great riddles, no matter whether he can accept the view of the spiritualists or believes in a case of split personality—though the latter cannot explain the origin of the knowledge or the surgical feats.

Perhaps something similar is involved as in the experiments of Dr. Vladimir Raikov with artificial reincarnation. Or was it "cosmic memory," cited by some investigators to account for many phenomena, with which Arigo had made contact? Was it the total experience of nature, which according to C. G. Jung rests in the collective unconscious, the depth layers of the human psyche? Or was it the potential intelligence of a dead man which survived physical death?

It looks as if two fundamentally different sources of information underlie Arigo and the Philippine surgeons. The latter are usually able to localize a disease paranormally. But I have hardly ever—except in diabetes and similar disorders—noted a diagnosis such as prevails in Western established medicine. This is because the Philippine healer, like the American healer Phil A., looks at a disease with different eyes from a Western physician and employs different procedures. But Arigo diagnosed in just the language of established medicine. For example, he would not only tell a patient sitting across from him that his blood pressure was too high, but would cite the exact figures, which on being checked by American physicians immediately were found correct. In the case of ocular disease, Arigo not only diagnosed correctly a disorder of the retina, as a good Philippine healer would, but used the exact medical term, "retinoblastoma." Hundreds of similar cases have been verified.

This is perplexing because Arigo was far less intelligent than Agpaoa or José Mercado. No one ever saw Arigo reading a book. He is said to have had only two years of schooling and to have left school because of insufficient ability. Yet he prescribed the most up-to-date pharmaceutical preparations for his patients, often in combinations that revealed the deepest understanding of physiological functions.

The theory that the accomplishments of the Brazilian were founded on latent knowledge from his own psychic depth layers, the magical realms, the collective unconscious, or something of the sort—plausible as it may be to a certain extent when applied to Philippine healers—seems patently absurd. For the psychic depth layers of the magic level or the collective unconscious most assuredly do not think in the language and terminology of established Western medicine.

Arigo "heard" the diagnosis and prescription in his right ear. When he did not hear the voice, he was unable to diagnose.

Several weeks before Arigo's fatal car accident Dr. Fritz "told" him that their collaboration would end at the beginning of 1971. And that is what happened.

Spiritualism is also rampant in the Philippines. Some healers with whom I spoke believe that they are guided by beings from a higher level of existence. The majority, however, did not attach a strong spiritualist interpretation to their healing powers, although they did believe in a beyond and in possibilities of contact between the living and the dead. As mentioned above, Agpaoa spoke of a protector who had been guiding him since childhood. Is he a being from the beyond, like Dr. Fritz? Agpaoa never gave an opinion on this point. But since he referred to the divine power which filled him, protector might also be an individual designation, coined by the healer himself, for his—and our—God.

12/FURTHER PROOFS
AND NEW ASPECTS

On February 14, 1973, I joined a large group organized by Sigrun Seutemann for a second trip to the Philippines. The group—composed for the most part of Swiss nationals—assembled in Zurich. Agpaoa's successful therapy had been publicized in Switzerland about a year earlier through the spontaneous cure of a Swiss patient; in March 1972 Sigrun Seutemann had taken a group of patients to consult Agpaoa. Among them was a businessman from Zurich, Karl Dobesch, who had been confined to a wheelchair for five years. The fact that a medical mistake had put him in the wheelchair in the first place is not an accusation, for human knowledge and skill are limited, and we cannot always foresee the results of our actions. He had suffered for years from allegedly incurable psoriasis, covering more than half his body. Large quantities of cortisone were prescribed, at a time when the tolerance limits for this substance were largely unknown and physicians were unaware of the consequences of overdosing. For Dobesch the consequences were osteoporosis (softening of the bones) and chondropathy (a cartilage disorder) in the joints, with severe prolapse of the meniscus. The cartilage of the knee joint was liquefied, and for the past five years the patient had been sitting bent over in the chair.

During Dobesch's first treatment by Tony Agpaoa, Dr. Hans Naegeli-Osjord was present, along with Seutemann and other witnesses. He reported to me as follows:

The first thing Agpaoa did to the patient, who was lying on the operating table, was to perform surgery on his

spine; sinew and muscle were clearly visible. He removed something like connective tissue. Then he operated laterally on the patella. All in all, he may have
taken four to five minutes. Then Tony left the room; we
remained. Suddenly Dobesch rose from the operating
table, got to the floor, and walked, upright, in a circle
around the room, came over to me, threw his arms
around my neck, and cried, "I can walk again!"

All those present were so surprised that no one said
a word. Then most of us felt tears in our eyes. Ten minutes later Dobesch, walking alone, went down the
stairs to the garden. His gait was a little unsteady, and
his joints creaked, but he could walk. . . .

In October 1972 Dobesch took a mountain hike lasting four hours. He is able to work almost a full schedule. His psoriasis has been remarkably reduced.

Dr. Naegeli-Osjord's report ends here. To this day
established medicine has no way of accounting for
Dobesch's cure.

The sensational cure encouraged many patients to
risk a consultation with Agpaoa. It is not characteristic of such a group travel that—as the mass media
continue to claim—"spiritualists, esotericists, hypochondriacs, and neurotics" fly to consult the "wonder
healer"; rather, the patients are generally so-called
hopeless cases, suffering from paraplegia, multiple
sclerosis, and other resistant disorders. It would be
insulting and inhuman to label such patients hypochondriacs and neurotics. Naturally not all patients
with such severe ailments can be helped, nor can one
expect many complete cures; but even alleviation
means great relief to the patient.

As in my first trip to the Philippines, we flew on a
DC-8. I sat next to a middle-aged paraplegic, Franz
P., father of three, who before his marriage had traveled all over the world as a sailor. He was not a day-
dreamer or hypochondriac but a realistic person with
good common sense, who refused to be resigned to his
fate. On April 17, 1970, he had been in an automobile
accident where he sustained a spinal injury, his
fourth and fifth dorsal vertebrae being collapsed and

the sixth dorsal vertebra also suffering impairment. After four months in a hospital he was released with the diagnosis of complete paraplegia and the prognosis of "incurable; no chance of improvement." He carried on his work from his wheelchair; he even drove a car—and a year later had a second accident. While he was stopped at a red light, a car drove into him from behind. This time the fourth dorsal vertebra was merged even more solidly with the fifth.

Franz P. had almost no sensation left in the lower half of his body. He was plagued by severe back pains, and according to his account he had a sore—an open wound—the size of a dinner plate on his back. He had severe abdominal cramps caused by misdirected muscular contractions emanating from the damaged spine. Because of these cramps, his abdominal muscles were unusually well developed and strong. The patient was neither a spiritualist nor a neurotic; he was not even religious. He did not believe in miracles and expected none—he just wanted to see if Agpaoa could help him a little more than traditional Western medicine had. Since he could not pay himself, Sigrun Seutemann had financed his flight.

There was also a young woman about twenty-seven years old who, after contracting infantile paralysis at the age of one, had spent practically her whole life in a wheelchair. From the time she was twelve, she could sit up in the chair only with a special brace. Nevertheless, she did flawless work as a computer technician. Could those who speak so glibly about hypochondriacs and neurotics show the same courage under similar conditions?

A young, pretty student, P., perhaps seventeen years old, had also had polio when she was one. After twelve operations she could get about laboriously with crutches, and she would not have achieved even this without the latest innovations of Western surgery. But now no further progress was expected. A year earlier P., with a group that included Karl Dobesch, had first traveled to consult Agpaoa; her second trip had been in August 1972; and now she was on her third trip. She now moved about more easily on her crutches, and she was very optimistic. A year earlier one leg had been much more atrophied than the other. During the year since her first trip to the Philippines her leg muscles had strengthened and equalized enormously.

Another traveler was a devoted middle-aged husband who was taking his wife to see Agpaoa for the second time (she suffered from multiple sclerosis). He had lifted her so much that he had damaged his back. Another young man, tall and strong, was paralyzed from the neck down; he had almost no voluntary movement left. Still other members of the large group suffered from so-called incurable diseases.

After a seventeen-hour flight we arrived in Manila in bright sunshine. When we entered the airport building we were greeted, as is the local custom, by pretty Filipino girls who placed flower leis around our necks. Two buses drove us to our hotel; we met in the evening in a reserved dining room, and Tony Agpaoa and his wife appeared and welcomed us. To Philippine background music we enjoyed an excellent meal. The evening was relaxed and informal and in no way esoteric. Nothing in the evening's arrangements indicated the creation of an atmosphere intended to prepare the patients psychologically for a miracle cure or an encounter with the divine power of a wonder healer. Only the wheelchairs called attention to the serious reasons for the patients' presence.

The following day Agpaoa began his work. In contrast to two years before, he was no longer concerned with attuning the patient's psyche to the operation. Formerly most patients watched several other operations before undergoing surgery themselves, usually removing any anxiety they might feel and strengthening their trust. Tony also used to do demonstration operations to persuade skeptical Europeans; but now he was intent on keeping spectators away as much as possible and concentrating exclusively on his work. This is understandable, since most days he saw more than thirty patients. The operations were performed in a hotel room. The healer Marcelo Jainar was also present and often took over the treatment.

I observed Agpaoa's activity for several hours on two days. I did not take moving or still pictures, so I could concentrate entirely on observing. I believe that I cannot have missed any significant detail.

Not to weary the reader with a renewed refutation of all possibilities of fraud, I want only to mention that Agpaoa wore a short-sleeved shirt and that the patients were usually brought from the waiting room by Sigrun Seutemann in random sequence, so that Agpaoa could not know until just before the operation what procedure he must employ, whether to operate on the patient's back or abdomen or ear.

Whenever a sizable group flies to the Philippines, it inevitably includes some people who "know," before they have seen an operation or after one or two of them, that it is all a matter of tricks. Thus someone claimed to have seen fish bladders concealed in some cotton. Of course he had nothing more urgent to do than report his "discovery" to the other patients. I was reminded of the unenviable position of lawyers in evaluating witnesses' depositions.

I watched Agpaoa at work for hours at a time. The cotton he used was taken from a large package, visible and accessible to everyone on a table placed against the wall. I kept a goodly quantity of it. Most of the operations I witnessed were performed without any possibility of trickery. It was a genuine paranormal occurrence, although I realized that Agpaoa's style of operating in many cases was not the same as it had been two years before. He tried to keep developing his skills for the benefit of his patients. In my opinion it is only rarely that he opens the body. What I had recently come to suspect on the basis of my study of ectoplasmic phenomena now bordered on certainty—that under the influence of the force fields in Tony Agpaoa's hands the most incredible materialization phenomena occurred. The most interesting operation during this stay was the brain-tumor surgery described in chapter 10.

After their operations most of the patients felt a

significant improvement, far exceeding what in my mind could be accounted for by faith healing.

The paralyzed Franz P., with whom I shared a table at most of our meals in Baguio, was cared for by a lady who considered the whole matter a trick; therefore, his attitude toward Agpaoa was somewhat ambivalent and more than a little skeptical. But after his first operation he said to me, "Anyone who claims that it's all just fraud and fantasy is talking plain nonsense." Agpaoa removed a significant amount of necrotic tissue from Herr P.'s back, but not without the patient's feeling considerable pain. After a day or two the bedsore had shrunk to around an inch in diameter. After his experiences in European hospitals Herr P. said this result would normally have required several weeks of hospitalization and treatment, during which he would have had to remain lying on his stomach. After more operations by Agpaoa, his chronic back pains disappeared; instead, he began to have a disagreeable tingling sensation in his legs, where recently he had no feeling to speak of. It looked as if nerve stimulation, which had been absent for two or three years, was returning. Mr. P. unfortunately had to return to Europe before I did. Some weeks later I spoke to his wife on the telephone. She told me his condition was continuing to improve and the flow of blood to the paralyzed limbs was visibly improving. Regardless of whether he continues to improve, I can say that the Philippine operations cannot be simply dismissed as the effect of suggestion or explained as the result of massage, as some Italian physicians have tried to do, for the patient had been treated by massage for three years in Europe.

The first polio victim mentioned above, who had been confined to a wheelchair for more than twenty-five years and forced to wear a steel brace for twelve years, was able after the first few operations by Agpaoa to sit upright in her chair without the body brace. She said that if there were no other beneficial results beyond this, she would consider the trip worthwhile. But she hoped for further progress and was prepared to come to the Philippines again. Unfortunately she was compelled by the exigencies of her job to return to Europe after a week.

Many patients with partial paralysis claimed to have gained significantly greater freedom of movement, but I do not draw conclusions about Agpaoa's operations on them, which would require thorough analysis of how much should be credited to suggestion. But I did see the student P., whose case history I related above, take her first steps without crutches a few days after her operation.

On the other hand, cases of advanced multiple sclerosis did not seem to show any significant improvement during the stay in the Philippines. Note that this disease often responds strongly to psychogenic effects, and the very failure to respond supports the view that the success of Agpaoa's operations involves more than suggestion.

Sigrun Seutemann told me of two other cases from earlier trips to the Philippines. According to available clinical findings, Mrs. D. from Lausanne suffered from acute polyarthritic degeneration; she had been treated intensively with cortisone for years. Almost all her joints were affected, and her blood count showed distinct changes. After her visit to the Philippines she was free of symptoms for three months. During the winter she had isolated light attacks of pain in the joints; normal biological medication was able to alleviate them, however. There was no longer any need for corticosteroids. Her blood level fell abnormally again but rose to almost normal readings.

Another case of severe arthritis was that of Mrs. Rina F., a Swiss woman, who had to take corticosteroids for eighteen years in order to endure the pain. After treatments by Agpaoa and Marcelo Jainar she can do entirely without medication. There is evidence of some circulatory damage and anomalies in the blood count—caused by the lengthy steroid treatment —but the polyarthritis is only fragmentary.

Seutemann has witnessed many other convincing feats by Agpaoa, but she does not publicize them, so as not to arouse false hope; severely ill patients generally do not properly evaluate sensational spontaneous cures, which leads time and again to serious disappointment. When the case of Karl Dobesch was publicized in a Swiss newspaper, four hundred paraplegics in wheelchairs sought out Sigrid Seutemann and her husband. The Seutemanns chose only a few of them—perhaps five—whom they conditionally advised to go to the Philippines.

I too beg the reader to correctly evaluate the cures cited in this book. The Philippine healers bring about astonishing results, but there is no way yet to quantify their success. The significance of psychic surgery, in my view, lies less in the cure of one or another sufferer who could not be helped in Europe, but in the fact that the surgery goes beyond the frame of reference of Western science; given further research, this will lead to new spiritual and scientific territory tending to revolutionize our whole picture of man. It is heartening that more and more scientists are beginning to take an interest in these phenomena. In February 1973 a number of scientists and researchers met in the Philippines. Among the visitors was an American, George W. Meek, member of the board of Life Energies Research, Inc., of New York, an association founded in 1968 to further scientific research into known and paranormal energies connected with life processes. It includes members from the fields of medicine, psychiatry, natural sciences, philosophy, and theology, who since 1953 have been meeting regularly to exchange ideas about the paranormal aspects of human experience. They have been particularly concerned with spiritual healing.

Meek is a sophisticated, knowledgeable man who has traveled all over the globe to study paraphenomena.[148] Marcus McCausland, head and founder of Health for the New Age, Ltd., London, a society with similar aims, was also in Manila.

Shortly after our arrival the Philippine healing society (Unio Espiritista Cristiana Filipinas) elected a new president: Joaquin Cunanan. He is highly respected in Manila; he has traveled in many parts of the world, including Germany. Cunanan drove George

Meek and me to meet some extraordinarily interesting healers in the Philippine lowlands.

After we had spent a week in the Philippines, Dr. Naegeli-Osjord as well as a professor of physics, Dr. Werner Schiebeler, and an engineer, Professor Benno Kirchgässner (both German) joined us. Mr. Cunanan invited us and other researchers to exchange experiences at a daily discussion hour. His opening speech began: "The human spirit is like a parachute. It is good only when it is open." Open-mindedness is the precondition for progress in investigating paranormal healing.

Most of the patients from other countries still sought out Tony Agpaoa; but reports of astonishing feats by other healers, such as Ricardo Gonzales in Baguio, were beginning to circulate.

In 1968 Dr. Motoyama met the American Dr. E.J.T. in Manila. He had come to the Philippines with his epileptic son Jeffery. The boy lost consciousness once an hour for a brief period—nine to ten seconds. The left side of his face had poor motility, and all of his face was expressionless. His electroencephalogram showed a distinct epilepsy focus in the left temporal lobe.

The little patient was treated by Blance before he was operated on by Gonzales in Baguio. A week later the father and son came to Tokyo, where the boy was examined in Motoyama's institute. The EEG showed a distinct improvement, the patient had not taken any medicine for five days, and during his five-hour examination he had no attacks. Two weeks later another EEG was taken in a Chicago hospital—the same one where Jeffery had been treated earlier. It confirmed the remarkable improvement.

A few weeks later, on October 22, 1968, the father reported to Dr. Motoyama that his son was well. The difference in facial expression and motility of the two sides of the face had disappeared. His behavior was much improved. He now reacted when he was told something. The number of attacks was reduced to two or three a day. Before the trip to Manila he took twenty-eight pills of his medication per day; now the dosage was sharply reduced. The EEG peaks in the left temporal lobe had disappeared. The physician of record was astonished at the patient's facial expressiveness, but no one had dared to tell him about the trip to the Philippines.

On November 27, 1968, the father wrote to Dr. Motoyama: "Since our return, the number of attacks has steadily decreased. In the last nine days he has not had one attack. His behavior keeps on improving, and he is almost back to being the normal boy he was before September 1966. He attends school fulltime, is mentally active, shows pleasure in learning, and follows instructions well. . . . Unfortunately our films of the operation were lost in the developing lab."[164,165]

A second successful operation by Gonzales was reported to Dr. Motoyama by a friend of the patient S.N., a forty-year-old Japanese who gradually lost mobility in his arms and legs. Examination at the Kurume Medical School showed spinal tumors exerting pressure on the nerves controlling arm and leg movements. An operation would be very difficult, and the prognosis was not favorable—that is, the patient was given little hope of a cure. He decided to fly to the Philippines, where he sought out Gonzales, who performed an operation in the manner of Agpaoa and removed tumors. Subsequent examination in the hospital associated with Kyushu University revealed no tumors. Since the patient had concealed the Philippine operations, the Kurume Medical School diagnosis was declared in error. But Dr. Motoyama got hold of X rays taken before and after the Philippine healer's operation which vouched for the correctness of the first diagnosis and the authenticity of Gonzales's operation. Motoyama showed slides of the X rays at Harold Sherman's ESP Congress in May 1972 in Hot Springs, Arkansas, as well as during a lecture on June 1, 1972, to the Society for Parapsychology at St. Louis. The best evidence, however, is the state of the patient. A month after Gonzales's operation he was again able to work on his farm and to ride his bicycle.[164,165]

Many cures take place quietly on the operating tables of the Spiritist churches, where psychic treatment and operations are generally performed at the end of religious services. Verification of these cases is usually not possible for Europeans, since the Filipinos, many of them seriously ill, seldom seek medical help either before or after psychic surgery; they simply do not have the money.

We can hear about the many achievements of psychic surgeons only by spending considerable time in the Philippines and traveling around to look up every possible healer. On this quest one often encounters cases where the success of the operation is obvious even without precise medical diagnosis.

It is very useful to get an introduction to the healers by Filipinos who know them well. The presiding officer of the Unio Espiritista Cristiana Filipinas, Joaquin Cunanan, took George W. Meek, a Swiss woman, and me to Urdaneta to meet the healer José Mercado.

The operations, which were quite varied, proceeded nonstop. Between operations Mercado washed his hands in a bowl placed on the table; he wore a short-sleeved shirt, and there was no possibility of sleight of hand.

The same morning Mr. Cunanan took us to see the healer Josefina Sison, who lived in a remote hamlet a few miles beyond Carmen in the lowlands. About fifteen local men and women were waiting in her simple wooden hut. The friendly patients immediately offered us their places on the benches.

Soon the healer, carrying her baby, bade us a cordial welcome. First her elderly assistant made a kind of prediagnosis by examining the patients' hands and palms. I noticed that almost all the patients had peculiar palm markings such as I had never observed among Europeans or urban Filipinos. I am sure a chirologist would have an interesting time studying them.

Then Josefina sat at the wooden table, her back to the window. We joined the patients in a semicircle around the table. Josefina prayed for about ten minutes and read from the Bible. She spoke the native language, so that we could not understand her. Then she began her work, remaining sitting—perhaps because she was expecting another child. Her dress bared not only her arms but part of her shoulders. Before operating she diagnosed through automatic writing. A cloth was spread on the table and the first patient took his place on the table, his head resting on the Bible, which served as a pillow. His abdomen was bared and some damp cotton placed on it. Josefina's open hands (nothing could be concealed in them) pressed against the abdominal wall, and after a little while a bloodlike fluid appeared. Before touching the body she often spread out her fingers so that one could clearly see that there was nothing hidden between them. In the course of the morning not only was tissue always produced, but the most unusual materializations were brought about. (To discuss them at greater length would go beyond the scope of this book.)

During all the operations Josefina did not leave her seat once. Between operations she washed her hands in a bowl. I watched her work from the front and from the side, so that I could see her sitting at the table and observe her from head to toe. Besides, people at times were peering in through the window directly behind her. She was not in the least disturbed by them. Operations followed rapidly one after the other.

We could not wait for the end of "office hours," since we had plans to move on. We took our leave of the healer, who seemed to radiate harmony, honesty, and inner peace such as I have seldom met with in anyone. A deep and genuine religiosity seemed to give her an almost unshakable spiritual equanimity. Even a fraction of it transferred to Westerners would probably decimate cardiac infarctions and ulcers. The thirty-year-old Josefina also radiated an inexpressible feminine charm. Meek said to me as we were leaving, "If that woman is a crook, there's nobody in the whole world you can trust."

After we had left the house I remembered something. I ran back and asked if I could have a little cotton, since my ears were somewhat sensitive while driving in an open car—which is true. The assistant was about to hand Josefina some cotton for her next operation and gave it to me instead. I have saved the cotton—to show anyone who wants to look for the dyestuff in it.

The skills of good healers seem to be stimulated by the patient's immediate needs. I am inclined to believe that the healer requires the patient's biofield, which has been disturbed by the disease, to begin his operation. That is why Philippine healers refuse to produce a wound in a healthy person without a good reason; possibly such a demonstration would not succeed if it were tried. Juan Blance was once asked to make his psychokinetic incision on a patient's skin after a plastic sheet, brought along for the purpose, had been placed over it; Blance refused. The healers want to help sick people; procedures that we consider scientific experiments, they look on as foolishness. After this encounter, when Blance made his usual incision from a distance, the observer managed quickly to interpose an artificial sheet. The plastic was undamaged, but the incision appeared on the skin.

The magnetic injections given by the healer Mercado without touching the patient's body seem to involve a different phenomenon. People who placed a sheet of paper under their shirt or a plastic sheet over their chest or another place that was to be "injected" afterward found tiny holes in the sheets.

Every paranormal healer develops a more or less individual style, to which he becomes accustomed. A demand for even a trivial change in procedure may place him in difficulties. The psychic-surgical achievements are probably controlled by a complicated system of conditioned reflexes from the subconscious;

ignoring the conditions that release these reflexes leads to failure in performance or requires a colossal expenditure of psychic energy by the healer.

The question of the authenticity of the Philippine operations has concerned a number of scientists since 1966. The first investigations were carried out by the Japanese scientist Dr. Hiroshi Motoyama with the pararesearcher Dr. Hiram Ramos of Manila. On September 19 and 22, 1968, these two, along with the pathologist Professor David de Léon, observed operations performed by the healer Juan Blance, including surgery on cysts on the nape of the neck, without using a knife. The doctors took blood and tissue samples during the operations. These were tested at the University of Tokyo and at Professor Léon's institute at Manila's Far Eastern University. Comparison with blood later withdrawn from the same patient showed that the operation blood was the patient's. Further support for the authenticity of Blance's operations was furnished by tissue analysis.

The substances produced during Blance's eye operations turned out to be useless for scientific evaluation. They quickly dissolved in formaldehyde; presumably they represented primitive materialization products. In all, Dr. Motoyama collected and analyzed twenty blood and tissue samples; on the basis of the test results he judged Blance's operations to be genuine.[164,165]

In 1970 Motoyama analyzed blood from two operations, including a cardiac operation performed on a sixty-year-old Japanese woman by the surgeon Gonzales of Baguio. Both operations were proved genuine by the results of the analyses.

In November 1972 Dr. Motoyama again came to the Philippines, on the initiative of Sigrun Seutemann, and obtained six or seven blood samples from Tony Agpaoa's operations, plus tissue samples. The thorough analysis included an immunobiological test. Most of the blood samples were demonstrably from the patient being operated on, which speaks for the authenticity of the operations.[166] In one or two cases the results were not clear. Generally Agpaoa and other surgeons of his school begin their operations with wet cotton, as is well known. Changes in the blood can occur through diluting it with water. As a result of the lower osmotic pressure in the thinned-out blood fluid, the corpuscles burst, and other undesirable effects set in. Furthermore, the possibility or probability of paranormal effects on the blood during these psychic operations must be considered.

In 1973 Dr. Werner Schiebeler observed as his German colleague, Professor Benno Kirchgässner, was given a magnetic injection by the healer Mercado. Mercado never touched the patient, although Professor Kirchgässner clearly felt a puncture, and blood began to well from the wound. The two scientists preserved the flowing blood: a forensic examination in Germany revealed that the fluid was human O-group blood. Professor Kirchgässner has B-type blood; nevertheless, there is no possibility that the healer committed any kind of trickery.

In February 1972 the Italian neurologist Professor Granone spent two weeks in the Philippines with a team of researchers and cameramen, thoroughly investigating nine healers. Dr. Theo Locher reported on this trip in the May 1973 issue of the *Schweizerisches Bulletin für Parapsychologie:*

> The application of spiritual injections by hand without touching the body . . . was confirmed. . . . During these injections the seven European members of the team felt something like needle punctures or electric shocks at the affected sites. Three members of the team were bleeding. The analysis of one of these blood samples (studied at the University of Turin, Italy) revealed that it was not human blood. In spite of telecameras, infrared film, and other monitoring of the puncture site, it was not possible to ascertain anything suspicious. Analysis of the blood flowing down the leg of another member of the group revealed a substance that was not blood, which remained completely incomprehensible to the members of the research team. A piece of paper placed under Dr. Moser's shirt showed three small holes at the site of the injection,

although the healer's hands were constantly monitored by the group's apparatus.[134]

Clearly, under certain conditions novel changes in the blood, as yet unamenable to our controls, appear. If this is so even with magnetic injections, where the patient is not touched, how much more readily can we expect such changes in direct psychic surgery, where the healer constantly touches and manipulates the patient, in some cases penetrating the body. Situations where materialization phenomena occur—as is probable in most psychic surgery—are incalculable by present-day investigative techniques.

It must therefore seem incomprehensible that the team led by Professor Granone interpreted the fact that blood samples taken from psychic operations could not be proved to be human blood as proof of fakery.[134]

Analogous changes probably occur in the tissue removed or materialized in paranormal operations. This leads in many cases to the false assertion that the tissues are no longer "fresh" and could not therefore have been taken from the body.[134]

No one will deny that fakery is possible in the Philippines, as it is the world over. But fakery in these drastic paranormal processes cannot be detected by conventional investigative methods, whose impracticability for judging paraphysical processes has been clearly shown. We must work out new methods of analysis and research for this purpose.

Criteria from the realm of the normal cannot simply be applied to the (presumably superordinate) realm of the paranormal; think of how many conclusions from Newtonian physics became inoperative when examined in the light of Einsteinian physics.

In February 1973, during one of his operations, Tony Agpaoa unexpectedly asked me to take some blood samples, and I did so from the next three patients. Unfortunately the samples were not analyzed in Germany. After they had been in the laboratory for several weeks, they were returned to me untested because the lab had too great a backlog of work. All three samples smelled of decayed blood.

Agpaoa also offered to let me remove a piece of tissue with a forceps during an operation; and at a later operation, behind Agpaoa's back, I fished a piece of tissue out of the garbage pail. The first sample was taken from an operation in the intestinal region on a thirty-two-year-old patient. Pathological findings obtained in Germany showed that the sample consisted of an autolytically altered segment of the small intestine with inflammation of the mucous membrane. Since I had told the analysts that the tissue was obtained during a lay operation, the report contained the cautious postscript: "The question whether the segment comes from a human being or an animal cannot be answered on the basis of histological analysis." If Agpaoa performed the operation fraudulently, he needed intestinal tissue from an animal with a close morphological resemblance to man, especially as the piece of tissue in question was rather large. The animal would have had to exhibit morbid changes in the small intestine—insofar as the autolytic changes did not come about during preservation in formaldehyde, a possibility I cannot exclude.

The second sample was from a patient who had been treated for three years in Europe on the basis of a mistaken diagnosis of multiple sclerosis until it became clear that she had a tumor in the region of the lumbar vertebrae. The tumor was surgically removed, but the patient was paralyzed as a result. Tony operated on her back. The report, based on a histological analysis of the sample, stated: "The submitted sample, a flat, cord-shaped, soft abdominal tissue excision, shows characteristic, evenly distributed close bundles of cross-striate skeletal muscles at the prepared cross section; at the edges it exhibits a fascial front. The musculature shows typical anisotropy in polarized light, no indication of an inflammatory reaction or of systemic degeneration. Diagnosis: Morphologically inconspicuous cross-striate skeletal muscle."

This finding seems reasonable. Possibly Agpaoa sought to lay bare some nerves, and in order to do so he removed basically healthy tissue. There would be no evidence of inflammation at this time, since the tumor operation had been performed long before. At the least, these samples show that he does not pass off plastic sheets, peppercorns, and seaweed as human tissue, as has been claimed on a German television program.

No one who wants to evaluate psychic surgery should bypass Motoyama's work or skip comparing the Philippine paranormal operations with reports from Brazil, of which the most thorough scientific investigations are those of the well-known physician and psi researcher Dr. Andrija K. Puharich, a former senior research scientist at New York Medical Center and president of the research group at Intelectron Corporation who gave up these associations some years ago so as to concentrate exclusively on para-research, including investigation of paranormal healing. He holds several academic degrees, belongs to a number of scientific organizations, is the author of several scientific articles and two books, and holds about fifty patents. Dr. Puharich, along with other American physicians, studied the healer Zé Arigo, noting the same basic phenomena observed among the Philippine healers. On October 30, 1971, at the Interdisciplinary Symposium of the Academy of Parapsychology and Medicine in Los Altos, California, Dr. Puharich showed a film demonstrating Arigo scratching the cornea of an eye with a sharp knife to show that no pain set in and no damage was done although the knife actually cut into the tissue. Medical examination immediately following showed that no wound remained and that the damage was instantly healed. We are reminded of Mirin Dajo. Dr. Puharich has said that the Philippine healers go one step beyond Arigo: they can separate tissue without using a knife—at times even without touching the body.

Arigo occasionally worked with knives so blunt that they could not cut butter, but he had no difficulty splitting tissue with them. The essential element was not the sharpness of the knife but probably, as with the Filipinos, a new form of energy, emanating from the fingers. The knife may be nothing more than a symbolic utensil or inductor which facilitates the process for reasons still unclear to us. Some South Amercan medicine men are said to get similar results with bamboo rods; Blance uses another person's finger to open the body.

If paranormal ways of separating and rejoining tissue are evident in the case of Arigo, why are some people so ready to express a blanket denial of even stronger phenomena among the Philippine healers?

Puharich has preserved some of Zé Arigo's operations on film, such as surgery on a cranial cyst in a woman. Though normally Arigo did not bother with such trivial ailments, sending the patients back to their doctor, he performed this operation for demonstration purposes. He cut with the bluntest of knives. And because the wound closed too quickly—remember Agpaoa, Mercado, Placido, and other Filipinos—vaseline was placed inside the incision.

Arigo said he would press the cyst out of the skull. The film shows sebaceous substance coming out of the wound and the capsule being cleansed—"an impossible action, from a surgical point of view," as Dr. Puharich put it. Then Arigo held out his hand and asked his "spiritual guide," Dr. Fritz, to remove the capsule. Then he pressed the capsule outward slightly and shortly afterward pulled it out without having separated it surgically from the skin or the periosteum of the skull.

The film is astonishingly reminiscent of what I witnessed in the Philippines, especially during 1971, when I visited Juan Blance as well as Tony Agpaoa. Blance, too, after opening the skin by a psychokinetic incision and, applying the cupping glass, pressed out tumors and metastases without cutting them surgically. Presumably such paranormal tissue separation involves sharply limited dematerialization processes at the interface of tumor and body, and the extrusion of the tumor is performed largely psychogenically.

There are other parallels between Philippine

surgery and Zé Arigo's methods. Puharich reports a
reliably documented case of advanced stomach cancer. The physicians gave the patient only a short time
to live. He went to see Arigo, taking his place in a
long line of three or four hundred waiting patients.
When Arigo arrived to begin his treatments, he
grabbed the patient out of the crowd and said, "You
come with me right away—you're really sick." In the
treatment room Arigo told the patient he had stomach
cancer and there was no time to lose. He prescribed a
number of medications for the next twenty-four hours
and ordered the patient to return the next day. The
next day he operated without a knife. He used his bare
hand—like Agpaoa, Mercado, and other Philippine
healers—to pass through the abdominal wall and
brought out a quantity of bloody tissue. Subsequent
X-ray examination showed that the cancerous growth
had been removed.[200]

In 1966 Harold Sherman and Henry Belk made
their trip to the Philippines; Sherman's book on
psychic surgery appeared in 1967. The nine years
since are too short a time for Western medicine to accept phenomena that fall so far outside the framework
of its experience. We must remember that it took ten
years after initial vehement rejection before C. L.
Schleich's local anesthesia was accepted; and his discovery did not require as great a change in thinking
as do the Philippine operations.

But more and more European scientists are becoming aware of these processes, thanks largely to the un-
tiring work of Sigrun Seutemann, who has strong
psychic talents and who can therefore skillfully judge
many details of the Philippine operations. We must
also cite the German physicist Dr. Werner Schiebeler,
who directed a fine film, commissioned by the Institute for Scientific Film in Göttingen, which earned
him the Bozzano prize at the parapsychology congress
in Genoa in the summer of 1974. And since early
1971 Dr. Hans Naegeli-Osjord, a Swiss medical specialist, has been advocating the authenticity of the Philippine phenomena throughout Switzerland regardless of

the difficulties and disadvantages accruing to him from this commitment.

In February 1973 a number of researchers and scientists, having made a thorough study of the phenomena, at the initiative of Joaquin Cunanan signed a declaration in Manila in which they attested that during their study tour of the Philippines they had observed healers who carried out genuine paranormal surgery. The Manila dailies gave banner headlines to the story and published the names of the signers:

Joaquin Cunanan, Manila
Professor B. Kirchgässner, West Germany
Marcus McCausland, London
George W. Meek, U.S.A.
Dr. Hiroshi Motoyama, Tokyo
Dr. Hans Naegeli-Osjord, Zurich
Professor W. Schiebeler, West Germany
Sigrun Seutemann, West Germany
Dr. Alfred Stelter, West Germany
Donald Westerbeke, U.S.A.

The declaration stressed that at present it was not possible to attest to the therapeutic results of the operations. The declaration did determine that the paranormal surgery of the Philippines involves paraphysical processes that cannot be subsumed in the ideological structure of Western science.

When the Healers Union elected Joaquin Cunanan to its presidency in February 1973, it chose an influential personality. Cunanan, a consultant of the accounting firm Joaquin Cunanan & Company, has taught at various universities, has been an official in the government of the Philippines and in the United Nations, and is a member of several professional and civic organizations. He has traveled extensively, with several trips to India, where on four occasions he received instruction in yoga from various gurus; he is the president of the Philippine Yoga Society, Inc. He has studied spiritualism in England and the United States. Cunanan succeeded in persuading the Philippine press, which for years had reported only pejoratively on the local healers, to publish lengthy articles on their astonishing feats.

During my third stay in the Philippines—in September 1973—many healers were exposed to a regular storm of patients. (These no longer came exclusively from the more deprived social classes but also included well-to-do patients.) Where Juan Blance used to see 50 to 70 patients a day in 1971, now there were days when he treated more than 400. Such an increase, of course, has its dangers. The patients may at times be treated with less than the necessary care, and any failures will generally be cheerfully publicized by the opposition. Further, excessive demands on the mediums can lead to a diminution of their psychic powers, increasing the temptation to bridge a slump with trickery. An upward evaluation of the healers tempts swindlers without genuine skill to call themselves healers. Nevertheless, my third stay in the Philippines was most interesting and productive.

The number of patients coming from abroad grew rapidly. Foreign travelers used to seek out Agpaoa almost exclusively. But in the summer of 1973 Doris Almeda, formerly a member of Lucy Agpaoa's travel agency, with the support of Joaquin Cunanan opened the Christian Travel Center, intended to put foreigners in touch with other healers. It is still active in the Hotel Bayview Plaza. Thanks to Cunanan and the Christian Travel Center, I met a number of fascinating healers. In the presence of an Australian physician I saw the surgeon Romy Bugarin perform a sensational lower abdominal operation on a Philippine woman doctor. Bugarin brought internal organs to the surface through the abdominal wall—in the physician's opinion, the uterus among others—and there were times when sizable areas of the abdominal wall seemed dematerialized.[262,263]

Now I was incontrovertibly convinced that dematerialization, materialization, ectoplasmic formations, and psychokinesis are the crucial factors in Philippine surgery. In the first eye operation I observed by the healer Alex Orbito of Manila, he removed the eye of a

Greek patient from its socket, largely by psycho-kinesis.[264] The Australian physician mentioned above, who was present at several of Orbito's eye opera-tions, had studied optical surgery in animals for six months; he was mystified by the procedures he ob-served here. He could not understand how it was possible to remove an eye from its socket without reaching behind the eyeball with one's hands or with an instrument. He took snapshots during the operation. I was standing close to the surgeon and observed the whole process at a distance of 8–10 inches. The white of the removed eye was bloodshot with little red veins; it is certain that we did not fall victim to a trick with a glass eye or the eyeball of an animal, as was subsequently claimed.

Let me warn the reader again not to misinterpret my accounts of psychic operations. I have already stated that we are not dealing with surgery in the Western sense. Psychic surgery includes a spectrum of paranormal processes in the treatment of disease, from psychic incisions, which in some cases remove immediate foci of illness as in Western surgery, to what is perhaps the most frequent phenomenon: ma-terialization of bloodlike fluids and primordial tissue —or of paranormal matter—on the patient's body. In such cases the body is probably not opened, even if the healers themselves believe it is. Sometimes the healers open the body in a spectacular manner but do not succeed in removing the cause of the disease thereby. Often they produce only minimal amounts of bloodlike substance on the closed body surface, which makes the skeptic even more skeptical, but more of-ten than not unexpected and astonishing cures result.

Professor Schiebeler, who has studied parapsy-chology and paraphysics for the last thirty years, states:

Surgery in the West removes mechanical causes of dis-ease, thus restoring normal bodily functions. Paranormal surgery of the so-called spiritist surgeons, on the other hand, does not simply remove a cause of disease me-chanically but for the most part initiates a process of healing with which we are still unfamiliar; the process often leads to partial or complete recovery within a very short time. From the standpoint of established medicine, therefore, the paranormal surgical processes appear in many cases to be simply secondary actions. But it must be said that a definite judgment is not possible given the current state of knowledge.[227]

Paradoxically, psychic surgery does not fall into the area of medicine at all but rather that of paraphysics. Many of those investigating these phenomena are not physicians but natural scientists. The physician's first reaction when he witnesses psychic surgery is often to conclude that these procedures are "not medical surgery." He thus easily falls prey to the error that deception must be involved. When the generalist makes a thorough study of the phenomena as a medical layman, he soon realizes that psychic surgery involves factors that cannot be categorized scientifically and that unlock new dimensions.

In four years I made five trips to the Philippines. During the last one, from October 1974 to March 1975, I worked especially closely with Dr. Hiram Ramos, the most experienced observer of psychic surgery in the Philippines. I owe him a great deal. I have met almost all the interesting healers of the northern Philippines, have observed many of them for several years, and have conducted experiments with several of them recently. Today my interpretations of some phenomena differ from those I made in early 1971. Some of the healers have changed their working methods too; some abilities seem to have become attenuated—for example, pulling teeth with the bare hands, a more or less everyday occurrence in 1971.

Outside the Philippines, healers seem to work with more expenditure of energy. Early in 1974 we invited Juan Blance to Germany, where he spent several weeks demonstrating his paranormal treatments. At first the phenomena appeared as in Manila, but they rapidly weakened, and after three weeks the healer suffered a near-fatal cardiovascular accident. Before the collapse he lost control over his psychokinetic powers; sometimes the psychokinetic incisions appeared at implausible sites—for example, on the hands of the assistant who was massaging the patient's feet instead of on the patient's chest, where Blance had directed it. We had, as it were, the apparition of minipoltergeists! The healer, who had been invited by the German practical healer I. Lutz, treated more than a hundred patients a day and totally exhausted himself. In Manila Lutz had performed the same paranormal feats as Blance in Blance's presence; in Germany, on her own, she cannot do them.

Opening the body is increasingly infrequent, at least among some healers. Most often, unusual materializations of bloodlike fluids or ectoplasmic substances appear on the patients' body surfaces, while presumably the body is not opened. Paranormal matter also appears on the patients' bodies under the hands of the healer. (One healer a year later managed only stale magic tricks, and soon thereafter disappeared altogether.)

During 1971–72 trickery was not a major factor in the work of the healers I observed; but it is increasing since 1973. Several healers use deceptive manipulation when they temporarily or permanently lose their materialization skills. When the loss is permanent, the healer soon drops from view.

Healers' condition is not constant: on certain days some healers can produce nothing—especially if they have indulged in sexual excesses. Some healers go through long periods when they cannot work at all as a consequence of loose living, money worries, family problems, and the like. Then they may resort to faked operations with dried animal blood or dyes, as the skilled observer can tell at a glance. When they regain control, their powers return in full. The fact that some healers now and then engage in simple sleight of hand, while at other times performing extraordinary materializations, is clear proof to me of the authenticity of the phenomena. Note that the reliable healers limited themselves to magnetic treatments whenever their powers were not at their height.

It would be a mistake to assume that it takes a professional magician to recognize the tricksters we occasionally encountered. On the contrary, so-called masters of magic, who have no understanding of paraphysics and do not believe in the possibility of paranormal phenomena, have made the most serious misinterpretations, not only in the Philippines but in connection with psychokinesis in the West. Such skeptics at times interpret even the most innocent motions of a healer as possible deceptive tactics. Years of observation of Philippine surgery cannot be superseded by a one-week visit by a conjurer. I was present, for example, in 1975, when a well-known magician, who had spent two days with Josefina Sison, claimed that he was now on to all her tricks. On the third day he demonstrated on my abdomen an alleged operation in Sison's style. Also present were Dr. Hiram Ramos, his coworker Maya, and George W. Meek. (The latter has since been engaged by the Academy for Parapsychology and Medicine in Los Altos, California, to investigate paranormal healing methods all over the world, especially in the Philippines.) I lay on the bed, my abdominal region bared. The magician dipped his hands in a bowl of water placed next to the bed and held them dripping and slightly curled over my abdomen, so that a tiny puddle of water quickly formed. He massaged my abdomen within this puddle, which quickly turned red—as the result of a dye capsule which he had presumably kept concealed between two fingers. This, he claimed, was what he had seen Josefina do. Dr. Ramos and I, who had watched Josefina carry out hundreds of operations, held a quite different opinion. Since 1974 Josefina works without the aid of cotton, in contrast to her earlier practice. Between operations, which are carried out in quick succession, she washes her hands in a bowl of water placed on a chair next to the table. But, unlike the imitation described, she sprays the drops of water off her hands before she touches the patient; the bloodlike fluid nevertheless appears, often in large quantities. Once, in my presence, George Meek asked her whether she can operate with entirely dry hands. In answer, she dried her hands after washing them and before touching the patient; the operation proceeded as usual. Also, each morning she begins the first operation of the day with dry hands, but a sizable amount of fluid is produced.

It was the opinion of the expert magician that, since Josefina invariably wore short-sleeved blouses and her hands never touched her own body in a suspicious way, the shreds of tissue produced during her operations were concealed beneath the rim of the washbowl. Before I left the Philippines in March 1975, Dr. Ramos and I made a final trip to the village of Villasis, about 150 miles north of Manila, where Josefina Sison works. I placed myself next to the healer, at the back of the table. Between the various operations her left hand did rest on the edge of the washbowl. When she quickly moved it to the patient's abdomen, I almost believed she was concealing a sizable piece of tissue in her palm. But one time her husband called to her from the doorway, and while she was distracted, I was able to carefully examine her hands, still resting on the patient's abdomen. As she spoke, her hands relaxed and flattened, and Dr. Ramos and I were able to see that nothing was concealed anywhere—even between her outspread fingers. Seconds later she concentrated on her work again without lifting her hands from the patient's body, and the paranormal process ran its usual course, producing great quantities of bloodlike fluid.

The next operation involved eye surgery, and Josefina, who normally worked sitting down, stood up so she could reach the patient's head more easily. Taking advantage of the opportunity to step even closer, I was able to use my left hand to touch the washbowl, placed to the healer's left. I covertly fingered the rim of the bowl while pretending to watch the treatment. I may not have felt every inch around the bowl, but I scanned the part of the rim where her hand general-

ly rested, without results. Further, there was no damp-
ness under the rim of the bowl, and there would have
been if she had removed a piece of chicken liver or
the like from it.

We generally see what we are looking for. A simple-
minded person, ready to believe in miracles, sees a
wide-open body even when a swindler has produced
a red puddle from pellets of dried animal blood and
damp cotton. And the skeptic is certain to find a
situation that he can interpret in the light of his
hypothesis of trickery and to label as fakery what is
real.

Western academic medicine, which until now has
scarcely paid any attention to paranormal phenomena,
continues to reject Philippine treatments and psychic
surgery as deception; although an increasing number
of open-minded physicians have recently expressed
interest in these phenomena, the American Medical
Association is waging a vigorous campaign against the
Philippine healers.

Early in 1975 Dr. William A. Nolen, an American
surgeon and writer, published *Healing, a Doctor in
Search of a Miracle*,[183] a book directed against paranormal healing in general and specifically against the
Philippine healers. Dr. Nolen spent two weeks in the
Philippines in June 1973. He begins his travel report
with words to the effect that "I hated the idea of going to the Philippines." And in fact his book gives
short shrift not only to Philippine healers but to the
Philippines altogether. He groans about the June
heat, complains of the hotel room costing a dollar and
a half in the lowlands because it did not have hot
water, criticizes the flushing mechanism that failed
in another hotel, objects to the flies that bothered him
at meals. He was disturbed by the water buffaloes on
the road that forced his car to a stop. The ride along
the narrow, winding mountain road to Baguio—for
me, a new adventure each time—was for him something he could survive only, as he writes, by feverish-
ly clutching his seat, holding his breath, closing his
eyes, and so on. All this is a manifestation of a negative basic attitude, which cannot but affect his in-

terpretation of what he observes. In fact he allows himself such errors and distortions in describing the healers that it is impossible to credit the book with objective value. Since he changed the names of some of the people in the book, his assertions can be checked only with great difficulty or not at all.

The work's intention is evidently to discourage travel to the Philippines and to its healers. I do not intend to argue against this motive; for Nolen is entitled to consider orthodox academic medicine as the only road to salvation. Then too, the streams of patients thronging to the Philippines have become so great as to create uncontrollable conditions and to tax the few genuinely good healers far beyond their capacity to perform. If Dr. Nolen sees it as his duty to intervene, I respect his conviction. But in so doing he should not report his findings in the Philippines with the poetic license of a novelist.

Thus he devotes a chapter to an interview with a Dr. Martinez in Manila, of whom he writes: "He is a stocky man in his mid-fifties, a practicing clinical psychologist. M.D.s in Manila refer patients to him for psychoanalysis, and obstetricians often send him pregnant women who need training in preparation for natural childbirth." Dr. Martinez, he goes on to explain, is also expert at hypnosis and has concerned himself for more than fifteen years with observing Philippine healers. The testimony of such a person must, of course, carry a great deal of weight with the readers of Nolen's book. "Dr. Martinez" can be none other than the above-mentioned Dr. Hiram Ramos, formerly professor of psychology at one of the universities in Manila, the greatest expert and most assiduous researcher in the field of Philippine healers and the leading pararesearcher in the Philippines. Dr. Ramos was interviewed by Dr. Nolen in 1973, but the description in the book in no way corresponds to the discussion, as I easily ascertained when I spoke to Dr. Ramos in March 1975. Our interview was recorded on tape, and what follows lists the discrepancies.

According to Dr. Nolen, Martinez/Ramos said that the so-called Philippine operations with blood and tissue were an invention of the now aged healer Eleuterio Terte. As long as thirty years ago Terte treated patients with prayer and magnetic stroking but then conceived the idea of imitating blood-releasing surgery, since surgical incisions are always greatly impressive to laymen, and the psychosomatic success rate could be improved by faked operations. Terte—a clever conjurer—had imitated surgical incisions by using chicken blood and animal entrails. Terte had next gone over to cotton and red dyestuff made from betel nuts. All healers kept betel nuts in their homes. Some made use of animal blood, others of dye fluids.

Dr. Ramos commented:

I have never made the claim, attributed to me in Dr. Nolen's book, that Terte conceived the idea of introducing deceptive operations as imitations of genuine surgical medical incisions. I would say that at the time Terte had no reason whatever to engage in any kind of deception. I have no doubt that there are some faked operations in the Philippines, but what they feign are genuine paranormal incisions and treatments. If healers keep betel nuts in their homes, that proves nothing. You will find betel nuts in most homes in the lowlands. Furthermore, I can't imagine how you could use betel nut dye to simulate blood.

Dr. Ramos continued:

There is no doubt of the fundamental possibility of genuine paranormal psychic surgery. Such phenomena may be age-old. There is a great deal of evidence—such as linguistic remnants—to indicate that the Spanish encountered local healers. It is possible that blood-producing paranormal surgery was already being practiced in the old days; I believe that the physiological and psychological effects of blood on the patient have been recognized and practiced for ages, as in the use of leeches, in bloodletting, and of course in paranormal techniques. However that may be, it was surely not Terte's idea to introduce an entirely new, psychosomatic type of treatment in the form of a placebo operation with chicken entrails and faked blood. He too—at least in the beginning—produced genuine paranormal phenomena.

On the question of deception in general Dr. Ramos added:

Even if there are healers who engage in fakery and are caught at it, that does not prove that everything is fakery. Even assuming, in the extreme case, that a healer acts deceptively nine out of ten times and performs only one genuine operation, this means that the one authentic surgery is of high interest to scientific investigators.

Further statements by Martinez/Ramos quoted in Dr. Nolen's book refer to Tony Agpaoa whom Nolen himself seems never to have visited his training by Terte, from whom he allegedly learned his tricks. his cunning in making money out of them the fortune he takes in, the value of his home in Kennon Road, the sum he spent on Dominican Hill near Baguio in 1973, and so on. On this subject Dr. Hiram Ramos told me:

I neither claimed that Agpaoa was a student of Terte nor did I assert the opposite. I do not know. Rather, I have heard the version that Tony Agpaoa discovered his healing powers for himself. The fact that Agpaoa is very wealthy today is not in dispute. But that, as Dr. Nolen writes, I claimed that Agpaoa would need only 1 percent of his income to turn his chapel into a Taj Mahal is, of course, the sheerest nonsense. Nor did I ever name such imaginary figures as $500,000 for his house or $7 million for the purchase of Dominican Hill, as is claimed in Nolen's book. Perhaps I used these numbers in pesos. [One United States dollar is worth six or seven Philippine pesos.] But the claims attributed to me are gross distortions.

Further, Dr. Ramos objected to Nolen's assumption that they both believed that healer Juanito Flores

deceptively used animal eyes in optic surgery and
that the psychokinetic incisions by Juan Blance and
David Oligani were sleight of hand. Nolen quotes
Martinez/Ramos as saying, "Blance and Oligani perform this incision from a distance. The trick consists
of previously making a very tiny scratch, which only
becomes visible when the site is subsequently kneaded
and massaged."

Dr. Ramos commented:

In principle, the phenomenon of opening the skin from a
distance is indubitably possible. In fact, the incision
sometimes becomes visible even before the finger motion
is executed in the air. Whatever form of energy it may
be with which the healers work, it does not maintain
a constant level. Sometimes, when the healer disposes of
strong psychic power, he is able to make these incisions
effortlessly from a distance. Blance has demonstrated
this skill to scientific witnesses under the most rigorous
test conditions. When this psychic power is decreased or
other energy-sapping factors are involved, the healer
requires direct manual touch of the patient. For the
most part he presses the thumb of his left hand or a
finger againt the particular place on the skin, though he
continues the gesture through the air even after the
incision is made. Superficial observation, of course, easily
leads to misinterpretation in such a case. Perhaps, too,
the healer may sometimes make use of mechanical aids
to carry out the incision. I cannot exclude such a possibility. But the description ascribed to me by Dr. Nolen
was never given by me.

Dr. Nolen further creates the impression that the
Manila scientist shares Nolen's opinion that the healer
David Oligani is an honorable, devout, and religious
man but that his operations are falsified and thus
cause him considerable conflicts of conscience. Nolen
quotes Martinez/Ramos as saying, "David, I think,
would like to get away from psychic surgery. He's
a truly religious man, and he'd like to heal people by
helping them to have faith in the Lord without all
this cotton and stuff. So far he hasn't been able to

make the break, but eventually I think he will. His conscience won't let him fake operations much longer."

Here is Dr. Ramos's comment:

That is a total distortion of what I said. I never claimed that Oligani's treatments or operations were faked—I have very positive feelings about Oligani. For me there is no discrepancy whatever between Oligani's inward attitude and his actions. I never claimed that Oligani was trying to get away from his allegedly faked operations because of religious convictions. What I said, rather, was that in Oligani's view purely spiritual healing is the highest form of the treatment of illness and that some days he felt the need to heal purely spiritually—that is, without any kind of "material operation." But that's altogether different from qualms of conscience about the use of deceptive methods.

Dr. Nolen's book contains many other distorted statements by Dr. Ramos, including those referring to the American Douglas Voeks, whom Nolen calls Donald Winslow. Voeks spent two years working with Placido Palitayan, where he allegedly learned the skills to perform paranormal operations. Nolen has Martinez/Ramos say, "The American is a master of deception and self-deception."

Dr. Ramos denies ever having said anything of the sort. "I never saw the American perform a 'material operation.' It seems entirely possible to me that he did indeed learn from Placido how to perform genuine psychic surgery, but I don't really know for sure one way or the other."

An equal distortion figures in Dr. Ramos's statements about the blood and tissue samples. The assertion attributed to Ramos that the blood and tissue produced by the healers are "of course not human tissue" is intended to give Nolen's readers the impression that Ramos, like Nolen, considers paranormal operations to be fakes.

Dr. Nolen considers the concept of an energy body a total "cop-out," and again the reader is led to believe that Dr. Ramos holds the same view. Nolen

first heard of the concept of an astral body in 1973, in
a conversation with the Apollo astronaut Edgar
Mitchell:

> I'd heard that explanation before from Dr. Edgar Mitchell
> when we had talked, briefly, of the psychic surgeons.
> It's a perfect cop-out, of course. How can anyone argue
> with a tissue report on an organ taken from the astral
> body? No one in this world, certainly, has ever ex-
> amined such tissue under the microscope. I can recog-
> nize an appendix from a human body, but I have no
> idea what the appendix from an astral body would look
> like.[183]

Obviously the process in the so-called astral re-
gions of the human body, which are still totally mysterious, cannot be explained away by a simple "one
times one is one" kind of logic. In recent years I have
seen increasing evidence that more and more physicians are coming to hold the belief that behind the
molecular cellular structure there must be a new kind
of energy or subtle structure in the form of an energy
body or astral body. Some of these physicians, outstanding surgeons, told me after a thorough study of
the Philippine phenomena: "These are not surgery
in the sense of our experience, but they cannot be
fakery either. I really do not know how to explain
them."

We are dealing with completely new paraphysical
phenomena in the realm of biological processes, quite
unfamiliar to Western scientists. They do not fall anywhere in the frame of reference of orthodox medicine,
and they lie outside the realms of physics and chemistry as practiced today. In a few decades daring innovations in biophysics may begin to explain them.
Inevitably, a physician who is not thoroughly experienced and knowledgeable in the field of medium-
ism and paraphysical phenomena, who is not open to
such matters and is not prepared to add completely
new concepts to his present fund of knowledge—who
could not even bring himself to visit the Philippines

except with the greatest reluctance—will arrive at totally erroneous conclusions.

No lay person tries to argue with me about radio-activity or nuclear chemistry. But there are countless people who insist on trying to enlighten me to the effect that the Philippine phenomena are complete nonsense and that pararesearch as a whole is superstitious rubbish. They have never visited the Philippines and have not the slightest idea of parapsy-chology.

Unfortunately the distortions and misinterpretations in Dr. Nolen's book cannot be completely explained by his lack of familiarity with paranormal processes as shown in the interview with Dr. Hiram Ramos. How much of what he says can we believe, given such cavalier treatment of the truth? Should we trust the five case histories Dr. Nolen cites as material wit-nesses against the Philippine healers? We cannot re-sist the impression that Dr. Nolen has changed not only the names but also the facts. This is true in the case of Neal Cook, an American.

In February 1973 I met an American, D.W., in Manila. In 1972 D.W. had learned that he was losing the sight of one eye; at the same time he developed diabetes. After several weeks of exploratory treatment in an American hospital a pituitary tumor was diag-nosed. An endocrine gland, the pituitary is located in the sella turcica of the sphenoid bone and is at-tached by a stalk to the floor of the brain. The tumor, which was pressing on the optic nerve, was also caus-ing the diabetes, since the endocrine function of the pancreas is controlled by a pituitary hormone. An operation was mandatory. It would take eight hours. The surgery was scheduled for July 19, 1972.

Shortly before that date D.W.'s daughter brought some friends home for the weekend. They showed a movie of supposed Filipino healers, and this was the first time D.W. heard the name of Tony Agpaoa. In their desperation, sufferers from some disease often grasp at straws. D.W. grasped for the telephone and asked to be connected to Baguio, where he was given

Agpaoa's private number. He spoke with Lucy Agpaoa,
who told him that Tony was in Manila and that to the
best of her knowledge he had not previously performed surgery on a brain tumor. D.W. then asked for
a postponement of his scheduled surgery and without
much ado took off for Manila. Agpaoa's first treatment
or operation took place on July 20, 1972, in a hotel
room. A second session followed two days later. When
I met D.W. in February 1973 in Manila—where he
was spending time on business—he told me that he
was feeling well, that his sight was normal, and that
his diabetes had disappeared.

Two years later, reading Dr. Nolen's book in Manila,
I encountered the case history of Neal Cook. I was
immediately struck by the amazing coincidence with
D.W.'s case. D.W.'s income had been doubled and
the number of his children cut in half, and a few other
insignificant changes had been made, but when I ran
across word-for-word quotations from an account of
his experiences D.W. had written and distributed in
1972, I no longer doubted that Neal Cook and D.W.
were one and the same. I was all the more shocked,
then, when I read in Nolen's book that after Agpaoa's
surgery the patient's condition had not improved in
the least, that the tumor continued to grow, and that
in the end the patient—disregarding his physician's
advice—sought out Agpaoa a second time. Another
"operation" by Agpaoa, for $1500, had been as useless
as the first, and in November 1973 the stubborn patient
had after all been forced to undergo brain surgery in
the United States. At present, Nolen stated, Neal Cook
was cured, had established a lavish foundation for
tumor research, and never mentioned the Philippines.

Dr. Nolen uses the case of Neal Cook as an example
of a highly intelligent and sophisticated person who
was taken in by a Filipino swindler. This representa-
tion shocked me deeply. I was trying to figure out how
to obtain D.W.'s address when friends in Manila told
me that he had arrived in town again. The following
day I met him in the offices of the Philippine Society
for Psychical Research, where, together with Dr. Antonio Araneta and Dr. Lava, a Philippine physician,

he was studying certain healers with a simple Kirlian machine. I immediately examined D.W.'s forehead and skull. His hair had grown a little grayer in the two years that had passed, but I could not find any scar pointing to a cranial operation. D.W. claimed to have been the only patient treated by Agpaoa for a pituitary tumor and said that since the treatment in July 1972 he had not had further surgery, either by Agpaoa or by Western surgeons. D.W. has a good mind and a critical spirit, and he is far from being an unrealistic fanatic. It was quite clear to him that Agpaoa's procedure did not constitute a guarantee of a permanent cure. He told me that Agpaoa himself had said at the time that he might need to repeat the treatment. D.W. does not exclude the possibility that conventional surgery might become necessary. But 2½ years after the treatment—in February 1975—no such necessity had arisen. The tumor had not been removed by Agpaoa's treatment, but it had not grown larger; in fact, it had shrunk somewhat. I further learned that Dr. Nolen had been thoroughly briefed on D.W.'s case and that he had been given a copy of D.W.'s report. D.W. is a trained biochemist, and at present he heads a major industrial enterprise. He devotes himself more and more to researching paranormal healing methods with modern scientific tools, and he is in touch with outstanding American researchers. On the subject of the book by Nolen, whom he had met, he said only, "I can't understand how William Nolen can play so fast and loose with the truth."

So much for Dr. Nolen's book. There is more to be said, but let the reader arrive at his own conclusions. I would like to note one other point, however. The majority of the Philippine operations have nothing in common with Western surgery. There has been genuine psychic surgery that removed diseased tissue by paranormal methods, but we see this phenomenon less and less often in the Philippines.

Dr. Ramos claims that until the early 1960s Agpaoa was by far the most outstanding surgeon among the Philippine healers. By the end of the 1960s

Ricardo Gonzales had developed outstanding skills in psychic surgery. Unfortunately he died under mysterious circumstances. Today most of the surgery performed by the Philippine healers consists of what Sigrun Seutemann calls procedures in "spiritual form." She seems to conceive the present form of the treatment administered by Agpaoa as a "visible form of spiritual healing." The Filipino healers do change something in the patient when they operate, though the change is not always on the material level. Are we seeing operations on the bioplasmic body, accompanied by mysterious materializations? Even when Western diagnostic tools cannot record any changes after Philippine surgery, a crucial change has taken place.

Perhaps the apparatus recently developed by Dr. Motoyama to measure the "subtle" levels of the human body will result in revealing explanations within the next few years. We know that something real occurs during the Philippine operations because the healers often see the "surgical scar" on a patient at once, although the ordinary person sees nothing. When dealing with a new patient, they can also tell whether one or more other healers have already "operated."[274] Juanito Flores explained to us that he could recognize José Mercado's work, or Alex Orbito's, or others' at once from the shape of the "scar," though the surgery might have taken place months before. In my case Flores immediately recognized an incision made by Orbito, though it had been performed five months earlier and I had forgotten all about it.

Psychokinesis—a familiar concept to everyone in the West nowadays, thanks to Uri Geller's feats of bending forks—seems at last to be establishing its authenticity. We must not be led astray by the claims that magicians can replicate these experiments. This is not true except insofar as the magician—perhaps without being aware of it himself—has also developed psychokinetic skills. Superficially, a magician can easily produce a similar phenomenon, but it cannot stand up to a thorough scientific investigation. Any one who still believes in a "fork trick" and the impossibility of psychokinetic bending of metal should study *Superminds*, by the English physicist Professor John Taylor.[274] Taylor tested not only Geller but a hundred others who discovered their own psychokinetic skills through Geller's performances. The existence of the phenomenon is no longer seriously contested. Discussion hinges solely on the question of the particular powers that become activated.

Present-day physics recognizes four basic forms of energy: the strong and weak interactions found in the realms of the elementary subatomic particles in and outside the nucleus, as well as electromagnetic interaction and gravitation—that is, the mass attraction we encounter in daily life.[67] It is my personal conviction that the bulk of paraphenomena cannot be explained on the basis of these four forms of energy. Some researchers may be inclined to explain psychokinetic phenomena by means of electromagnetic energy, but this will hardly account for the phenomena of materialization, the fundamental possibility of which I no longer doubt after five years of studying Philippine healers. Materializations confront our scientific thinking with its most serious challenge.

About two hundred years ago the French chemist Antoine Lavoisier demonstrated the principle of conservation of matter. This was supplemented in 1840 by the law of the conservation of energy, formulated by the German physician and chemist Julius Robert von Mayer. In the twentieth century Albert Einstein postulated the possibility of the reciprocal conversion of matter and energy—that is, the equivalence of matter and energy—forcing us to abandon the nineteenth-century concept of matter as immutable and permanent. Today physics often considers matter to be a special form of energy. But mediumistic materialization phenomena meet with physicists' vehement rejection; for the conversion factor for the transformation of matter into energy, according to Einstein, is given by the square of the speed of light—that is, it is astronomically high. In transforming matter into energy, an enormous amount of energy is released, as in an atomic bomb. During normal chemical reactions the transformation of energy at the electron shells is on the order of 1 electron volt (an energy unit) per atom or molecule. This can result in a quite noticeable manifestation of energy—as in a gas explosion! But if the smallest atom—that of hydrogen —were dissolved into energy, an energy mass of nearly 1 billion electron volts would be released. Evidently this cannot be the process by which Philippine healers materialize sizable amounts of organic tissue or bloodlike fluids—it would take far too much energy.

Explaining these materializations, which do exist, will upset our basic scientific beliefs, then, to a degree greater perhaps than that of any previous scientific revolution. Though ignored by the official sciences, French and German chemists have carried out numerous tests with plants and animals with a significant bearing on the problem of the energy released during materialization and dematerialization. Building on the work of the German chemist Albrecht von Herzeele in the nineteenth century, Dr. Rudolf Hauschka, a contemporary German chemist, has observed the germinating process and the weight of plant seeds that have been sealed in glass tubes with distilled water. The results show an unmistakable alteration in the mass which, according to Hauschka, far exceeds allowable margins of error. Can these changes be materialization phenomena in the realm of the biological processes? In this context we are reminded of the Soviet researchers' theory of bioplasma.

The works of the French chemist C. Louis Kervran are closely related. He claims to have demonstrated transmutations of chemical elements in plant and animal life, such as phosphorus into sulfur and potassium into calcium.[110] These are not just changes on the periphery of atoms, as in the usual chemical reactions, but in the nucleus of the atom—which is possible in modern physics, but requires an energy expenditure millions of times greater than what takes place biochemically and biophysically in living organisms, according to present knowledge.

Physicists and nuclear chemists transmute elements in large, expensive accelerators where small, charged particles are brought to very high energies in order to "smash" the atoms. The idea that a daisy can transform silicon into calcium must seem absurd to every nuclear physicist and chemist, especially since calcium has an atomic number six times higher than silicon and this calls for even more than the usual enormous "atom-smashing" energies.

Kervran is not alone in his claims. Professor Pierre Baranger, director of the Institute for Organic Chemistry at the École Polytechnique in Paris, has proved transmutations in the biological sphere based on the work of von Herzeele, and other researchers seem to confirm his results.[134]

Acceptance of biological transmutations by the physical sciences will throw a new light on the phenomena of materialization, which have been a subject of heated dispute for a hundred years, and thus also on the controversial Philippine operations. It is probable that psychokinesis and materialization, dematerialization, and rematerialization hold unsuspected possibilities for the medicine of the future. But we must first learn to thoroughly investigate and evaluate these mysterious paraphysical processes.

We have probably already missed a most favorable moment for such an investigation. During my first visit to the Philippines, in January and February 1971, the healers were for the most part very open and willing to demonstrate their skills, making themselves available for scientific experiments. Today, as a consequence of great hostility and many accusations of trickery in the Western media, they have become mistrustful of scientists and other observers. Furthermore, they receive so many foreign patients that they often lack the time and interest to put themselves at the disposal of scientific investigators.

However, there are several plans for more extensive scientific investigations of Philippine psychic surgery. Supported by Sigrun Seutemann, Tony Agpaoa bought Dominican Hill from the Catholic Church in the summer of 1973. On this unique site, high above Baguio, a large hotel to house visitors and patients has been erected. Seutemann also plans to establish a modern research laboratory to investigate paranormal phenomena.

In 1973 the Philippine Society for Psychical Research, with a research center in Manila, was founded. Dr. Antonio Araneta, Jr., and the Manila physician Dr. Lava run it as a "nonprofit organization dedicated to the advancement of research in the field of psi phenomena, particularly as this concerns healing and the restoration and maintenance of health. In establishing its Research Center, the Society intends to further document and authenticate the occurrence of these phenomena, to provide a broader accumulation of facts to serve as a basis upon which cooperative research, especially with our medical societies, could be undertaken."

Surely this is a very ambitious goal, for official Philippine medicine takes its direction closely from American academic medicine—Philippine physicians are without a doubt among the best in the Far East. The study of medicine at Philippine universities is in no way inferior to instruction given in modern Western universities, and practical and theoretical training are of a high quality. Established Philippine physicians employ the latest tools of Western science and technology and are extraordinarily skillful surgeons. A unique chance nevertheless remains for the Filipinos to enrich their scientifically outstanding medical services with the potential of psi medicine. Such a combination would be unique in the world.

REFERENCES

Abbreviations used:

JASPR   Journal of the American Society for Psychical Research (New York)

JoP   Journal of Paraphysics (Downton, Wilts., England)

JP   Journal of Parapsychology (Durham, N.C.)

ZPG   Zeitschrift für Parapsychologie und Grenzgebiete der Psychologie (Freiburg, West Germany)

1. Adamenko, Viktor, "Controlled Movement of Objects in Bioelectric Fields," Moscow Conference, July 1972.
2. ――――, "Electrodynamics of Living Systems," *JoP*, Vol. 4, No. 4, 1970.
3. ――――, "Informational Bioelectronics," *JoP*, Vol. 7, No. 1, 1973.
4. ――――, "Living Detectors," *JoP*, Vol. 6, No. 1, 1972.
5. ――――, "The Phenomenon of Skin Electricity," *JoP*, Vol. 6, No. 1, 1972.
6. ――――, "St. Elmo's Fire. Symposium of Psychotronics," *JoP*, Vol. 5, No. 4, 1971.
7. ――――, "Seminar on the Problems of Biological Plasma," *JoP*, Vol. 5, No. 4, 1971.
8. ――――, "The Tobiscope: Its Use in Hypnosis," *JoP*, Vol. 6, No. 1, 1972.
9. Andrés, P., W. Kiefer, and T. Locher, "Prager Kongress über Psychotronik," *Schweizerisches Bulletin für Parapsychologie*, No. 2, Nov. 1973.

10. Agpaoa, Antonio, et al., *The Gifts of the Spirit,* Baguio, 1971.

11. ———, *The Living Legend,* Baguio, 1972.

12. Aksakov, Aleksandr, *Animismus und Spiritismus,* 2 vols., Leipzig, 1894.

13. Andreas, Peter, and Gordon Adams, *Was niemand glauben will,* Berlin, 1967; see also *Between Heaven and Earth,* London, 1967.

14. Bach, C., "Die Handlinien in der medizinischen Diagnostik," *Erfahrungsheilkunde,* No. 1, 1960.

15. Bardon, Franz, *Der Schlüssel zur wahren Quabbalah,* Freiburg im Breisgau, 1957.

16. Bauhofer, Alfred, *Wunderheiler auf den Philippinen,* Salzburg, 1971 (privately printed).

17. Baumgartner, Friedrich, "Die Grosse Mission der Parapsychologie in unserer Zeit," in Allan Kardek, *Du, ich, und die anderen,* Remagen, 1970.

18. Bender, Hans, "Glaubensheilung und Parapsychologie," in Bitter (see below).

19. ———, *Parapsychologie. Ihre Ergebnisse und Probleme,* 2d ed., Bremen, 1971.

20. ———, *Telepathie, Hellsehen und Psychokinese,* Munich, 1972 (paperback).

21. ———, *Unser sechster Sinn,* Stuttgart, 1971 (also available in paperback).

22. Berndt, G. H., *Buch der Wunder und Geheimwissenschaften,* 2 vols., Leipzig, 1900.

23. Bischko, Johannes, *Einführung in die Akupunktur,* Heidelberg, 1972.

24. Bitter, Wilhelm, *Magie und Wunder in der Heilkunde,* Munich, no date (paperback).

25. Blavatsky, Elena, *Die Geheimlehre,* Berlin, 1958; see also *Isis Unveiled,* Los Angeles, 1931.

26. Boswell, Harriet A., *Master Guide to Psychism,* New York, 1969.

27. Böttcher, Helmut M., *Der Mensch stirbt viel zu früh,* Cologne, 1961.

28. Bozzano, Ernesto, *Les énigmes de la psychométrie,* Paris, 1927.

29. ———, *Übersinnliche Erscheinungen bei Naturvölkern,* Bern, 1948.

30. Brenner, Charles, *Grundriss der Psychoanalyse*, Frankfurt am Main, 1968.

31. Bro, Harmon H., *Traumdeutungen in Trance*, Geneva, 1969; see also *Edgar Cayce on Dreams*, New York, 1968.

32. Buchinger, Otto, *Das Heilfasten*, Stuttgart, 1947.

33. Burr, H. S., *Blueprint for Immortality*, London, 1972.

34. Busse, Ernst, and Paul Busse, *Akupunkturfibel*, Munich, 1965.

35. Carrel, Alexis, *Der Mensch, das unbekannte Wesen*, Munich, 1955; originally published as *Man, the Unknown*, 1935.

36. ———, *Tagebuch eines Lebens*, Munich, 1957.

37. Cassirer, M., "Bioplasmic Energy: New Science of the Future?" *JoP*, Vol. 7, No. 1, 1973.

38. Cazzamalli, F., "Ausstrahlung von Gehirnwellen bei telepsychischen Phänomenen," *Zeitschrift für Parapsychologie*, 1926.

39. Chauchard, Paul, *Hypnose et suggestion*, Paris, 1951.

40. Clair, David, "Spiritism in Brazil," *Psychic*, Dec. 1970.

41. Correll, Werner, *Lernpsychologie*, Donauwörth, 1970.

42. ———, *Pädagogische Verhaltenspsychologie*, Munich, 1969.

43. ———, *Programmiertes Lernen und Lernmaschinen*, Braunschweig, 1965.

44. Cunanan, Joaquin, *Readings on Spiritualism*.

45. ———, *What Can Yoga Do for You?* Tarlac, Philippines, no date.

46. Daco, Pierre, *Les prodigieuses victoires de la psychologie moderne*, Verviers, Belgium, 1960.

47. ———, *Les triomphes de la psychoanalyse*, Verviers, Belgium, 1965.

48. David, Albert Roy, "Biomagnetics, Biological Electronics," Green Cove Springs, Fla., no date (unpublished manuscript).

49. David-Neel, Alexandra, "Psychic Phenomena in Tibet," *Psychic*, Dec. 1970.

50. Day, G. W. L., *Die Wasser zu Damaskus*, Garmisch-Partenkirchen, 1962.

51. Deck, Josef, *Grundlagen der Irisdiagnostik*, Ettlingen, 1965.

52. Devi, Indra, *Ein neues Leben durch Yoga*, Geneva, 1966.

53. Dosch, Peter, *Lehrbuch der Neuraltherapie nach Huneke*, Heidelberg, 1970.

54. ———, *Wissenswertes über die Neuraltherapie nach Dr. Huneke*, Heidelberg, 1972.

55. Duke, Mark, *Akupunktur*, Bern and Munich, 1973; also *Acupuncture*, New York, 1973 (paperback).

56. Dunsford, Ivor, and C. C. Bowley, *ABC der Blutgruppenkunde*, Munich, 1969; see also *Techniques in Blood Grouping*, 2 vols., Springfield, Ill., 1968.

57. Ebon, Martin, "Freud and the Paranormal," *Psychic*, Dec. 1970.

58. ———, *Psychic Discoveries by the Russians*, New York, 1972.

59. Edwards, Harry, *Geistheilung*, Freiburg im Breisgau, 1968; see also *Healing Intelligence*, New York, 1971.

60. ———, *Wege zur Geistheilung*, Freiburg im Breisgau, 1963; see also *The Power of Spiritual Healing*, London, 1963.

61. Edwin, Ronald, *Uhr ohne Zeiger*, Lucerne, 1957; originally published as *Clock Without Hands*, Indian Hills, Colo., 1956.

62. Eisenbud, Jule, "Gedanken zur Psychofotografie und Verwandtem," *ZPG*, Vol. 14, No. 1, 1971.

63. ———, "Mental Suggestion at a Distance," *Psychic*, Feb. 1971.

64. ———, *The World of Ted Serios*, New York, 1967.

65. Eliade, Mircea, *Schamanismus und archaische Ekstasetechnik*, Zurich, 1954; also available as *Shamanism: Archaic Techniques of Ecstasy*, Princeton, N.J., 1964.

66. Ellen, Arthur, *Ich hypnotisierte Tausende*, Geneva, 1973; see also *Intimate Casebook of a Hypnotist*, New York, 1968 (paperback).

67. Feynman, Richard, et al., *Lectures on Physics*, Vol. 1, 1971.

68. Finkelnburg, Wolfgang, *Einführung in die Atomphysik*, 12th ed., Berlin, 1967.

69. Fodor, Nandor, *Encyclopedia of Psychic Science*, New York, 1966.

70. Ford, Arthur, *Bericht vom Leben nach dem Tode*, Bern and Munich, 1972; see also *Life Beyond Death*, New York, 1972 (paperback).

71. Freedom-Long, Max, *Geheimes Wissen hinter Wundern*, Freiburg im Breisgau, 1965.

72. ———, *Kahuna-Magie*, Freiburg im Breisgau, 1966.

73. Friedlander, Gerhart, and Joseph W. Kennedy, *Nuclear and Radiochemistry*, London, 1956.

74. Fritsche, Herbert, *Hahnemann, die Idee der Homöopathie*, Berlin, 1944.

75. Fuller, John, *Surgeon of the Rusty Knife*, New York, 1974.

76. Geisler, Hans, "Der Fall Tony Agpaoa," *Esotera*, Oct. 1971.

77. Geley, Gustave, *De l'inconscient au conscient*, Paris, 1919.

78. ———, *Hellsehen und Teleplastik*, Stuttgart, 1924.

79. ———, *Materialisationsexperimente mit M. Franek-Kluski*, Leipzig, 1922.

80. ———, *Die sogenannte supranormale Physiologie und die Phänomene der Ideoplastie*, Leipzig, 1920.

81. Gerloff, Hans, *Die Heilungen von Lourdes im Lichte der Parapsychologie*, Büdingen-Gettenbach, 1959.

82. ———, *Das Medium Carlos Mirabelli*, Tittmoning, 1960.

83. ———, *Die Phantome von Kopenhagen*, Munich, 1955.

84. Graham, K., and Anita M. Watkins, "Possible PK Influence on the Resuscitation of Anesthetized Mice," *JP*, Vol. 35, No. 4, 1971.

85. Grazziani, Giuseppe, "Die Pflanze, die vor Schreck schrie," *Esotera*, Dec. 1972.

86. Groenefeld, Gerhard, "Delphine—Intelligenzler unter Wasser," *Westermanns Monatshefte*, Oct. 1972.

87. Grunewald, Fritz, *Die physikalischen Erscheinungen des Okkultismus*, Berlin, 1925.

88. ———, *Physikalisch-mediumistische Untersuchungen*, Pfullingen, 1920.

89. ———, *Versuche über Materialisation und Telekinese*, Leipzig, 1924.

90. Gubisch, Wilhelm, *Hellseher, Scharlatane, Demagogen?* Munich, 1961.

91. Gurwitsch, A. G., and L. D. Gurwitsch, *Die mitogenetische Strahlung*, Jena, 1959.

92. H.U.E., "Auf Agpaoas Operationstisch," *Esotera*, April 1971.

93. Heisenberg, Werner, "Naturwissenschaftliche und religiöse Wahrheit," *Kontakt*, April 1973.

94. ———, *Schritte über Grenzen*, Munich, 1971; also available as *Across the Frontiers*, New York, 1973.

95. Herbert, B., "Alexei Krivorotov: Russian 'Healer,'" *JoP*, Vol. 4, No. 4, 1970.

96. ———, "Electric PK," *JoP*, Vol. 6, No. 4, 1972.

97. ———, "Spring in Leningrad: Kulagina Revisited," *JoP*, Vol. 7, No. 3, 1973.

98. ———, and M. Cassirer, "Parapsychology in USSR," *JoP*, Vol. 6, No. 5, 1972.

99. Heyer, G. H., "Magie und Wunder in der Heilkunde," in Bitter (see above).

100. Hofmann, Heinz, *Experimente als Brücke zum Übersinnlichen*, Freiburg im Breisgau, 1965.

101. ———, "Od- und Erdstrahlen-Experimente," *Esotera*, Dec. 1972-Jan. 1973.

102. Hummel, K., *Blutgruppenserologische Grundbegriffe*, Frankfurt am Main, 1969.

103. Hutton, J. B., *Healing Hands*, London, 1966.

104. Inyushin, Viktor M., "Biological Plasma and Interaction of Organisms at a Distance," Symposium on Psychotronics, Prague, Sept. 1970.

105. ———, "Biological Plasma of Human and Animal Organisms," Symposium on Psychotronics, Prague, Sept. 1970.

106. ———, "Report from Alma-Ata," in Herbert and Cassirer (see above).

107. Issberner-Haldane, Ernst, *Die medizinische Hand- und Nageldiagnostik,* Freiburg im Breisgau, 1963.

108. Jordan, Pascual, *Atom und Weltall,* Braunschweig, 1956.

109. Karagulla, Shafica, *Breakthrough to Creativity,* Los Angeles, 1967.

110. Kervran, Louis, *Biological Transmutations,* Bristol, 1972.

111. Kherumina, R., "Introduction à l'étude de la connaissance parapsychologique," *Revue métaphysique,* Nos. 1–3, 1948.

112. Koch, Robert, "Schamanen und Medizinmänner," *Esotera,* Oct. 1971.

113. Koestler, Arthur, "Physik und Synchronizität," *ZPG,* Vol. 16, No. 1, 1973.

114. ———, *Die Wurzeln des Zufalls,* Bern and Munich, 1972; also available as *The Roots of Coincidence,* New York, 1972 (paperback, 1973).

115. Koot, D. J., and B. Herbert, "Kirlian Photographs," *JoP,* Vol. 5, No. 4, 1971.

116. Kriege, Theodor, *Fundamental Basis of Iris-diagnosis,* London, 1969.

117. ———, *Krankheitszeichen der Iris,* Osnabrück, 1969 (privately published).

118. Krippner, Stanley, "Acupuncture and Hypnosis in the USSR," *JoP,* Vol. 6, No. 2, 1972.

119. ———, et al., "The Moscow Meetings on Biological Energy (July 1972)," *JoP,* Vol. 7, No. 2, 1973.

120. Krmessky, Julius, "A New Force Revealed," Symposium on Psychotronics, Prague, Sept. 1970.

121. ———, "Radiation from Organisms," *JoP,* Vol. 3, No. 4, 1969.

122. Kuhlman, Kathryn, *God Can Do It Again,* Englewood Cliffs, N.J., 1969.

123. Kulagin, V. V., "Nina Kulagina," Symposium on Psychotronics, Prague, Sept. 1970.

124. Langelaan, George, *Die unheimlichen Wirklichkeiten,* 2d ed., Bern and Munich, 1969.

125. Leadbeater, C. W., *Die Chakras,* Freiburg im

Breisgau, 1968; also available as *The Chakras*, New York, 1972 (paperback).

126. ———, *Der sichtbare und der unsichtbare Mensch*, Freiburg im Breisgau, 1968; also available as *Man Visible and Invisible*, New York, 1969 (paperback).

127. ———, and Annie Besant, *Gedankenformen*, Freiburg im Breisgau, 1968; also available as *Thought Forms*, abridged ed., New York, 1969 (paperback).

128. LeCron, Leslie, "Hypnosis and ESP," *Psychic*, Aug. 1970.

129. ———, *Selbsthypnose*, Geneva, 1965; also available as *Self-Hypnosis*, New York, 1970 (paperback).

130. Leeb, Günther, "Den westlichen Parapsychologen zur Nachahmung empfohlen," *Esotera*, Sept. 1972.

131. Lempke, Klaus, "Der Heiland mit den flinken Fingern," *Stern*, No. 29, July 11, 1971.

132. Leonidov, L., "The Kirlian Effect," *JoP*, Vol. 4, No. 5, 1970.

133. Levinson, G. I., *Die Philippinen—gestern und heute*, East Berlin, 1966.

134. Lobstein, Lizzie, "Es gibt mehr Dinge am Himmel und auf Erden. Erinnerungen an eine Reportage beim brasilianischen Wunderheiler Zé Arigo," *Argentinisches Tageblatt*, Jan. 24, 1971.

135. Locher, Theo, "Antwort an einen Mediziner," *Schweizerisches Bulletin für Parapsychologie*, Vol. 6, No. 1, 1971.

136. ———, "Drei berühmte medial Begabte," *Schweizerisches Bulletin für Parapsychologie*, Vol. 6, No. 1, 1971.

137. ———, "Geistoperationen?" *Schweizerisches Bulletin für Parapsychologie*, Vol. 8, No. 1, May 1973.

138. ———, "Geistoperationen—echt oder Betrug?" *Schweizerisches Bulletin für Parapsychologie*, Vol. 6, No. 2, 1971.

139. ———, "Psychotronische Energie existiert!" *Schweizerisches Bulletin für Parapsychologie*, Vol. 7, No. 2, 1972.

140. Lutten, L. P., *Maurice Mességué, der grosse Heiler*, Gelnhausen, 1964.

141. Maltz, Maxwell, *Psychocybernetics*, Englewood Cliffs, N.J., 1960.

142. Mann, Felix, *Acupuncture: Cure of Many Diseases*, London, 1971.

143. ———, *The Meridians of Acupuncture*, London, 1971.

144. Mann, Thomas, "Okkulte Erlebnisse," in *Autobiographisches*, Frankfurt am Main, 1968.

145. Maxey, E. Stanton, "Acupuncture: Consider the Ion. A Theoretical Explanation," 1972 (unpublished manuscript).

146. McKnight, Harry, "Silva Mind Control through Psychorientology," Institute for Psychorientology, Laredo, Tex., 1972.

147. Meek, George W., "Medicos Pay Tribute to Psychic Surgery," *Psychic News*, No. 2128, 1973.

148. ———, and B. Harris, *From Seance to Science*, London, 1973.

149. Miller, Robert N., "The Positive Effect of Prayer on Plants," *Psychic*, April 1972.

150. Mitchell, Edgar, "New Developments in Personal Awareness," in *The Dimensions of Healing*, Los Altos, Calif., 1972.

151. ———, "Outer Space and ESP," address to the ESP Congress in Hot Springs, Ark., May 27, 1972 (unpublished manuscript).

152. Monroe, Robert A., *Der Mann mit den zwei Leben*, Düsseldorf, 1972; see also *Journeys out of the Body*, New York, 1971 (paperback, 1973).

153. Montgomery, Ruth, *Born to Heal*, New York, 1973 (paperback).

154. Morselli, Enrico, *Psicologia e "spiritismo,"* 2 vols., Turin, 1908.

155. Moss, Thelma, "Psychics, Saints, and Scientists," color film, Cos Cob, Conn.

156. ———, "Searching for Psi from Prague to Lower Siberia," *Psychic*, June 1971.

157. ———, and Ken Johnson, "Radiation Field Photography," *Psychic*, July 1972.

158. Motoyama, Hiroshi, "Chakra, Yoga, Meridians, Points of Acupunture—Points Where Western Medicine, Chinese Medicine and Yoga Meet Each Other,"

lecture at Washington University, St. Louis, June 2, 1972 (unpublished manuscript).

159. ———, *Hypnosis and Religious Superconsciousness*, Tokyo, 1971.

160. ———, "Interview with a Faith Healer, *Religion and Parapsychology*, Vol. 1, No. 3, Aug. 1973.

161. ———, *The Non-Physical in the Correlation Between Mind and Body*, Tokyo, 1972.

162. ———, "Physiological Characteristics of the Psychic Person."

163. ———, *The Present Situation of Parapsychology in the World*, Tokyo, 1969.

164. ———, *Psychic Surgery in the Philippines*, Tokyo, 1972.

165. ———, "A Scientist Looks at Psychic Surgery," address to the ESP Congress in Hot Springs, Ark., May 28, 1972 (unpublished manuscript).

166. ———, personal communication to the author.

167. Mrkvicka, J., and Zdenek Rejdak, "Latent Abilities of the Human Cybernetic System," *JoP*, Vol. 5, No. 5, 1971.

168. Muldoon, Silvan J., and H. Carrington, *Die Aussendung des Astralkörpers*, Freiburg im Breisgau, 1974; also available as *Projection of the Astral Body*, New York, 1970 (paperback).

169. Murphy, Gardner, "A Carringtonian Approach to Ian Stevenson's 'Twenty Cases Suggestive of Reincarnation,'" *JASPR*, Vol. 67, No. 2, 1973.

170. Murphy, Josef, *Die Macht Ihres Unterbewusstseins*, Geneva, 1967; see also *Psychic Perception*, Englewood Cliffs, N.J., 1971 (paperback).

171. ———, *Die Wunder Ihres Geistes*, Geneva, 1964; see also *The Miracle of Mind Dynamics*, Englewood Cliffs, N.J., 1964 (paperback).

172. Naegeli-Osjord, Hans, "Auf Agpaoas Operationstisch," *Esotera*, May 1971.

173. ———, "Firedancing and Firewalking," *JoP*, Vol. 4, No. 1, 1970.

174. ———, "Logurgie auf den Philippinen," *Imago Mundi*, Vol. 4.

175. ———, "Ohne Messer, ohne Narkose, ohne Schmerzen," *Nueue Zürcher Zeitung*.

176. ———, "Psychic Healing and Psychic Surgery in the Philippines," lecture at Washington University, St. Louis, June 2, 1972.

177. Nager, Katherina, "Es handelt sich nicht um Betrug!" *Esotera,* No. 7, July 1973.

178. ———, "The Moscow Congress," *JoP,* Vol. 3, No. 4, 1969.

179. Neumann-Hellwig, Nora, *Wunderheiler und wunderbare Heilungen,* Steinebach and Wörthsee, no date.

180. Neundorf, Robert, "Parapsychologie: Allerlei Fälle von Spuk und Zauberei. Aberglaube mit wissenschaftlichem Anstrich," *Die Zeit,* Oct. 20, 1972.

181. Nicol, J. Fraser, "Old Light on 'New' Phenomena," *Psychic,* June 1971.

182. Nikolaev, Yuri S., "Moscow Hospital for Schizophrenics," *JoP,* Vol. 6, No. 5, 1972.

183. Nolen, William A., *Healing, a Doctor in Search of a Miracle,* New York, 1974.

184. Ostrander, Sheila, and Lynn Schroeder, *Psi. Die wissenschaftliche Erforschung und praktische Nutzung übersinnlicher Kräfte des Geistes und der Seele im Ostblock,* Bern and Munich, 1971; originally published as *Psychic Discoveries Behind the Iron Curtain,* Englewood Cliffs, N.J., 1970; also available in paperback (Bantam Books), New York, 1971.

185. ———, "Psychic Enigmas & Energies in the USSR," *Psychic,* June 1971.

186. Pakraduny, T., ed., *Die Welt der geheimen Mächte,* Innsbruck, 1952.

187. Passian, Rudolf, *Abschied ohne Wiederkehr?* Pforzheim, 1973.

188. ———, "Die philippinischen Geisterchirurgen," *Formengesetze,* Autumn 1971.

189. Pauwels, Louis, and Jacques Bergier, *Aufbruch ins dritte Jahrtausend,* 5th ed., Bern and Munich, 1970; see also *Morning of the Magician,* New York, 1968 (paperback).

190. ———, *Der Planet der unmöglichen Möglichkeiten,* Bern and Munich, 1968.

191. Pollak, Kurt, *Die Heilkunde der Antike,* Düsseldorf, 1968.

192. ———, *Wissen und Weisheit der alten Ärzte*, Düsseldorf, 1968.

193. Powell, Arthur E., *The Astral Body and Other Phenomena*, London, 1926.

194. Powers, Melvin, *Fortgeschrittene Methoden zum Erlernen der Selbsthypnose*, Freiburg im Breisgau, 1965; see also *Practical Guide to Self-Hypnosis* and *Self-Hypnosis: Its Theory, Technique, and Application* (paperbacks).

195. Presman, A. S., *Electromagnetic Fields and Life*, London, 1970.

196. Prokop, Otto, ed., *Medizinischer Okkultismus, Paramedizin*, Jena, 1962.

197. ———, and G. Uhlenbruck, *Lehrbuch der menschlichen Blut- und Serumgruppen*, Leipzig, 1965.

198. Pschyrembel, Willibald, *Klinisches Wörterbuch*, Berlin, 1964.

199. Puck-Kornezki, "Die heilenden Nadeln," *Westermanns Monatshefte*, Aug. 1972.

200. Puharich, Andrija K., "The Work of the Brazilian Healer Arigo," address to the Interdisciplinary Symposium, Los Altos, Calif., Oct. 30, 1971 (unpublished manuscript).

201. Quilisch, Werner, *Homöopathie als Therapie der Person*, Ulm, 1957.

202. Raikov, Vladimir L., "Artificial Reincarnation Though Hypnosis," *Psychic*, June 1971.

203. Ravitz, Leonard J., "Application of the Electrodynamic Field Theory in Biology, Psychiatry, Medicine, and Hypnosis," *American Journal of Clinical Hypnosis*, Vol. 1, No. 4, 1959.

204. ———, "Electromagnetic Field Monitoring of Changing State Function," *Journal of the American Society of Psychosomatic Dentistry and Medicine*, Vol. 17, No. 4, 1970.

205. Reich, Wilhelm, *Die Entdeckung des Orgons*, Frankfurt am Main, 1972 (paperback); also available as *The Discovery of the Orgone*, New York, 1942, 1948, 1961.

206. Reichenbach, Karl von, *Aphorismen über Sensitivität und Od*, Vienna, 1866.

207. ———, *Odisch-magnetische Briefe*, new ed., Ulm, 1955.

208. Rejdak, Zdenek, "Alles Lebendige leuchtet," *Westermanns Monatshefte*, June 1972.

209. ———, "The Kulagina Films," *JoP*, Vol. 3, No. 3, 1969.

210. ———, "Nina Kulagina's Mind over Matter," *Psychic*, June 1971.

211. ———, "Psychotronics," *JoP*, Vol. 2, No. 2, 1968.

212. ———, "Telekinesis or Fraud?" *JoP*, Vol. 2, No. 3, 1968.

213. Rhine, Joseph B., and J. G. Pratt, *Parapsychologie. Grenzwissenschaft der Psyche*, Bern and Munich, 1962; originally published as *Parapsychology: Frontier Science of the Mind*, Springfield, Ill., 1957.

214. Rhine, Louisa E., *Mind over Matter, the Story of PK*, New York, 1970.

215. Richet, Charles, *Grundriss der Psychologie und Parapsychophysik*, Stuttgart, 1923.

216. Rodrigues, Henrique, "Der bioplasmische Körper alles Lebendigen," *Esotera*, April 1973.

217. Rogo, D. Scott, "Photographs by the Mind," *Psychic*, April 1970.

218. Rohracher, Hubert, *Einführung in die Psychologie*, Vienna and Munich, 1960.

219. Roman, A. S., and V. Inyushin, "Problems in Bioenergetics—the Influence of Autosuggestion," *JoP*, Vol. 6, No. 1, 1972.

220. Roth, Jürgen, *Geheilt wie durch ein Wunder*, Vienna, 1972.

221. Ruchpaul, Eva, *Hatha Yoga. Kenntnis und Technik*, Heidenheim, 1969.

222. Ryzl, Milan, *Parapsychologie*, Geneva, 1970.

223. Schellbach, Oscar, "Erkennen, Schaffen, Vollenden," *Kontakt*, 1950–52.

224. ———, "Es gibt wirklich Wunder," phonograph record, Baden-Baden, no date.

225. ———, *Mein Erfolgssystem*, 21st ed., Baden-Baden, 1970.

226. ———, *Werkstatt der Seele*, Hamburg, 1930,

227. Schiebeler, Werner, *Paranormale Heilmethoden auf den Philippinen*, Göttingen, 1974.

228. ———, "Das Rätsel der Hebeversuche," *Schweizerisches Bulletin für Parapsychologie*, Vol. 7, No. 1, 1972.

229. ———, private communications to the author.

230. Schindewolf, Ulrich, *Physikalische Kernchemie*, Braunschweig, 1959.

231. Schleich, Carl Ludwig, *Besonnte Vergangenheit*, Reinbek, 1961.

232. Schmitz, Karl, *Was ist, was kann, was nützt Hypnose?* Munich, 1964.

233. Schrenck-Notzing, Albert von, *Experimente der Fernbewegung*, Stuttgart, 1924.

234. ———, *Materialisationsphänomene—ein Beitrag zur mediumistischen Teleplastie*, Munich, 1923.

235. ———, *Die Phänomene des Mediums Rudi Schneider*, Leipzig, 1933.

236. Schultz, J. H., *Das autogene Training*, Stuttgart, 1966.

237. Schütz, Erich, and Karl E. Rothschuh, *Bau und Funktion des menschlichen Körpers*, Munich, 1966.

238. Seidel, Franz, "Neue Ergebnisse und Erkenntnisse der Psi-Forschung," *Esotera*, Feb. 1973.

239. Sergeyev, G.A., "Detection of PK by Semi-Conductors," *JoP*, Vol. 7, No. 2, 1973.

240. ———, "KNS Phenomenon," Symposium on Psychotronics, Prague, Sept. 1970.

241. ——— and V. V. Kulagin, "Psychokinetic Effects of Bioplasmic Energy," *JoP*, Vol, 6, No. 1, 1972.

242. ———, G. D. Shushchkov, et al., "The Piezoelectric Detector of Bioplasma," *JoP*, Vol. 6, No. 1, 1972.

243. Seutemann, Erwin, and Sigrun Seutemann, "Agpaoa—Wunderheiler oder Scharlatan?" *Esotera*, Sept. 1971.

244. Sherman, Harold, *Aussersinnliche Kräfte*, Freiburg im Breisgau, 1966.

245. ———, article in *ESP Research Associates Foundation for Exploration of the Origin and Nature of Man's Sixth Sense*, Vol. 5, No. 5, 1972.

246. ———, *Gebet—heilende, helfende Macht*, Freiburg im Breisgau, 1965; originally published as *How to Use the Power of Prayer*, New York, 1959.

247. ———, *How to Take Yourself Apart and Put Yourself Together Again*, Greenwich, Conn., 1971.

248. ———, *Wonder Healers of the Philippines*, Los Angeles, 1967.

249. ———, *Wundervolle Kräfte in dir*, Freiburg im Breisgau, 1970.

250. ———, *Your Mysterious Powers of ESP*, New York, 1969.

251. ———, *Your Power to Heal*, New York, 1972.

252. Sigma, Rho, "Ein Werkzeug jenseitiger Ärzte," *Esotera*, No. 10, Oct. 1973.

253. Sinclair, Upton, *Radar der Psyche*, Bern and Munich, 1973; originally published as *Mental Radio*, Springfield, Ill., 1930.

254. Sonnet, André, *Der Mensch ist voller Geheimnisse*, Berlin, 1959; see also *The Twilight Zone of Dreams*, New York, 1961.

255. Spath, I. M., *Yoga—Wege der Befreiung*, Zurich, 1951.

256. Speicher, Günther, *Ihrer Zeit voraus*, Düsseldorf, 1967.

257. Spragget, Allen, *Kathryn Kuhlman, the Woman Who Believes in Miracles*, New York, 1970.

258. Stearns, Jess, *Der schlafende Prophet: Edgar Cayce*, Geneva, 1968; originally published as *Edgar Cayce, The Sleeping Prophet*, New York, 1967 (paperback).

259. Steiger, Brad, *The Psychic Feats of Olof Jonsson*, Englewood Cliffs, N.J., 1971.

260. Steinbuch, Karl, *Falsch programmiert*, Stuttgart, 1968 (also in paperback).

261. Stelter, Alfred, "Agpaoa im Deutschen Fernsehen," *Esotera*, Nov. 1971.

262. ———, "Paraphänomene im Fernen Osten," *Kontakt*, Oct. 1974–May 1975.

263. ———, "Umstrittene mediale Chirurgie."

264. ———, "Was ist Psi?" *Kontakt*, No. 12, Dec. 1973.

265. Stevenson, Ian, "Some New Cases Suggestive of Reincarnation," *JASPR*, Vol. 66, Nos. 3–4, 1972.

266. ———, *Twenty Cases Suggestive of Reincarnation*, New York, 1966.

267. Strauch, Inge, "Die geistigen Heilungen von Dr. rer. pol. Trampler," in Bitter (see above).

268. Süssman, Georg, and Nikolaus Fiebiger, *Atome, Kerne, Elementarteilchen*, Frankfort am Main, 1968.

269. Tajon, R. V., "Healers Have Become Tourist Attractions," *Philippine Panorama*, Vol, 2, No. 34, Aug. 26, 1973.

270. Tanagra, A., "The Nature of Telekinetic Energy," *JoP*, Vol. 6, No. 2, 1972.

271. Taniguchi, Masaharu, *Die geistige Heilkraft in uns*, Pfullingen, 1962.

272. ———, *Leben aus dem Geiste*, Pfullingen, 1964.

273. Tart, Charles, *Altered States of Consciousness*, New York, 1969.

274. Taylor, John, *Superminds*, London, 1975.

275. Tenhaeff, W. H. C., *Aussergewöhnliche Heilkräfte*, Olten and Freiburg im Breisgau, 1957.

276. Thorsen, Paul, *Die Hypnose im Dienste der Menschheit*, Freiburg im Breisgau, 1957.

277. ———, *Methodik und praktische Anwendung der Hypnose*, Freiburg im Breisgau, 1961.

278. Thorwald, Jürgen, *Die Geschichte der Chirurgie*, Stuttgart, 1965; see also *The Triumph of Surgery*, New York, 1960.

279. ———, *Macht und Geheimnis der frühen Ärzte*, Munich, 1968; also available as *Science and Secrets of Early Medicine*, New York, 1963.

280. Thurston, H., *Die körperlichen Begleiterscheinungen der Mystic*, Lucerne, 1956; originally published as *Physical Phenomena of Mysticism*, New York, 1952.

281. ———, *Poltergeister*, Lucerne, 1955; originally published as *Ghosts and Poltergeists*, New York, 1954.

282. Tietze, Thomas R., "Eusapia Palladino," *Psychic*, Feb. 1972.

283. Tiller, William A., "Autogenic Training in the USSR," *JoP*, Vol. 6, No. 4, 1972.

284. ———, "The Psychokinetic Phenomena of Alla Vinogradova," *JoP*, Vol. 6, No. 2, 1972.

285. Tirala, L. G., *Massenpsychosen in der Wissenschaft*, Tübingen, 1969.

286. Tischner, Rudolf, *Fernfühlen und Mesmerismus*, Munich, 1925.

287. ———, *Franz Anton Mesmer. Leben und Wirkung*, Munich, 1928.

288. ———, *Das Medium D. D. Home*, Leipzig, 1925.

289. Titze, Kurt, *Bali, Timor, Philippinen*, Munich, 1968.

290. Tolentino, Guillermo, *Unio Espiritista Cristiana Filipinas*, San Diego, Calif., 1972.

291. Tompkins, Peter, and Christopher Bird, *The Secret Life of Plants*, New York, 1974.

292. Torrevillas-Suarez, Domini, "Foreign Scientists Look at Psychic Healing," *Philippine Panorama*, Vol. 2, No. 43, Oct. 28, 1973.

293. ———, "The Healers of Pangasinan," *Philippine Panorama*, Vol. 2, No. 39, Sept. 1973.

294. ———, "The Spiritual Healers," *Philippine Panorama*, Vol. 2, No. 34, Aug. 26, 1973.

295. Turner, Gordon, *An Outline of Spiritual Healing*, London, 1970.

296. Tyrrell, G. N. M., *Mensch und Welt in der Parapsychologie*, Bremen, 1972; see also *Apparitions*, New York, 1970 (paperback).

297. Valentine, Tom, *Psychic Surgery*, Chicago, 1973.

298. Vasiliev, Leonid, *Experimentelle Untersuchungen zur Mentalsuggestion*, Bern and Munich, 1965.

299. Vaughan, Alan, "In Pursuit of the Whole at the Human Dimensions Institute," *Psychic*, April 1972.

300. ———, "Interview: Captain Edgar Mitchell," *Psychic*, Oct. 1971.

301. ———, "Interview: Montague Ullman, M.D.," *Psychic*, June 1971.

302. Ventura, Sylvia M., "Faith-Healing: Magic or Miracle," *Woman's Home Companion* (Manila), Sept. 20, 1973.

303. Vergin, Ferdinand, "Psychotherapie vom Geistigen her," *Kontakt*, July 1972.

304. Verweyen, J. M., *Das Geheimnis von Konnersreuth*, Stuttgart, 1932.

305. ———, *Die Probleme des Mediumismus*, Stuttgart, 1928.

306. Vinokuraia, Svetlana, "Life in a Magnetic Web," *JoP*, Vol. 5, No. 4, 1971.

307. Völgyesi, Franz A., *Menschen- und Tierhypnose*, Zurich, 1963.

308. Waelder, Robert, *Die Grundlagen der Psychoanalyse*, Bern and Stuttgart, 1963.

309. Warcollier, R., *La Télépathie à très grandes distances. Le compte rendu officiel du III Congrès international des Recherches psychiques*, Paris, 1927.

310. Watson, Lyall, *The Romeo Error*, London, 1974.

311. Weimann, Theodor, "Die Parapsychologie," in Pakraduny (see above).

312. Weiss, G., "724 Fragen an den Patienten," *Kontakt*, Feb. 1973.

313. Westlake, Aubrey T., *Medizinische Neuorientierung*, Zurich, 1963.

314. White, John W., "Acupuncture: The World's Oldest System of Medicine," *Psychic*, July 1972.

315. Wiener, Norbert, *Kybernetik*, Düsseldorf, 1968 (also in paperback); originally published as *Cybernetics*, New York, 1951 (also in paperback).

316. Wimmer, W., "Parapsychologie and Kurpfuschertum," *Deutsche medizinische Wochenschrift*, No. 2, 1973.

317. Wise, Charles C., Jr., "Some Problems of Spiritualist Healing," *Spiritual Frontiers*.

318. Wood, Rebecca, "A Discussion with J. R. Wosley," *Psychic*, July 1972.

319. Worral, Ambrose, and Olga Worral, *Explore Your Psychic World*, New York, 1970.

320. ———, *The Gift of Healing*, New York, 1965.

321. Worral, Olga, "Healing by Unconventional Methods," in *The Dimensions of Healing*, Los Altos, Calif., 1972.

322. Wright, Harry B., *Zauberer und Medizinmänner*, Zurich, 1958.

323. Wyss, Dieter, *Die tiefenpsychologischen Schulen von den Anfängen bix zur Gegenwart*, Göttingen, 1970.

324. Yagodinsky, Victor, "The Magnetic Memory of the Virus," *JoP*, Vol. 6, No. 4, 1972.

325. Yesudian, S., and E. Haich, *Sport und Yoga*, Munich, 1949; see also *Yoga and Health*, New York, 1954 (also available in paperback).

326. Zweig, Stefan, *Heilung durch den Geist*, Frankfurt am Main, 1931.

ABOUT THE AUTHOR

ALFRED STELTER was born in 1926 in western Prussia. He has a doctorate in physics and chemistry and teaches these and related subjects at the Dortmund Technical University. He is an expert in parapsychological phenomena and has explored this field in extended trips and stays in the United States, Russia, Europe, East Asia and in the Pacific Islands.

PSYCHIC WORLD

Here are some of the leading books that delve into the world of the occult—that shed light on the powers of prophecy, of reincarnation and of foretelling the future.

- [ ] YOGA, YOUTH & REINCARNATION
  by Jess Stearn   10056—$1.75
- [ ] THE GOLD OF THE GODS
  by Erich Von Daniken   8477—$1.75
- [ ] SETH SPEAKS
  by Jane Roberts   8462—$1.95
- [ ] THE DEVIL'S TRIANGLE
  by Richard Winer   8445—$1.50
- [ ] PSYCHIC DISCOVERIES BEHIND THE
  IRON CURTAIN by Ostrander & Schroeder   7864—$1.50
- [ ] GOD DRIVES A FLYING SAUCER
  by Robert Dione   7733—$1.25
- [ ] NOT OF THIS WORLD
  by Peter Kolosimo   7696—$1.25
- [ ] WE ARE NOT THE FIRST
  by Andrew Tomas   7534—$1.25
- [ ] CHARIOTS OF THE GODS?
  by Erich Von Daniken   5753—$1.25
- [ ] LINDA GOODMAN'S SUN SIGNS
  by Linda Goodman   2777—$1.95
- [ ] BEYOND EARTH: MAN'S CONTACT
  WITH UFO'S by Ralph Blum   2564—$1.75
- [ ] EDGAR CAYCE: THE SLEEPING
  PROPHET by Jess Stearn   2546—$1.75
- [ ] THE OUTER SPACE CONNECTION
  by Alan Landsburg   2092—$1.75

Buy them at your local bookstore or use this handy coupon for ordering:

Bantam Books, Inc., Dept. PW, 414 East Golf Road, Des Plaines, Ill. 60016

Please send me the books I have checked above. I am enclosing $_____
(please add 35¢ to cover postage and handling). Send check or money order
—no cash or C.O.D.'s please.

Mr/Mrs/Miss_____

Address_____

City_____State/Zip_____

PW—10/76

Please allow three weeks for delivery. This offer expires 10/77.